FIRE ON THE WATER

SCOTT MacGREGOR
ILLUSTRATED BY GARY DUMM

INTRODUCTION BY PAUL BUHLE

Abrams ComicArts • New York

Editor: Charlotte Greenbaum
Designer: Max Temescu
Managing Editor: Connor Leonard
Production Manager: Alison Gervais

Cataloging-in-Publication Data has been applied for
and may be obtained from the Library of Congress.

ISBN 978-1-4197-4116-6
eISBN 978-1-68335-825-1

Color by Scott MacGregor
Cover color by Laura Dumm

Printed and bound in China
10 9 8 7 6 5 4 3 2 1

ABRAMS The Art of Books
195 Broadway, New York, NY 10007
abramsbooks.com

CONTENTS

INTRODUCTION

This graphic novel brilliantly explores a much misunderstood and maligned phenomena in the USA: working class life. The blue-collar experience has long been subject to endless caricature, most of it unfriendly, or at least condescending. Historians of race and community—their work linked, in turn, to specific ethnic histories—see things more fully. Their rich, dense historical studies were supported by the work of older scholars such as David Montgomery and Herbert Gutman, themselves influenced by E. P. Thompson and his totemic *Making of the English Working Class* (1966). A fresh scholarship of African American life, followed by work on Latinos, Asian Americans, and Native Americans, told a story of exploitation, repression, and upward struggle. Ruthless plunder had been an ever-present reality of the nation's rise to global supremacy. Gains on the part of ordinary people had been made not through philanthropy but from struggle and often bloody sacrifice. These history lessons pointed to continued conflicts ranging from social and health conditions to the very sustainability of life.

These struggles occupy most of *Fire on the Water*, a cautionary tale of American industrial life during the 1910s. Cleveland had by this time repeated the old ecological tragedy of treating a primary water source, in this case Lake Erie, as a dumping ground for refuse of every kind. The results were predictable as those of vanished cities across the world (and as close to Ohio as Cahokia Village in Illinois) that built up a population with commerce, cut down the surrounding green zones, slaughtered nearby game for the tastes of the ruling group, then faced illness and ultimately decimation of the protein-starved poor classes. American technology, with the swift rise of industrialism, allowed an escape from this dire fate, but at a great cost.

Let us set the scene a little more firmly. Long before the era of this graphic novel, Ohio became a racial battleground. The "Butter Nut" districts of the state had openly sympathized with the Confederacy, and after the Civil War, as white and black regional in-migrants from Kentucky met a growing stream of Europeans looking for work, a dire pattern of discrimination emerged. Scholars of Cleveland have analyzed how the differentiation made between white and nonwhite in-migrants (setting "skilled" categories of better work by race rather than the skill itself) relegated jobs, housing, and all the rest to the supposedly superior race. Racial segregation crossed all lines of work and domestic life, established earlier for Irish and native-born, then reinforced with the newer arrivals of the 1870s from Central and Southern Europe. Even the recent European immigrants suffered, often working in the worst of conditions and achieving the lowest standards of living. Some fortunate immigrants managed to rise in American society, but they were never the majority. When necessary, the threat of black labor to replace them was used by the bosses to drive their wages and conditions downward.

Meanwhile, the "public works" required for urban life—infrastructure, public transportation, and so on—had come to play a central role in the rapid growth of cities, and therefore a central role for the urban workforce. American cities rising up from the frontier, with an expanse of presumably available land (often snatched up in preparation of public purchase), had room for vast and hasty, experiments. In particular, the work of municipal visionaries after the turn of the century created miles of tunnels offshore, beneath the lake, in order to get safe drinking water. It would have been a shining triumph of engineering wisdom if not for the tragedy of human sacrifice to make it possible—and the stupidity of needless pollution that ruined the lake in the first place.

Something similar could be said, of course, for the creation of railroads and of urban architecture growing into skyscrapers. The sacrifice of human life was viewed as a small cost, the men who built these projects were expendable. Meanwhile, older established ethnic groups—Germans, Welsh, or Scottish—took full advantage of their positions within the working class. In Cleveland, the tunnel diggers, also known as sandhogs, were at the bottom of the hierarchy and often had the shortest life spans of all immigrant workers. They were "fortunate" enough to risk their lives on a daily basis and earn a measly salary. Such is the life brilliantly depicted by Scott MacGregor and Gary Dumm in these pages.

Fast-forward to Cleveland half a century later. Here, during the 1960s–80s, the city loses its historic industries. "Urban decay" is the subject of endless journalism and editorializing, most of it sympathetic to business rather than the people. As if to compensate, the setting gained its vernacular prose and visual storytellers: Harvey Pekar and a small circle of local comics artists, most especially Gary Dumm. Dumm "owns" Cleveland and Cleveland owns him, not only by virtue of personal residence but the location of his Irish-and-other, blue-collar family, stretching as far away as Pennsylvania but not much further, for generations. An illustrator for his community-college newspaper, prolific artist (with his wife, fellow artist Laura Dumm) of local scenes and interests, Gary has the feeling for the city and its residents in his very bones.

Author Scott MacGregor, who initiated the project, is a suitable partner in the work. A native Clevelander (whose own great grandfather was an Irish immigrant and a sandhog) and talented photographer, Scott MacGregor began a long-term friendship and intermittent collaboration with Gary Dumm in 1976 and produced his own one-shot comic (drawn by Gary and others) four years later. In the decades following, MacGregor wrote essays on local history, illustrated by Dumm and collaborator Greg Budgett, for the alternative press and placed his photos in the Irish American press. In retirement, after four decades as a medical practice manager, he found a way to make the vision of a graphic novel work, and *Fire on the Water* was begun.

MacGregor has made the graphic novel a model study in the world of work and of its perils, also to recover the lost history of African Americans like Garrett Morgan, who were effectively erased by racial prejudice. These characters come alive in their travails, in their daily habits, their home lives, their slang, and, above all, their willingness to risk life and limb in order to make a living. MacGregor has also captured the corruption innate to the political-economic system of the burgeoning Gilded Age metropolis, as one hand dirties another and fortunes are made almost, but not quite, in public sight.

The keenness of the narrative, no less than the illuminating artwork, shows us what comic art can do when freed from the limits of the superhero model and used to tell the story of one city, inside and out. In my view, *Fire on the Water* will stand out as an exceptional example of how to tell history so that all can understand it.

—Paul Buhle (Retired Senior Lecturer, Brown University)
(June, 2019)

Scott MacGregor dedicates this book to—

Kate, Patrick, and Maureen . . .
. . . and to Gary Dumm, who traversed his own "tunnel to hell"
while battling cancer during the creation of this book
and bravely won back the daylight.

Gary Dumm dedicates this book to—

The memory of my parents, Margaret and George Dumm, who both, in vastly different ways, allowed and gave me the strength to dream big.

Laura Dumm, who's helped me to recover from cancer while in the middle of our four-year journey, working together on the nuts and bolts of producing this big graphic novel.

Scott MacGregor, who trusted me implicitly to collaborate artistically and lend shape and definition to his dream.

PREFACE

Cleveland was a wicked little town back in the day. A popular jumping off point on the railway between New York and Chicago, the well-situated city had earned its nickname as "the best location in the nation." Then as now, Cleveland is symbiotically tethered to Lake Erie, its invaluable water mother and the conduit most responsible for bringing the world to its doorstep. The city's serpentine Cuyahoga River, though infamously polluted for decades, has survived and remains an integral resource for the city's hopeful present and future.

Cleveland is one of those great American cities that grew up during the industrial era personalized by self-made tycoons. Their smoke-belching industries turned buildings and respiratory systems black with soot and banks green with money. Success in steel, oil, and manufacturing translated into significant enviromental pollution, which triggered a mammoth struggle for this Great Lakes city to provide clean drinking water for its growing population. Though generally forgotten, well into the 20th century Clevelanders were sickened or died from outbreaks of typhoid fever, cholera, and other illnesses stemming from the same waters their city's very existence depended upon.

Long before effective pollution controls were in place, the city's water supply was fed from long intake pipes that were placed incrementally farther and farther away from its fetid Erie shoreline. They worked like big hypodermic needles sucking lake water of hideous quality back toward the thirsty masses onshore. To simply clean up and restrict the pollution had never entered into the prevailing wisdom of the day, much less threaten the conventions of those in power and control. Instead, the municipal visionaries ordered the construction of intake tunnels originating miles offshore and underneath the lake in order to channel relatively potable water toward the city's filtration plants.

The tunnel projects attracted waves of Irish, Italian, and Bohemian immigrants from places with names like Achill Island, Mezzogiorno, and Krakow. Among their ranks were experienced European tunnel men who had dug through the Alps, cut coal mines in Wales, or built the New York subways. Many of the workers were just fellas living far away from home and trying to feed their families any way they could. They were desperate to have any job no matter how dangerous it was. It's important to understand that there was no such thing as a "safety net" during the ruthless times in which these stories dwell. If you didn't work, you didn't eat.

Forever optimistic and expert on the rules of calamity, the tunnel workers (aka "sandhogs") had the right stuff. They were affable, willing to work for low wages, and their vulnerable circumstances were fully exploited by the potentates that controlled the city. In Cleveland for the long run, these immigrant groups settled into urban neighborhoods and ramshackle villages that grew up along the city's river underbelly. The ghettos they created were sharply divided along ethnic lines and known by names that sound romantic today. And yet, Big Italy, Dutch Hill, and Irishtown Bend were not the types of neighborhoods where you would bump into a Rockefeller. They were the dank, desperate enclaves of the blue-collar working poor who would eventually become the bedrock of Cleveland's future.

Water, water, every where,
Nor any drop to drink.

—Samuel Taylor Coleridge

CHAPTER 1: "THE MAN IN THE MOON"

BENJAMIN BELTRAN PREFERRED TO FLY IN HIS DREAMS...

IT WAS EASIER THAN WALKING AND THE VIEW WAS WONDERFUL...

BUT, NO WALKING MEANT NO SCUFFLING...
...AND NO SCUFFLING MEANT THAT HE WAS DREAMING...

HEY! WAKE UP MAN–

HEY! WAKE UP–TIME TO GO TO WORK! WAKE UP!

C'MON, CHIEF! IT'S SHOWTIME. GRAB YOUR HELMET AND GET YOURSELF READY–I'LL GO INTRODUCE YA!

THIS IS A STORY ABOUT ORDINARY MEN...

...WHO TUNNELED DEEP WITHIN THE EARTH AND STRUCK THE RAREFIED AIR OF HISTORY...

JULY, 1916—AT THE AMERICAN FIRE CHIEFS CONVENTION—ATLANTA, GEORGIA...
GENTLEMEN, GATHER 'ROUND AND ENJOY A COLD GLASS OF BEER!
TODAY YOU WILL WITNESS A DEMONSTRATION OF THE GREATEST FIREFIGHTING INVENTION OF THIS YOUNG CENTURY!
BELTRAN SAFETY CO. CLEVELAND, OHIO
LIVE DEMONSTRATION OF THE BELTRAN SMOKE HELMET
HERE IS A MAN— NOT JUST ANY MAN—BUT ONE WHO IS EXTRAORDINARY AND BRAVE! HE HAS MADE THE JOURNEY ALL THE WAY FROM HIS INDIAN RESERVATION ON THE GREAT LAKES! MEN, I GIVE YOU...
CHIEF HURON! OF THE SENECA INDIAN NATION!
AND HE'S WEARING MY LATEST INVENTION, THE BELTRAN SMOKE HELMET! IT'S AN INNOVATION THAT WILL REWRITE HISTORY!
THAT'S NO INJUN!

HE'S THE MAN IN THE MOON!

HA-HA HARDY-HAR HA-HA!

YES...YES...YOU MAY LAUGH AT OUR EXPENSE...

...BUT PROGRESS HAS MANY FACES AND AFTER WITNESSING THE WONDERS OF THIS GREAT INVENTION...

IT IS I, BENJAMIN BELTRAN, WHO WILL HAVE THE LAST LAUGH!
BELTRAN SAFETY CO. CLEVELAND,

...AND YOU WILL TELL YOUR MAYORS AND YOUR CITIZENRY HOW THE BELTRAN SMOKE HELMET WILL SAVE LIVES–MAYBE EVEN THEIR LIVES!
CHIEF HURON! LIGHT THE FIRES! LET'S SHOW THEM WHAT THIS AMAZING DEVICE CAN DO!!
THE BELTRAN
PLACE YOUR ORD

GENTLEMEN, I INVITE YOU TO SURROUND THE SMOKE TENT.

LOOK AT YOUR WATCHES AND MARK THE TIME. CHIEF HURON—PROCEED INTO THE DEMONSTRATION TENT!!

AND WHILE YOU COUNT THE MINUTES, I WILL RELAX AND READ MY MORNING PAPER...
3 DEAD CLEVELAND TUNNEL ACCIDENT
ALLIES STA IN ADVANC

20 MINUTES LATER...

GENTLEMEN, WE CAN ALL AGREE THAT NO ORDINARY MAN COULD SURVIVE IN SUCH THICK SMOKE FOR 20 MINUTES. I WILL NOW PROVE US ALL WRONG!!

OK, CHIEF! THE TIME IS UP!
KOF
KOF
CHOKE

BOYS, GET READY TO WITNESS SOMETHING THAT YOU'LL REMEMBER FOR THE REST OF YOUR LIVES!
CHIEF HURON, EXIT THE DEMONSTRATION TENT, IF YOU PLEASE!
CHIEF HURON- IS ALIVE AND WELL- THANKS TO THE BELTRAN SMOKE HELMET! THE FIREFIGHTERS' BEST FRIEND!!!
CLAP!
CLAP!
CLAP!
GASP!!
GASP!!
NOW...IF YOU WILL STEP INTO MY OFFICE-I WILL BEGIN ACCEPTING YOUR ORDERS FOR THIS LIFESAVING DEVICE!
SMOKE HELMET
ORDERS HERE!

HEY CHIEF!...(HIC!)... I KNOW YE! YER FROM CLEVELAND,OHIO...'TIS ME!...CAPT. CASEY! THE FIRE CHIEF UP THERE!
I'VE NEVER SEEN YOU BEFORE!

SURE YE HAVE! IT WAS AT THE ERIE FIRE CHIEFS' PICNIC AT ELKS FIELD! Y'WERE SHOWIN' OFF YER SMOKE HELMET.

EXCEPT YE DIDN'T HAVE THAT WHITE FELLA WIT Y'A AND YE T'WEREN'T MADE UP LIKE SOME FECKIN' RED SAVAGE!
...NOW, LOOK HERE, CAPTAIN. MOVE ALONG BEFORE YOU CAUSE ME TROUBLE.

YER HIMSELF, RIGHT? YER BEN BELTRAN, THE NEGRO INVENTOR FROM CLEVELAND?
THIS MAN IS DRUNK! I NEVER SAW HIM BEFORE IN MY LIFE!

Y'KNOW...YOU SURE DON'T SOUND LIKE SOME RED MAN...DON'T LOOK LIKE NO RED MAN T'EITHER!

HEY, CHARLIE!! I HEAR'D TELL THIS INDIAN IS THE REAL BELTRAN 'CEPTING HE AIN'T NO INDIAN, ARE YE, BOY?

YOU IDIOT! THESE WHITE MEN WON'T BUY MY HELMET NOW.

HOLD ON, BOYS—THIS MAN IS WELL-KNOWN IN OHIO. HE'S THE REAL INVENTOR O' THIS SMOKE HOOD THING!

THIS AIN'T OHIO, THIS HERE'S **GEORGIA!** AND YA SOUND IRISH! I S'POSE YO' ONE OF THEM KNEELIN' MICK **CATHOLICS...ZAT RIGHT?**
I TRULY AM, ME FINE YOUNG FELLOW...
...I WAS BAPTIZED **PATRICK JOSEPH CASEY** FROM COUNTY MAYO. WHAT OV' IT?

WE AIN'T GOT MUCH USE FOR CATHOLICS 'ROUND HERE! 'SPECIALLY SOME **PIG-FARMING MICK.**
AT LEAST I KNOWS **PIG SLOP** WHEN I SEES IT!

UH...CHIEF CASEY! WE'S A BIT OUTNUMBERED AND YOU AS **DRUNK** AS A GODDAM SKUNK!

YEA! I'M DRUNK ALRIGHT...AND **I'M IRISH,** TOO!

SOME OF US DO OUR **BEST** FIGHTIN' WHEN WE'RE **DRUNK.** IT'S KIND O' TRADITION, EH?

THWAP!!

...OOH I GAVE 'IM A **GOOD ONE,** EH, BELTRAN?
SHUT UP, YA GODDAM **FOOL!**

UGH!!

HEY!
WHAT THE...?
WHYYY
YOU!!
WHAP!
GET OFFA ME!
BAP
UHN!
OOF!!
BAP!
WHOA!
KRAK!
WOOSH!
JAYSUS!
FIVE MINUTES LATER...

THERE—THOSE MEN! T'WAS THAT NIGRA WHO CAUSED ALL THE TROUBLE!
YOU! C'MERE, BOY! YOU COMIN' WITH US!

A FEW HOURS LATER...
LOOKS LIKE YOU GETTING OUTA HERE, BOY! SOMEONE MADE YER BAIL!

IF I WAS YOU I'D PACK UP YOUR STUFF AND SKEDADDLE. A NIGRA DRESSED LIKE A REDSKIN! WHATCHA THINK THAT'LL GET YA?

MORE THAN WHAT A 'NIGRA' GETS!

LISTEN, BOY. NUTHIN' A NIGRA MAKES WILL EVER AMOUNT TO ANYTHIN' 'CEPT MAYBE TROUBLE! THAT'S WHY YOU IS OUTA HERE! MOVE IT!

3RD PRECINCT
POLICE
CHIEF CASEY! I 'SPOSE I SHOULD BE THANKIN' YOU FOR BAILIN' ME OUT?

WEREN'T ME, BEN, I'M BROKE. T'WAS HARRY HERE–HE CALLED YER COLORED PEOPLE CLUB UP IN CLEVELAND–THEY BAILED YE OUT, BOYO!

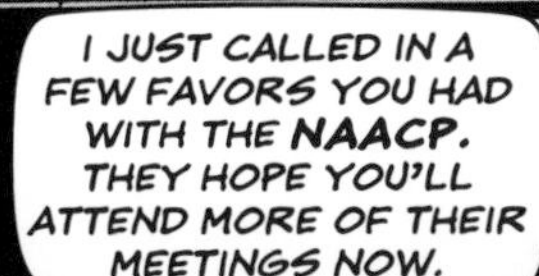
I JUST CALLED IN A FEW FAVORS YOU HAD WITH THE **NAACP.** THEY HOPE YOU'LL ATTEND MORE OF THEIR MEETINGS NOW.

LOOK...UH..., BELTRAN...I AM SORRY FOR WHAT I DONE TO YEZ. YE HAVE ME SOLEMN PROMISE TO MAKE THIS UP TO YE SOMEHOW. I'LL TALK TO **MAYOR SALMON** UP IN CLEVELAND! MEBBE THE CITY WILL **BUY** SOME O'YER HELMETS.

THAT'LL BE THE DAY! JUST HELP ME AND HARRY LOAD UP OUR INVENTORY ON THE TRAIN AND WE'LL BE ON OUR WAY!

THAT'S JUST IT, BEN–WE HAVEN'T GOT ANY INVENTORY–WHAT DIDN'T GO UP IN SMOKE WAS **TAKEN** BY ALL THOSE THIEVIN' FIRE CHIEFS!

...THE SMOKE HELMETS?
GONE WITH THE SUMMER BREEZES, BEN.

GODDAMN!...WELL, ONE WAY OR T'OTHER I **HOPE** THEY **DO** THE **BASTARDS** SOME **GOOD!**

SIGH!...ME AND ME BIG **IRISH** MOUTH...

CHAPTER 2:
"DIG 'TIL WE DROP"
TWO WEEKS LATER JULY 24, 1916 WATERWORKS CRIB #5 OFF THE COAST OF CLEVELAND, OHIO...

D'YA TINK THEY'LL LET US DIG TONITE, EAMONN?
NOW, HOW THE FECK DO I KNOW...?

YE KNOW, EAMONN, WHEN THE WATER IS STILL LIKE DIS–IT REMINDS ME OF THE 'SOUND.'
AN' WHAT 'SOUND' WOULD THAT BE?

ACHILL SOUND–BACK HOME. 'TIS ALWAYS STILL AND QUIET LIKE DIS.
I'D LIKE A NICKEL FER ALL YOU MAYO BOYS IN CLEVELAND! YER THICK AS THIEVES!
ACCH!! WHAT I WOULDN'T GIVE RIGHT NOW FOR THE HANDSHAKE OF A DONEGAL MAN!

THE MORNIN' CREW HIT A GAS POCKET...A REAL CORKER, SAYS THAT FELLA SWEENEY...
AHHH! CAN'T BE ANY WORSE THAN YOU AFTER A PLATE O' BEANS!

...HEH, HEH! WELL LAD, I S'POSE I BEEN KNOWN TA LIGHT A LAMP OR TWO IN ME TIME.
JAYSUS, MAN, YE COULD LIGHT UP A WHOLE VILLAGE!

WELL, WIT' THE WAY I'M FEELIN', 'TIS ALRIGHT IF WE STAY TOPSIDE TONITE!
YEA? ... AN WHYZ DAT?

I MEAN I'M DREADIN' SOMETIN'...LIKE DEATH IS 'BOUT TO POUR ME A FECKIN' PINT...
EAMONN!! ENUF O' THAT TALK - DO A SIGN O' DA CROSS!

HEH-HEH-GOD STOPPED LISTENIN' T'ME JOKES A LONG TIME AGO, LAD!

...SIGN O' DA CROSS ANYWAY MAN-IT WON'T KILL YA...!

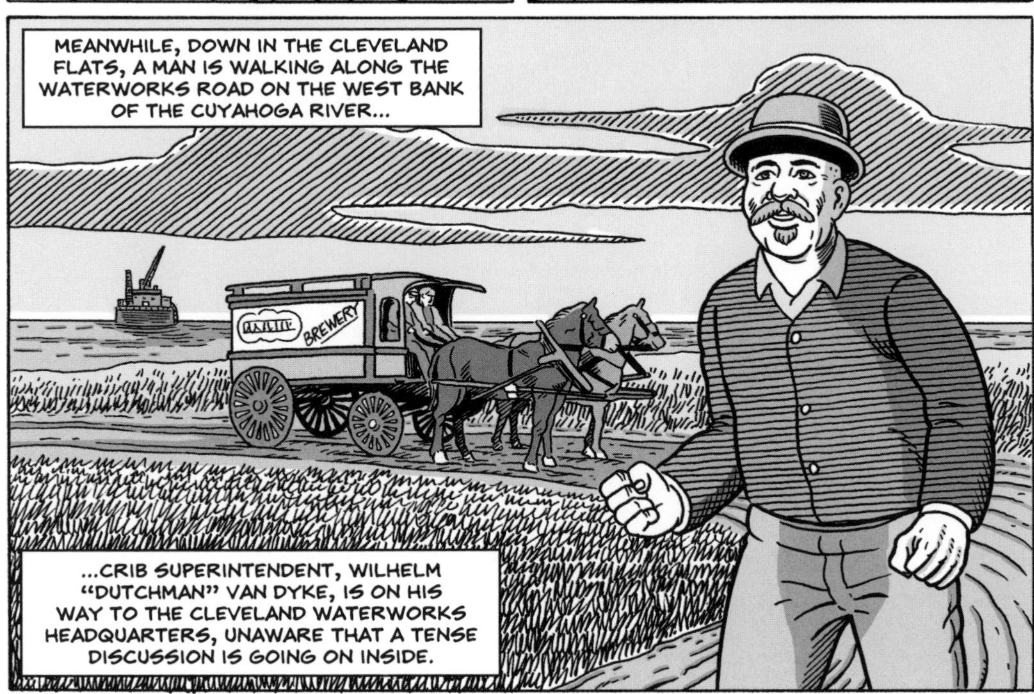
MEANWHILE, DOWN IN THE CLEVELAND FLATS, A MAN IS WALKING ALONG THE WATERWORKS ROAD ON THE WEST BANK OF THE CUYAHOGA RIVER...
BREWERY
...CRIB SUPERINTENDENT, WILHELM "DUTCHMAN" VAN DYKE, IS ON HIS WAY TO THE CLEVELAND WATERWORKS HEADQUARTERS, UNAWARE THAT A TENSE DISCUSSION IS GOING ON INSIDE.

THE OFFICE OF CHARLES B. NORTON—DIRECTOR OF THE CLEVELAND WATERWORKS...
TAKE IT EASY, MAYOR! ALL I SAID WAS WE NEED A DAY TO DETERMINE THE SIZE OF THE GAS DEPOSIT. I JUST NEED SOME TIME!
DEALER

...YOU DON'T HAVE MUCH LEEWAY HERE, NORTON. YOU CAN'T RUN FINGERS THROUGH YOUR OWN HAIR, **MUCH LESS RUN THE WATERWORKS!**
I COULD REPLACE YOU IN THE BLINK OF AN EYE...AND WELL I SHOULD!

THIS PROJECT IS BEHIND BECAUSE WE KEEP HITTING THESE DAMN GAS DEPOSITS. OUR GEOLOGISTS ARE **WORTHLESS!**

ACCH! IT'S ALWAYS A GEOLOGIST, A GAS POCKET, OR A DRUNKEN MICK! I DON'T GIVE A RAT'S ASS FOR YOUR EXCUSES! YOU GET THAT OPERATION MOVING OR IT'S YOUR TIT IN THE RINGER—**NOT MINE!**
MAYOR, DO YOU WANT A **REPEAT** OF WHAT HAPPENED TEN YEARS AGO? ARE WE THAT STUPID?
HMMPH! THE BOYS AT **MCCRACKEN STEEL** SAY GAS IN THE TUNNEL IS AS COMMON **AS BUGS IN A JUNGLE!**

THAT'S WHAT THIS IS ABOUT ISN'T IT? **MCCRACKEN'S GODDAM KID?**
SURE HE'S UPSET! I WOULD BE TOO, IF MY KID CAUGHT THE **TYPHOID** FROM PLAYING IN A SWIMMING POOL! I WANT MEN IN THAT TUNNEL—**TONITE! YA GET ME?!**
DEAL

YEAH—WELL YOU BETTER BELIEVE IT'S GONNA COST **YOU PLENTY!**

JUST GET IT DONE!- OR IT'S GOING TO COST YOU PLENTY!

SHIT! SO—HOW BAD IS IT, WILLY?
AHH!...A'NUDDER GODDAM MICK FIRE DRILL.

I SAY "GODDAM IRISH"! THEY RUN VEN THEY SHOULD VALK!
WHA?

LOOK DUTCH, WE GOTTA GET THIS TUNNEL BACK ON TRACK OR IT'S THE END OF BOTH OF US.
...THE END O' YOU MAYBE! HEH, HEH... NOT THE END OF VILLY!

WELL, CAN THEY START DIGGING AGAIN OR NOT?
I TAKE BUNCHA AIR SAMPLES AND SENT THEM TO LAB.

LAB TESTS TAKE DAYS! I NEED AN ANSWER NOW!
YAA—VELL, THERE'S SOME GAS IN TUNNEL, I'VE SEEN VORSE.

FORGET IT THEN- IF THERE'S GAS WE HOLD.
YAA?...AN' IF VE HOLD EVERYTIME VE SMELL GAS- TUNNELS NEVER GET DUG!

OK, THEN WHO WILL LEAD A CREW DOWN TONITE?
CLARKE!

AND IF HE REFUSES?
HE VON'T.

PRETTY SURE OF YERSELF, I'D SAY.
VITH THAT LEG O'HIS–HE'S IN NO POSITION TO ARGUE!

AND HE NEEDS THE MONEY–HIS VIFE VILL HAVE A BABY SOON.

D'YA THINK HE'S FORGOTTEN...HELL... HAVE YOU FORGOTTEN CRIB #3 ALREADY?

CRIB #3 VAS TEN YEARS AGO! VE LEARNED A LOT FROM DOT, AND NOBODY HAS DIED SINCE!
BULL-SHIT! WE HAVEN'T LEARNED ANYTHING! THIS WHOLE OPERATION IS AN ACCIDENT WAITING TO HAPPEN!

DO YOU REMEMBER HOW MANY MEN WE LOST ON THE #3 CRIB, WILLY?
NO, I PUT IT OUT OV MY MYNDT!

WELL, I REMEMBER–FIFTEEN MEN DEAD–MOST OF 'EM BURNED BEYOND RECOGNITION.

HMMM...? VAT IS DIS WRITINK ON THE NEWSPAPER??
WE HAVE TO PLAY THIS SMART, WILLY. WE HAVE TO DO THIS JUST RIGHT!

SO, LISTEN UP! OFFICIALLY, MY ORDER STANDS TO SUSPEND WORK UNTIL FURTHER NOTICE!
YAA? AND "UNOFFICIALLY"?

...UNOFFICIALLY...

UNOFFICIALLY, I HAVE A WIFE, A MISTRESS, AND FOUR DAUGHTERS! ...AND ALL SIX OF THEM THINK I'M A GIANT BILLFOLD.

MAYOR SALMON WANTS HIS TUNNEL DUG...

AND THAT'S WHAT I AIM TO DO!
VE STILL GET DER BONUS ALSO!

...(SIGH) SEVENTY MEN...

SEVENTY MEN, WILLY. THAT'S HOW MANY WE'VE LOST OVER THE YEARS -DIGGING IN PLACES THAT GOD DOESN'T CARE ABOUT.

DON'T CHANGE DER SUBJECT. DO VE GET DER BONUS OR NODT?

STOP THINKING ABOUT YOUR DAMN BONUS AND START WORRYING ABOUT KEEPING MEN ALIVE TONITE.

HMMPH! NO BONUS. AND IT'S YOU THAT VILL BE VORRIED.

WHAT YA SAY?
YOU HEARD ME!

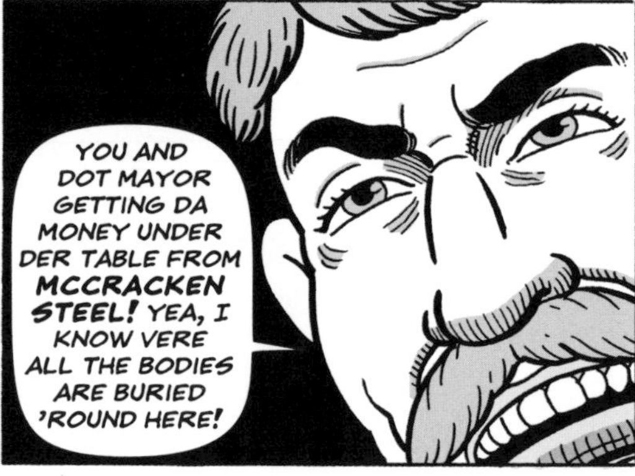
YOU AND DOT MAYOR GETTING DA MONEY UNDER DER TABLE FROM MCCRACKEN STEEL! YEA, I KNOW VERE ALL THE BODIES ARE BURIED 'ROUND HERE!

Y'KNOW WILLY—WHEN PEOPLE FLUSH THEIR TOILETS, IT ALL ENDS UP DOWN HERE!

YAA? SO VAT?!

SO, IT'S NO SURPRISE I'M STANDING NEXT TO A PIECE OF SHIT!
GET THE HELL OUTA HERE!

CHARLES NORTON WATERWORKS DIRECTOR
SLAM

MEN

BEFORE LEAVING, WILLY STOPPED IN THE MEN'S LAVATORY TO DO HIS "BUSINESS."

Norton
$1,000. Bonus
Money
DEALER
1916
R-R-R-I-I-I-P-P!!
GERMANS ADVANCE
HA! I STOLE YER NOTES, NORTON! EVERYTHING YOU AND MAYOR TALK ABOUT IN YOUR OWN HANDWRITINK!
YESSIR...DIS MIGHT COME IN HANDY SOMEDAY!
WITH MARCHING ORDERS IN HAND AND A BULGING MONEY BELT AROUND HIS WAIST, VAN DYKE HEADED DOWN THE ROAD THAT LED HIM TO THE PIERS OF WHISKEY ISLAND.
VE DIG ALRIGHT! BY GOD, VE DIG 'TIL VE DROP!

CHAPTER 3:
"GOBSHITE!"
Gaton's Saloon
CLEVELAND'S IRISHTOWN BEND DISTRICT ON THE CUYAHOGA RIVER ONE HOUR BEFORE VAN DYKE'S MEETING WITH NORTON.

...DA? DA? IT'S TIME TO WAKE UP, DA...

WAKE UP, DA—MA SAYS FOR ME TA WAKE YEZ.

DA?
GRRRRRR—
WHO WAKES ME?

'TIS ME, DA.
WHO? WHO IS IT? WHO WAKES ME? GRRRRR...

ME, DA! 'TIS ME! LILLIAN, YER DAUGHTER!
COME CLOSER CHILD—I CAN'T SEES YA.
CAN YE SEES ME NOW—DA?
...CLOSER, CHILD.

CAN YE SEES ME NOW? HEE-HEE!
...CLOOOSER!

...CLOOOSER!
CAN YE SEES ME?

I GOT YA!
AHHH! HELP ME, MA! HELP ME! DA IS TURNED TO A FEARSOME ANIMAL!!

HERE NOW! WHAT IS THE RUMPUS GOING ON IN HERE?!

'TIS DA... HE'S TURNED TO A HUNGRY BEAR!
HE IS A WILD CREATURE... IT'S TRUE.

I LIKE TA SAY, "FEARSOME"! F-E A-R-S-O...
AYE-AND THERE'S A FEW "FEARSOME" CHORES WAITIN' FER YA.

AWWW, GEEZ!
LET HER SIT AWHILE. I LIKE HER BY ME SIDE KICKIN' THOSE PLUMP LITTLE LEGS.

PLUMP?!

THAT IS TO SAY THAT YER GOT TWO HEALTHY LEGS. SOMETHIN' I WISH I HAD.

ALRIGHT, LITTLE ONE. GO TEND TO YER BUSINESS WHILE I HELP YER DA GET READY FOR WORK.
AWWW, GEEZ..!

ON WIT YA NOW, YOUNG MISS!

OH DEAR...IT'S LATE. GET YERSELF UP- I'LL BANDAGE AND SPLINT YER LEG
AYE.

RODGER CLARKE, SHIFT FOREMAN ON CRIB #5, GAZED DOWN THE RIVER ROAD AND PONDERED HIS UNCERTAIN FUTURE.

...BUT ALL HE COULD SEE WERE SPECTERS FROM HIS PAST.
...GALLAGHER!!
OH... OH GOD!
OPEN UP! OPEN UP, DAMN YE!

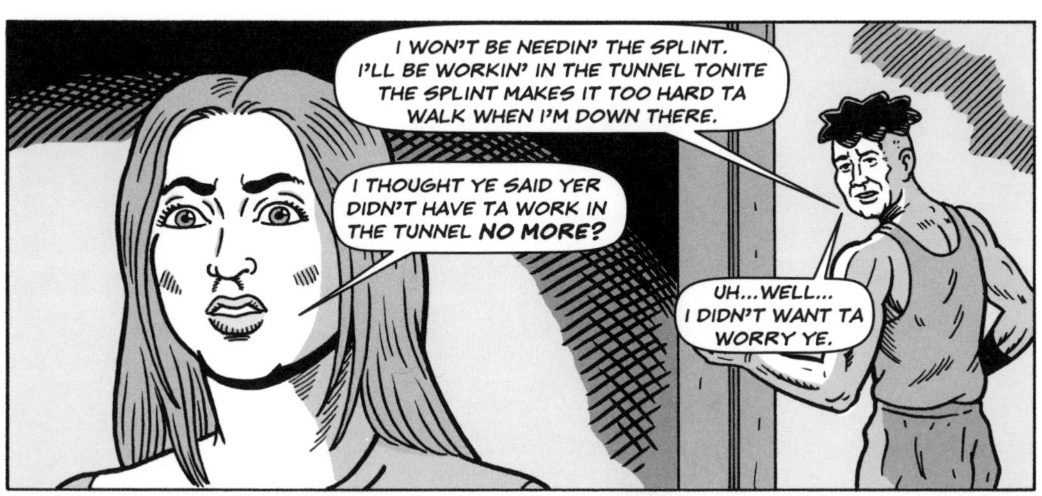
I THOUGHT YE SAID YER DIDN'T HAVE TA WORK IN THE TUNNEL NO MORE?
I WON'T BE NEEDIN' THE SPLINT. I'LL BE WORKIN' IN THE TUNNEL TONITE THE SPLINT MAKES IT TOO HARD TA WALK WHEN I'M DOWN THERE.
UH...WELL... I DIDN'T WANT TA WORRY YE.

YE SHOULDN'T LIE ABOUT IT. IT HURTS ME WHEN YE DO.
AHH...NOT TA WORRY...WE'RE BEHIND SCHEDULE AND DUTCH NEEDS ME TO KEEP A CLOSE EYE ON THE MEN– IT'S THE EASIEST JOB ON THE CRIB!
AHH, I MIGHTA KNOWN IT WAS THAT CREATURE.
THERE'S NOTHIN' I CAN SAY...HE'S THE BOSS.

HE'S A GOBSHITE! HE COMES FROM THE LOWER REGIONS...
WELL, THAT MAY BE SO, BUT HE'S MY GOBSHITE. I WOULDN'T BE HERE IF IT WEREN'T FOR HIM.

AYE...AND HE'LL NEVER LET YE FORGET IT WILL HE? TELL ME...WHAT'S IN IT FER YA?

WELL... THERE IS TALK OF MONEY, YES.
THERE'S ALWAYS TALK...THE CRIB IS FULL OF TALK...FER THE LOVE O' PETE, YER LEG ISN'T FIT FER TUNNEL WORK!...
I DON'T LIKE IT WHEN YOU ARE MAD–BOTH OF YOU!

(SIGH)...GALLAGHER...! AH, HOW I WISH YE WAS HERE, BOYO.

POUND!
POUND!
POUND!

NOW WHO'S THA' POUNDIN' ON OUR DOOR?

STAY HERE-I'LL SEE WHO IT IS
PROBABLY THAT TOAD... SWEENEY!

POUND!
POUND!
POUND!
TAKE 'ER EASY-TAKE 'ER EASY!

...HMMPH...SWEENEY. WHAT'S THE WORD?
I DELIVER YEZ THIS MESSAGE-IT'S FROM THE DUTCHMAN. HIS BLOOD IS UP.

WAZZUP?
THE CRIB'S BEEN DOWN SINCE MORN' WIT GAS IN DA TUNNEL. THE MAYOR Z'ABOUT SHITTIN' A BRICK, AND IT'S UP TO DUTCH TO GET IT GOIN'.

AH...UP TA ME IS MORE LIKELY THE CASE.

tonite - Wet Rags

THE MAYOR'S BEEN PUTTING THE SCREWS ON NORTON TA GET DIGGIN' EVER SINCE THAT MCCRACKEN KID CAUGHT THE TYPHOID!
YEA?
ACHH! WE LOSE A KID DOWN HERE EVERY OTHER DAY! YA DON'T SEE NOBODY GIVIN' A HOLY GODDAM ABOUT WORKIN' PEOPLE'S KIDS...AM I RIGHT?

WHAT? WHAT YER SAY?
I SAID THE LITTLE BRAT PROBABLY HAD IT COMIN'!
YEA—YEA, SURE, SWEENEY. I'M SURE HE DID. WE'LL SEE YA.

I GOTTA HIDE 'DIS MONEY QUICK!
WHO WAS IT, RODGER?

UHH...JUST SWEENEY.

A FEW MOMENTS LATER...
...WHAT DID SWEENEY WANT?
IT SEEMS THE ELEVEN-YEAR-OLD SON OF JOHN MCCRACKEN GOT SICK ON CITY WATER.

THE MCCRACKEN? MCCRACKEN STEEL?
AYE—HE CAUGHT THE **TYPHOID** PLAYIN' IN A SWIMMIN' POOL, OF ALL THINGS.

IS THE SPOILED LITTLE THING **DEAD,** THEN?
NAWW! JUST PLAYED OUT...AND TURNING HIS BEDSHEETS BROWN, I'M SURE.

SO, I S'POSE MCCRACKEN IS PUTTIN' PRESSURE ON THE MAYOR TO GET THE TUNNEL DONE.
I DON'T LIKE THE SOUND O' THIS.

IT MEANS **EXTRA DOUGH** FER ALL OF US, AN' WE DESERVE IT! ...I'LL KNOW MORE WHEN I SEES THE SIZE OF WILLY'S **MONEY BELT...** WHEN THE DIGGIN' STOPS THAT BUMP ON HIS BELLY GROWS LIKE A **SUMMER SQUASH!**
YE MEAN MEN WORK WHEN THE TUNNELIN' ISN'T SAFE? RODGER, **YER SCARIN' ME!**

SHHH!...DON'T YA WORRY. IT'S EASY MONEY. HE SLOWS DOWN THE DIGGIN' SO HE CAN WORRY MORE DOUGH OUTA THE BOSSES.
HE'S A OPERATOR, THAT EVIL EEDJIT.

AHH...YOU WATCH. WE'LL PROBABLY BE PAID FER PLAYIN' CARDS ALL NIGHT!!
WHAT ELSE DOES HE KEEP IN THE MONEY BELT B'SIDES MONEY?

HE SQUARRELS AWAY EVERYTHING IMAGINABLE–I THINK HE EVEN KEEPS HIS FALSE TEETH IN IT.
HEE HEE!
AHH! NOW THERE'S YER BEAUTIFUL SMILE GOIN' THERE.

AYE–I'M A LUCKY MAN TA HAVE TWO BEAUTIFUL WOMEN TA LOOK AFTER ME!

I NEED A CUP O' SOMETHIN' BEFORE I GO. HOW 'BOUT SOME TEA?

TEA IT IS! YOUNG LIL AND I WILL SET SOME WATER TA BOIL!

IT'S TOO HOT TO BE BOILIN' WATER!
THE WATER ALWAYS GET BOILED, SO'S WE DON'T CATCH THE TYPHOID!
MA, LET'S GET A SWIMMIN' POOL!
DO YE EVEN KNOW WHAT A SWIMMIN' POOL IS?
I DON'T... BUT IT SOUNDS WONDERFUL!
NOT SO WONDERFUL FOR THE LITTLE MCCRACKEN BOY, I FEAR.
SWEET GIRL—YE NEVER ASKS US FOR ANYTHIN'. IT'S SUCH A CONTENTED, GOOD HEARTED NATURE YE HAVE!
TELL YE WHAT. AFTER THE NEW TUNNEL BRINGS US THE CLEAN WATER, WE'LL SET TO BUILDING YE A SWIMMIN' POOL.
REALLY?!
AH, SURE WE COULD! ALL'S IT TAKES IS A FEW STICKS O' WOOD AND SOME OIL CLOTH!
DA! DA! MA SAYS WE CAN MAKE A SWIMMIN' POOL!!
JUST THEN, A SIGHT THROUGH THE WINDOW TRIGGERED MARY'S FEARFUL INTUITION...

...SHE SAW TWO CRIB WORKERS WALKING DOWN RIVER ROAD...

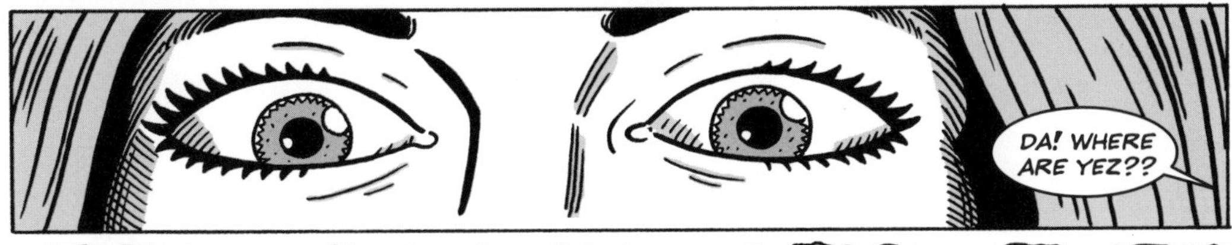
DA! WHERE ARE YEZ??

...WHEN SUDDENLY A PREMONITION TRANSFORMED THEM INTO...

...THE WALKING DEAD!

MA! DA FELL DOWN ON THE FLOOR!

JAYSUS, MARY, AND JOSEPH! I DIDN'T HEAR YA FALL!

I DIDN'T FALL! THE LEG BEGAN TO GIVE OUT SO I SAT DOWN AND MADE IT TA THE BED.

WHY NOR YE CALL ME!??

HEY, SPRITE. RUN AND FETCH MY SPLINT LIKE A GOOD LASS.

BECAUSE I DON'T WANT OUR DAUGHTER TA SEE ME CRAWLIN' ON ALL FOURS.

RODGER...WHAT ARE WE GONNA DO?
I'M GOING TO PUT ON THIS SPLINT AND GET TO THE DOCK.

THEY'LL FIRE ME Y'KNOW—I CAN'T MISS ANY MORE TIME.

YOU WORK FOR MORDERERS. MORDERERS AND DUTCH DIVILS.

WELLL...YE KNOW WHAT THEY SAY, LOVE: "THE IRISH AND THE DUTCH, THEY DON'T AMOUNT TA MUCH!"
HEE-HEE! IRISH AND DUTCH JUST WON'T AMOUNT TA MUCH!

A CUP O' TEA LATER...
YE BE A GOOD GIRL AND HELP YER MA NOW. I DEPEND ON YA, LASSIE.
I WILL.

MARY, DONCHA' WORRY 'BOUT ME. YER BEAUTIFUL EYES ARE LIKE A CANDLE IN THE WINDOW. THEY'LL GUIDE ME BACK TO YEZ.
WHA...? MY POET WARRIOR IS AWAKE.

FAREWELL, ME LACE CURTAIN IRISH PRINCESSES– I'LL SEE YEZ IN A COUPLE DAYS.
YOU JUST BRING YERSELF HOME– SAFE AND SOUND, MR. SMOOTH TALKER!
I LOVE YOU, DA!
TOOOOOOOOOOT!

SHITE! I LEFT THE MONEY IN HER KNITTIN' BAG!

WHAT IF SHE FINDS IT?
A-OO-GA!

AHHH! WHO'D BE KNITTIN' ANYWAY–IN THIS TARRIBLE HEAT WAVE?!

CHAPTER 4: "IT'S A MIRACLE!"

WHISKEY ISLAND AT THE MOUTH OF THE CUYAHOGA RIVER, 7:30 PM...

YEA, I SEEN HIM...BUT, I HAVEN'T SEEN ENOUGH **MONEY** YET.
I GIFF YOU $100 ALREADY–'NUTHER $50 COMINK AFTER I SEE SOME TUNNELIN' DONE TONITE!
HA!

MEBBE YOU SHOULD BE LUCKY YOU CAN VORK AT ALL!!

YEAH, MEBBE I SHOULD–I SHOULD BE LUCKY, BUT I'M NOT, WILLY!

I'LL TAKE SOME MORE OF THEM **DOLLARS** NOW!

I HADN'T GOT DOT MUCH VITH ME...
THAT'S SHITE! WITH THE WAY YER MILKING THAT MONEY BELT–YUD THINK IT WAS THE **VILLAGE TIT!**

AHH...YES
YOU ARE CARRYING
SOMETHIN' EXTRA
TONITE AREN'T YA,
BOYO?!
ARGHH!
GET 'CHER
HANDS UFF
OV ME!

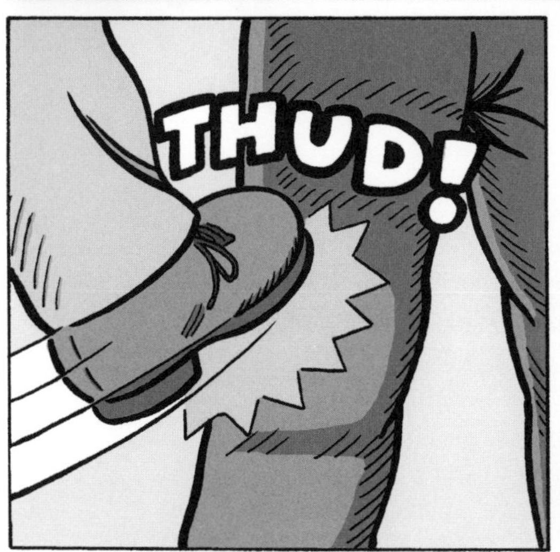
THUD!

UNH!!

YOU'LL
TAKE $50,
"BOYO"!

BUT NOT
A PENNY
MORE UNTIL
I SEE SOME
DIGGING...!

A FEW MOMENTS LATER.
I DON'T CARE WHAT YE HAVE ON ME–DO THAT AGAIN AN' I'LL BOX YER EARS IN FOR YE!
HA! YOU ARE HAFF THE MAN I AM. ARE YOU LOSING YOUR NERVE, CLARKE?

NO! BUT ONCE I PAY OFF THE MEN, THERE WON'T BE ENOUGH LEFT TA MAKE ME GO INTA THAT HOLE!
AHH! YOU HEFF VORKED IN DOT TUNNEL FOR A LOT LESS!

I'M NOT RISKIN' ME LIFE AN' THE LIFE O' THE CREW FER PEANUTS! THAT TUNNEL IS FULL O' GAS!
THERE'S ALVAYS GAS IN THE TUNNEL! PUT A VET RAG 'ROUND YER FACE UND KEEP DIGGING!

THE #3 CRIB ALREADY LEFT YER MIND? EH?
TEN YEARS AGO IT VAS! I DON'T CARRY DOT CROSS. I SAY LET THE DEAD...LET THEM ALL REST IN PEACE!

...YEAH, THEY REST WILLY, THEY REST... BENEATH BLANKETS OF CLAY...

TELL ME, WILLY... HOW D'YA DO IT? HOW D'YA **FORGET** CRIB #3?

I WANT YE TO TEACH **ME**...

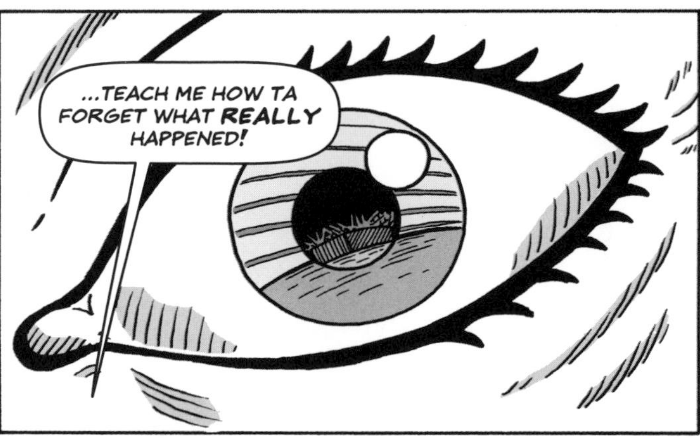
...TEACH ME HOW TA FORGET WHAT **REALLY** HAPPENED!

RETURNING TO A TIME TEN YEARS EARLIER WHEN CLARKE AND A TEAM OF SANDHOGS BEGAN THEIR FATEFUL SHIFT ON THE CRIB #3...
MR. GALLAGHER! WHO CARRIES THE BIRDS?

RINI CARRIES 'EM. HE AND LAVELLE WILL GO ON AHEAD.

WHAT IF... UH, THE GAS GETS 'EM?
YER A GREAT ONE FER THE "WHAT IFS," LADDIE.

THERE ARE NO "WHAT IFS" IN THE TUNNEL TRADES... CERTAINLY **NOT THIS TUNNEL!**

AWWW-**SHITE!** LOOKS LIKE WE GOT **THE DUTCHMAN** ON THE AIRLOCK TODAY, LADS.
THE MAN'S A **GOBSHITE!** TRUST HIM LIKE A 10-CENT WATCH!

THE TUNNEL AIRLOCK...

THE TUNNELS WERE PRESSURIZED AND AIR REFRESHED BY A STEAM ENGINE COMPRESSOR LOCATED ON THE CRIB'S TOP DECK. TOO MUCH PRESSURE MEANT THE BENDS ONCE YOU ASCENDED UP THE MAIN SHAFT. TOO LITTLE OR LOSS OF PRESSURE COULD CAUSE THE TUNNEL TO COLLAPSE OR FILL WITH METHANE GAS AND WATER.

DON'T TELL ME IT'S YOU ON AIRLOCK DUTY?!
VAT UFF IT?

NUTHIN'... IT'S JES' I TRUST A RAT MORE THAN A SKUNK TO BE WATCHIN' ME BACK!
AWW...GO AVAY BEFORE I THUMP YOU!

THUMP AWAY, TRY IT!
EASY NOW! HE'S NOT WORTH LOSIN' A JOB OVER!

RINI! LAVELLE! GRAB UP DEM BIRDS AND GET READY TO ENTER THE TUNNEL!

YOU! GO 'BOUT 'CHER BUSINESS!
SETTLIN' SCORES WITH DOGFISH LIKE YERSELF IS TURNIN' INTA A BUSINESS 'ROUND HERE!

WE'LL STAY IN THE COMPARTMENT UNTIL WE GET THE SIGNAL FROM RINI AND LAVELLE.
PUT THIS 'ROUND YER NECK.

YE KNOW WHAT TO DO. LAVELLE, YE LET RINI GO FIFTY PACES IN FRONT O' YA. RINI, KEEP YER EYE ON DEM BIRDS.

WHEN YE KNOW IT'S SAFE, GIVE THREE SHORT BURSTS ON THE WHISTLE.

...BUT IF A BIRD DROPS OR IF RINI DROPS–PUT THE WHISTLE IN YER MOUTH...

...AN' BLOW IT LIKE YEZ ON FIRE–CUZ AT ANY SECOND–YA WILL BE!

REQUEST PERMISSION TO GO AHEAD OF RINI!
NO–NO, MIND ME ORDERS, PATRICK. BESIDES, IS YE THAT GOT THE BETTER LUNGS AND RINI IS THE BEST SKEDADDLER!

WOULD YE SAY IT'S TRUE RINI? YE CAN RUN LIKE THE WIND–CAN'T YE?
AWWW! STUPIDO MICKS!!
GOOD MAN.
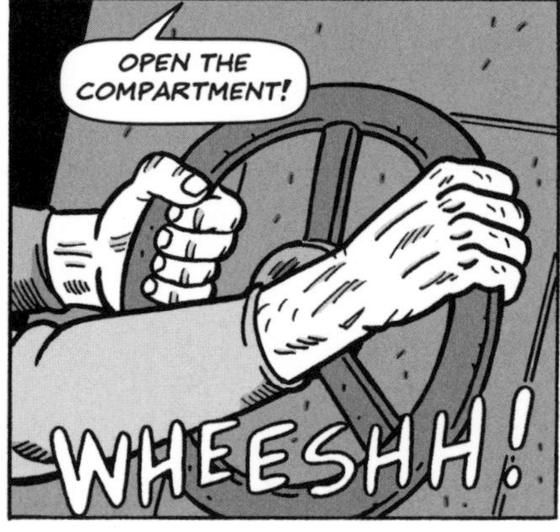
OPEN THE COMPARTMENT!
WHEESHH!

REMEMBER! IF ALL'S CLEAR, GIMME THREE BURSTS OF THE WHISTLE, AND WE'LL VENTURE IN BEHIND YEZ.

PRESSURE IS EQUALIZED! I'M OPENING THE HATCH!
SHOOSH!

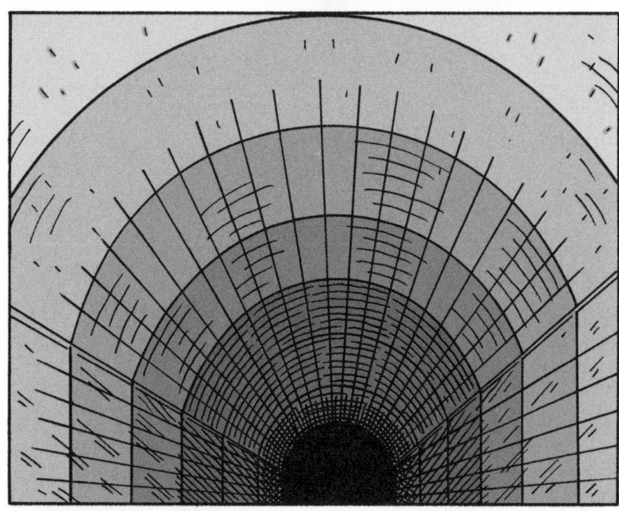

ENTERING THE TUNNEL, MR. GALLAGHER!

WE'LL WAIT FOR YOUR SIGNAL.

AT THE SAME TIME ON THE PLATFORM ABOVE, CARELESSNESS HAD CAUSED THE ALL-WOODEN CRIB STRUCTURE TO CATCH FIRE WITH DOZENS OF MEN INSIDE.

CRIB#3

WHAT'S BURNIN'??!!

JAYSUS CHRIST, **KAMINSKI!!**– WAKE UP, MAN!!– YER BOILER HAS SET US **AFIRE!!**

LORD AND SAVIOR!!

BLEET!
BLEET!
BLEET!

YEP! THERE'S LAVELLE'S SIGNAL! TIME TA GO TA WORK!

SOMETHIN' BOTHERIN' YE, MR. GALLAGHER?
IT'S THAT DUTCHMAN! I DON'T TRUST HIM, I TELL YA. NOT FER A SECOND!

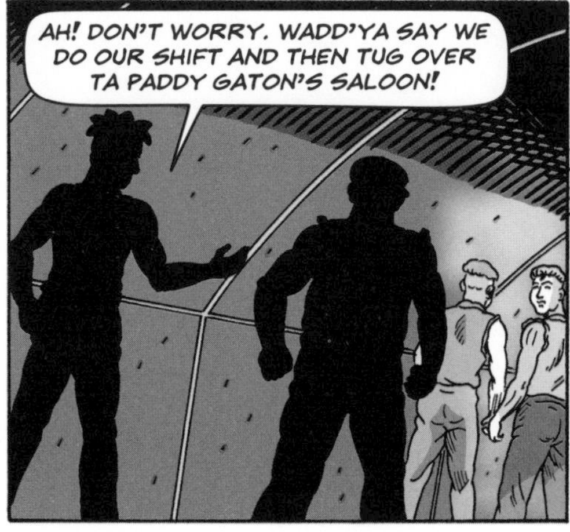
AH! DON'T WORRY. WADD'YA SAY WE DO OUR SHIFT AND THEN TUG OVER TA PADDY GATON'S SALOON!

EH? YE MAY HAVE SOMETHIN' THERE!

BACK AT THE AIR LOCK...
HMMPFF! BIG MAN!!

THE MAN IN CHARGE OF THE AIR LOCK HAD A BORING BUT IMPORTANT JOB. WHEN WORKMEN ENTERED AND LEFT THE DIG SITE, THEY STEPPED INTO A CHAMBER WHERE THE HIGH AIR PRESSURE INSIDE THE TUNNEL WAS EQUALIZED. A REVERSAL OF THIS PROCESS ALLOWED THE MEN TO SAFELY EXIT THE TUNNEL AND RETURN TO THE CRIB.

WHILE MEN WERE DIGGING, THE AIR LOCK OPERATOR HAD TO STAND DUTY UNTIL RELIEVED OR UNTIL THE LAST MAN WAS OUT. GALLAGHER HAD KNOWN THE DUTCHMAN WELL FROM PAST TUNNEL PROJECTS AND HAD REASON TO WORRY ABOUT HIM.

Z-Z-Z-Z-Z SNORE... Z-Z-Z-Z
TROUBLE SEEMED TO FOLLOW VAN DYKE ON EVERY PROJECT HE WORKED. GALLAGHER CALLED HIM A "JONAH INSIDE THE TUNNEL WHALE." HE DIDN'T TRUST HIM ANY FURTHER THAN HE COULD SKIP HIM LIKE A STONE ACROSS LAKE ERIE.

REMEMBER, MEN: SAFETY FIRST!
ZZZZZZZ

HERE WE ARE, BOYOS! AND...THE WORK, SHE BE WAITIN' FOR US!
MR. GALLAGHER ...OVER HERE!

MEANWHILE—SMOKE FROM THE FIRE ABOVE HAD REACHED THE AIRLOCK...

THERE WAS ONLY ONE WAY TO COMMUNICATE IN THE TUNNEL AND THAT WAS BY MESSENGER. WHEN WILLY FIGURED OUT THE CRIB PLATFORM WAS ON FIRE, HE HAD TO MAKE A CHOICE...

...HE COULD EITHER RUN DOWN THE TUNNEL TO WARN THE MEN AND RISK GETTING TRAPPED WITH THEM, OR HE COULD ABANDON HIS POST AND GET OUT BEFORE IT WAS TOO LATE!

IN THE END WILLY DID WHAT WAS BEST FOR WILLY, JUST AS GALLAGHER HAD FEARED.
AAGG! COUGH! COUGH!!

I GO UP AND HELP PUT OUDT DER FIRE...

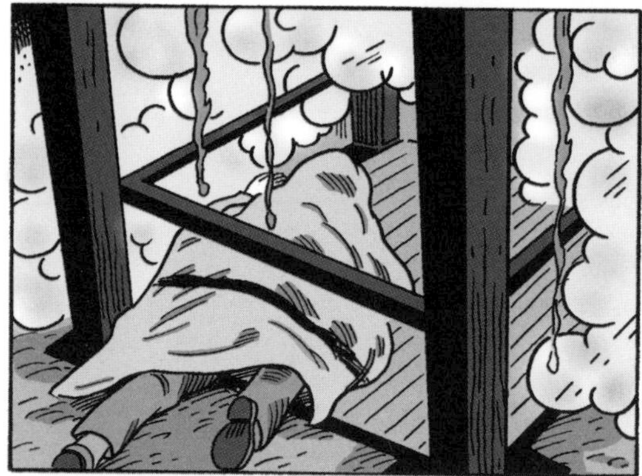

...THEY SAFER INNA TUNNEL... DER TUNNEL IST SAFEST PLACE!
UP

MA-MAAAAAAAAAA!!!

ALMOS' THERE, SUZETTE! 'NUTHER 100 PACES, THAS' ALL.

HOWZ' A CARROT FER YER TROUBLES, SUZETTE? YE WAIT HERE WHILE I WAKE UP THE DURTY DUTCHMAN!

WHAT?... WHAT THE?!...

OH, NO!...FIRE!! DEAR GOD...FIRE! FIRE!

WE HAVE TA TURN YER HARNESS 'ROUND FAST, SUZETTE! WE MUST WARN THE BOYS!!

MOVE IT, SUZETTE!! HE'YAHH!!

TWEET!
TWEEET!

TWEEE! TWEEET!

AHHHHHHHHHH!

VAN DYKE'S COWARDICE HAD SAVED HIM FROM A CRUEL **DEATH DOWN UNDER**. BUT WITHIN MOMENTS, HIS EYES WERE MET WITH THE HORROR OF FIERY CARNAGE ENGULFING THE ENTIRE CRIB!

KRR-R-ACCK!

GOEDE HEMEL!!!

EEEEEEK!!!

HEPP!!!!!!HEPPPP ME!!!!!!!
AAAAGGGGGGG!!!!!!!

WILLY CRASHED HIS BODY THROUGH THE FLAMING WALLS OF THE CRIB, TURNING HIS TREACHEROUS DESERTION INTO A **"FAIT ACCOMPLI."**
I MADE IT! I'M OUDT!!

THAT AIR COMPRESSOR IS GONNA **BLOW ANY SECOND!!!**
WATTA 'BOUT DA MEN IN DA TUNNEL!?

DOOMED... THEY'RE ALL DOOMED.

MEANWHILE, DOWN IN THE TUNNEL, THE SANDHOGS NOTICED A SUDDEN CHANGE IN AIR PRESSURE...
OOF! JAYSUS!
ACH! ME EARS JUST POPPED!
AHH! ME TOO!

IT'S OK, BOYS. THEY'RE PROB'LY TINKERIN' WITH THE COMPRESSOR AGAIN! MR. CLARKE! FRONT AND CENTER PLEASE!

TWEEET!! TWEEET!!
GET DOWN TO THE AIRLOCK. THERE MIGHT BE TROUBLE BREWIN'
I HEAR SOMETHIN'! WHOSE WHISTLE IS THAT?

WHAT THE FECK AM I LOOKIN' AT?
IT'S LAVELLE!.. BUT—WHAT THE..?

TWEEET!!
TWEEET!!

JAYSUS, MAN!! WHAT IS IT—WHAT HAS HAPPENED??

FFFFFFF–FI... FFFFFFFF–FI!!

GATHER YERSELF, MAN!! SPIT IT OUT!

FFF—
FIRE!!!!!!!!
FIRE AT THE
AIRLOCK!!!

FIRE?
FIRE?!
WADD'YA
MEAN FIRE?!

HOLD ON BOYS—THIS IS
NO TIME TO PANIC!

...AND WHAT O'
THE DUTCHMAN?
NO...NO
SIGN O' HIM
NOWHERE.

BASTARD! HE
DESERTED US!

LISTEN,
SON—TELL ME
EXACTLY WHAT
YE SEE'D.
THE SHAFT
IS THICK WITH
SMOKE!! BUT
NONE IN THE
TUNNEL SO
FAR.

RINI! YOU
GET BACK
HERE!! DON'T
BE A FOOL!

MAMA!!
STOP MEN!! WE MUST STICK TOGETHER!!!
ANNABETH!!
MY BABIES!!
JANIE, MY LOVE!!

LISTEN, LAD– NO MATTER WHAT– YE STICK WIT' ME AND WE'LL GET OUT SOMEHOW.
I'M WIT YA–I'M WIT YA!
OH MY GOD– THE TUNNEL IS FLOODING!!

THE WATER IS SEEPIN' IN BECAUSE THE COMPRESSOR STOPPED.
WON'T BE LONG 'TIL SOMETHIN' ELSE STARTS SEEPIN' IN!

AYE–THE GAS!

HUH? GA–GAS??

STICK WIT' US, BOY! LAVELLE! C'MON BACK!!!
DEAR GOD SAVE ME!!!
LET 'IM GO. LET 'IM GO. B'FORE LONG WE MAY ENVY THE DEAD!
WE CAN'T STAY HERE MUCH LONGER. THE WATER IS FLOWIN' IN!
THERE'S HIGHER GROUND IN THE SERVICE TUNNEL. C'MON, HELP ME WIT' THE STIFF ONE. WE GOTTA MOVE FAST!
ECCH!
AYE, SHE'S GETTIN' A BIT RIPE FER SURE!
NO- NOT THAT! CAN YE TASTE SOMETHIN'?
ACCH! EWW-YEA-I DO NOW!
'TIS THE GAS ISN'T IT?
PTOOO!
'TISN'T LADIES' PERFUME, BOYO!

WHA...WHAT ERE' WE GONNA DO?
CLARKE, ME BOY, ...I T'INK WE WILL GO O' STROLLIN'
... STROLLIN' THRU THE GLOAMIN'...
I RECKON THE MEN REACHED THE AIRLOCK BY NOW...
ONCE THEY PRY IT OPEN AND THE REMAINING PRESSURE IS RELEASED-WE'LL HAVE FIRE AND SMOKE FROM ONE END OF THIS WORM HOLE TO THE OTHER!
AH YEA! THIS'LL HAVE TO DO. HELP ME WITH THESE CARTS, BOYO!
WHAT HAPPENS IF THE FIRE TOUCHES ON THE GAS?

AYE, YES. WELL THAT IS THE RUB, IS IT NOT?
'TIS TOO HARD TO IMAGINE AND TOO HORRIBLE TA TINK.
SQUEEZE IN BEHIND THE LEFT CART AND I'LL GO BEHIND THE RIGHT.
WHAT?
MIND WHAT I SAY. INSIDE! TIGHT AS A TICK, BOYO.
ECCH! THE GAS IS GETTIN' WORSE!
AYE! COULD BE WORSE. WE COULD BE STUCK AT THE AIRLOCK WIT' THE REST!

BACK AT THE AIR LOCK
WE GOT IT! IT'S OPEN!
WOOOSSSHH!
LISTEN TO ME! WE CAN'T DECOMPRESS THIS FAST!
EVERY MAN FOR HIMSELF! COMIN' THROUGH!
C'MON BOYS, WE GOTTA...WE... WE...AUGHHH!.
UUGHH! ME ARMS!
UGH! CAN'T HARDLY BREATHE!
I TOLD YA NOT TO DECOMPRESS THIS FAST! WE'RE GETTIN' THE BENDS!
ARRGHH!

THE FORCED OPENING OF THE AIR LOCK DOOR CAUSED A RUSH OF PRESSURIZED AIR TO ESCAPE RAPIDLY FROM THE TUNNEL, WHICH FED THE HUNGRY FLAMES ABOVE!
LOOK AT THE CRIB!! LOOK AT THE FIRE!!!
...SANDHOGS IN THE TUNNEL! THEY AIN'T GOTTA CHANCE NOW!
LET'S PRAY FOR THE SOULS OF THE DEPARTED...
BACK AT THE AIRLOCK...
OH GOD! THE GAS! STOP THE GAS...!
METHANE GAS AND OXYGEN SIPHONED OUT OF THE TUNNEL AND RUSHED UP THE SHAFT TO THE FLAME-ENVELOPED CRIB. THE FATAL MIXTURE RESULTED IN A CATACLYSMIC EVENT.
KA-BLAM!
WHIRLWINDS OF FLAME FINISHED OFF THE CRIB AND THEN BID A HASTY RETREAT BACK DOWN TO THE TUNNEL BELOW!

THE SANDHOGS TRAPPED IN THE AIRLOCK NEVER HAD A CHANCE.
OH...! PEL L'AMORE DI SAN PIETRO!
A SHORT TIME LATER...
I DON'T TASTE THE GAS ANYMORE!
LIGHT THE DAVY!
IS THE DONKEY STILL BREATHIN'?
YAA- A TROOPER SHE IS!
AYE, 'TIS A COUNTRY CHOCK FULL O' REMARKABLE ASSES.
D'ZAT INCLUDE ME AN' YOU, MR. GALLAGHER?
IT DOES.

AGG! THE GAS IS BACK.
COUGH! WE GOTTA FIND LOW GROUND! COUGH! AN' GET BELOW THE GAS LAYER.
GIMME THE DAVY—I'LL GO SEE HOW BAD THE FLOODIN' IS BEHIND US.
COUGH! WHAT D'YER SEE?!
I HOPE YER A SWIMMER, MR. CLARKE—WE GOT CHEST-DEEP WATER AHEAD!
BAM!
WHAT?!
OH NO!... GAS EXPLOSION!!
WHOA! STEADY GIRL!

NO!!
DEAR GOD-NO!!!
CLARKE!!
AUGHHH!!!!!
I'M ON ME WAY!
STOP HER! SHE'LL DROWN!
PUT YOUR ARMS AROUND ME NECK— THA'S A GOOD LAD!

BACK INTO STEERAGE CLASS WE GO, **BOYO!**

AS THE CRIB BURNED AWAY, TUGBOATS TRANSPORTED ALL KNOWN SURVIVORS TO THE DOCKS ON WHISKEY ISLAND.

THE DECK HANDS OF SHIPS SAILING UP THE CUYAHOGA RIVER SHOUTED OUT NEWS OF THE DISASTER THAT TURNED WHISKEY ISLAND INTO A SCENE OF CHAOS AND FEAR. TERRIFIED WIVES AND MOTHERS FLOODED THE SCENE SCREAMING THE NAMES OF THEIR LOVED ONES, NOT KNOWING IF THEY WERE DEAD OR ALIVE.
ING & SONS
MANUFACTURING
BRAND & SONS

STANLEY WALSH!
HUEY O'NEILL!
VINCENT DONOFRIO!
DAVID KOCINSKI!

FEARFUL OF ONE PERSON'S SCRUTINY, VAN DYKE HID IN THE SHADOWS AS THE HUMAN DRAMA PLAYED OUT ON THE DOCKS.
WHEN ALL WAS QUIET, HE ATTEMPTED HIS ESCAPE...

...BUT HIS WILY RETREAT WOULD NOT GO UNNOTICED!

DUTCHMAN!!!

MMM-M-M-MISSUS GALLAGHER?
WHERE BE OUR HUSBANDS?! WHERE'S JOHNNY GALLAGHER?!!

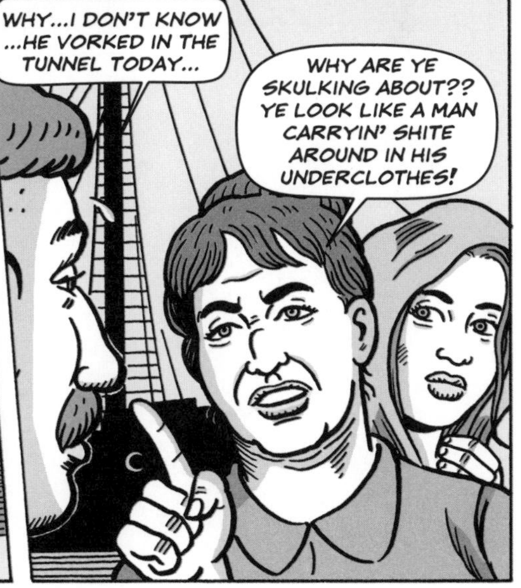
WHY...I DON'T KNOW ...HE VORKED IN THE TUNNEL TODAY...
WHY ARE YE SKULKING ABOUT?? YE LOOK LIKE A MAN CARRYIN' SHITE AROUND IN HIS UNDERCLOTHES!

I'M NODT SKULKING! I'VE CHUST HAD A TERRIBLE EXPERIENCE!
AND CAME OUT ALIVE LIKE USUAL. MY JOHNNY TOLD ME IF EVER SOMETHIN' GOES AMISS— TRACK DOWN THE DUTCHMAN—HE'LL HAVE THE DIRT!

I...I...I DON'T...
AND LOOK AT THIS POOR GIRL SHAKIN' LIKE A LEAF...AND WITH CHILD NO LESS! WHAT O' HER HUSBAND? WHERE'S RODGER CLARKE!!??

MR. VAN DYKE...DO...DO YOU KNOW WHERE MY RODGER IS? WILL THERE BE ANOTHER BOAT MAYBE?? NO ONE IS SAYIN' ANYTHIN'...

BOTH YOUR MEN VERE IN THE TUNNEL VHEN THE FIRE STARTED. ALL THOSE THAT COULD GET OUT VERE ON THE BOAT.

THEY'RE ALL DEAD. NO VON COULD SURVIVE DOT INFERNO.
IF HE WAS IN THE TUNNEL, MAYBE HE IS STILL ALIVE?

HEARTLESS CREATURE! CAN'T YE SEE THE POOR THING IS BARELY HANGING ON? GO ON! GET OUTA HERE!!

MY JOHNNY TOLD ME ABOUT YE! YER A JONAH! YOU'LL KILL 'EM ALL B'FORE YER THROUGH!!!

YOU KNOW MORE THAN YER TELLIN'!!!... I'M PUTTIN' YE DOWN IN ME BOOK– YE DIRTY GOBSHITE!!

DARLIN'...LET'S GET YE HOME AN' INNA BED.

DON'T YE WORRY, DEAR. KEEP YER FAITH IN GOD!

...IF RODGER STICKS WITH ME JOHNNY–HE'LL MAKE IT OUTA THERE... YOU MARK MY WORDS!

AUGHHHHHH!
AAAUGGH!! JAYSUS, MARY, AND JOSEPH! THE PAIN IS EXQUISITE!
STEADY NOW! IT'S A BAD BREAK, BUT THE BONE DIDN'T COME THRU THE SKIN. YER LUCKY!
ACHHH! I'M MANY THINGS, MR. GALLAGHER, BUT "LUCKY" DOESN'T COME TA MIND!
LISTEN, SON, I WENT UP THE SERVICE TUNNEL FER THE SPLINTIN' WOOD...
...THE GAS IS THICK...TOO THICK! WE CANNO' GO THAT WAY.
OUR ONLY HOPE IS TO GO THROUGH THE FLOODED PART O' THE TUNNEL...
...D'YA THINK YE CAN DO IT WITH THAT LEG O' YERS?
BROKE LEG OR NOT... I'D SAY THE CHOICE HAS BEEN MADE FOR US!
BESIDES, I CAN'T SWIM ANYWAYS.

WE'VE REACHED THE FLOODED SECTION, BOYO.
AUUGH!! LET ME DOWN, MR. GALLAGHER. THE PAIN IS TOO MUCH, TOO MUCH!
I GIVE YE A MINUTE'S REST- WE MUST KEEP MOVIN'.
I'M FINISHED. WE'LL NEED A MIRACLE TA GET ME THRU ALL THAT WATER!
SAVE YERSELF, MAN! GET OUT WHILE YE STILL CAN!
YER JUST FULL O' CLEVER IDEAS, AREN'T YE? LET ME DO THE T'INKIN' AND YOU CAN DO THE HAIL MARYS!
WHAT WE NEED IS SOMETHIN' TO FLOAT ON. WE NEED A RAFT!
HOW MANY HAIL MARYS D'YA NEED FER THAT?
HMMM...NOW WHAT IS THAT?
I CAN'T MAKE IT OUT...

THAT'S IT, GALLAGHER! SAVE YERSELF! I DON'T BLAME YA!
SHADDUP, YA FECKIN' IDJIT! I SEES SOMETHIN'!
HMM...? IS THAT WHA' I T'INK IT IS...?
WHAT IS IT? WHAT D'YER SEE?
I T'INK WE HAVE OUR MIRACLE, MR. CLARKE!
'TIS A GREAT DAY FER THE FENIANS!
WHAT YER FOUND?
A RAFT! I FOUND US OUR RAFT!

'TIS THE MULE THAT DIED LAST NIGHT! SHE CAME FLOATIN' UP FER DUTY.
THA'S IT. HOP ABOARD THE HMS DUTCHMAN. THA'S A GOOD LAD!
OOOH! ME LEG IS ON FIRE!
OH, GALLAGHER! LOOK! JES' LOOK AT 'EM ALL!
DON'T LOOK AT 'EM, SON— OR ELSE YOU'LL BE T'INKIN' OUR SITUATION HAS TURNED HOPELESS!

AT CITY HALL, THEN-MAYOR JOHNSON MET WITH THE PRESS...
I AM DECLARING THE SITUATION ON CRIB #3 HOPELESS!

THESE MEN SURVIVED THE ACCIDENT AND THEY REPORT A SCENE FROM HADES! TELL 'EM, BOYS...

THE CRIB IS A TOTAL LOSS.
ALL SURVIVORS ARE ACCOUNTED FOR.

WHAT ABOUT YOU, MR. VAN DYKE? YOU WERE THERE... WHAT DID YOU SEE?

I VAS ASLEEP VEN THE FIRE STARTED.
I JUMP INTO THE VATER...DAT'S ALL I REMEMBER!

BOYS, WHAT WE HAVE HERE IS A GREAT HUMAN TRAGEDY!
THE FIRES ARE STILL CRACKLING, BUT THE CRIES OF THE FATED VICTIMS HAVE BEEN SILENCED...

"...JUST AS SOON AS IT IS SAFE, WE WILL SEND IN A RECOVERY TEAM TO REMOVE THE HONORED DEAD."

RODG...RODGER...
(PANT PANT) I
T'INK I SEE IT!
THE AIRLOCK!
HANG ON, SON!
ERRGH! STEADY AS SHE GOES, LAD!
KEEP YER IRISH UP, RODGER! JAYSUS T'ISN'T BUYING THE DRINKS FER US YET!
OOOHH!
I HAVE TO CARRY YE, LAD. THIS'LL HURT LIKE HELL.
HERE WE GO ERPSY-DAISY!
AUGHHH!

GALLAGHER WAS SO DETERMINED TO SAVE CLARKE HE BARELY NOTICED THE ACRID SMELL OF BURNT FLESH AND HUMAN WRECKAGE THAT SURROUNDED HIM.
AAAAUGGG!— JAYSUS GOD!
OOF! HUH, I GUESS I'M FEELIN' A BIT WOOZY...WHOA!
OOOH, ME ARM! I MUSTA PULLED A MUSCLE.
UGH! WHAT'S HAPPENIN'? MY CHEST! I CAN'T BREATHE!
OOF! OH NO! OH NO!
AAGGHH!

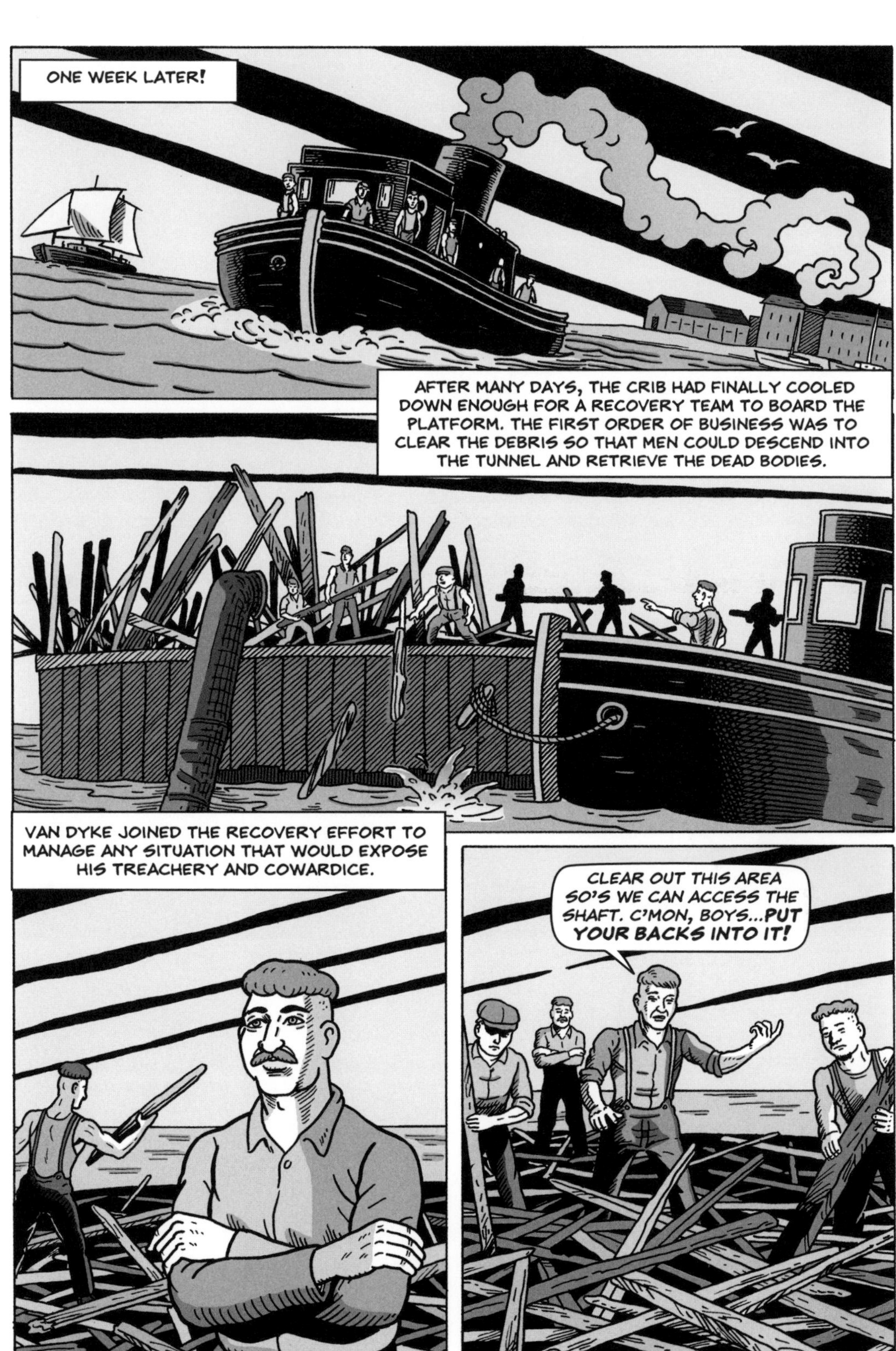
ONE WEEK LATER!
AFTER MANY DAYS, THE CRIB HAD FINALLY COOLED DOWN ENOUGH FOR A RECOVERY TEAM TO BOARD THE PLATFORM. THE FIRST ORDER OF BUSINESS WAS TO CLEAR THE DEBRIS SO THAT MEN COULD DESCEND INTO THE TUNNEL AND RETRIEVE THE DEAD BODIES.
VAN DYKE JOINED THE RECOVERY EFFORT TO MANAGE ANY SITUATION THAT WOULD EXPOSE HIS TREACHERY AND COWARDICE.
CLEAR OUT THIS AREA SO'S WE CAN ACCESS THE SHAFT. C'MON, BOYS...PUT YOUR BACKS INTO IT!

TWO HOURS LATER...
THAT'LL DO IT! HAND ME THAT BLOCK O' WOOD THERE!

LISTEN CLOSELY, BOYS! IF SHE SPLASHES WE'LL KNOW THE TUNNEL IS FLOODED!

ANY O' YOUSE HEAR A SPLASH?
BING!
BANG!
CLUNK!

SOUNDED LIKE IT HIT DRY LAND TO ME!
TRY IT AGAIN.

OK, LISTEN WITH ALL YOUR EARS THIS TIME—READY?
BANG! BANG!

HEY! I DIDN'T EVEN DROP IT YET.
MEBBE THE FIRST PIECE IS STILL FALLING!

WHAT'S ALL THE RUMPUS?
NOISES, SIR! NOISES IN THE SHAFT!

AHH! MOST LIKELY YOU HEAR DEBRIS FALLING IN THE SHAFT.
O'MALLEY! HAND ME THAT HOOK SPANNER!

BANG!
BANG!
BANG!

JUST AS I THOUGHT— IT WAS FALLING DEBRIS. C'MON, GET BACK TO...
BANG! BANG! BANG!

THAT'S NO DEBRIS!! SOMEONE IS DOWN THERE!!
WELL I'LL BE HANGED!

BANG! BANG! BANG! BANG!

BANG! BANG! BANG! BANG!

WE GOTTA LIVE ONE!!
YOU MEN THERE— GET A RIGGING FIXED OVER THIS HOLE!!
MR. O'MALLEY—FIRE THE CRIB ROCKETS!! SIGNAL THAT TUG TO GET BACK HERE!!
JUMP TO IT, BOYS!! MOVE IT!

SUPERINTENDENT, I VOULD LIKE TO VOLUNTEER TO GO DOWN THE SHAFT.
YOU READ MY MIND, VAN DYKE. YOU HAVE MORE EXPERIENCE AT THIS THAN THE REST OF US!

VAN DYKE... WHO DID'YA SAY WAS ON AIRLOCK DUTY THAT DAY?
RODGER CLARKE!!

THE RUSH OF AIR PEOPLE WITNESSED TELLS ME THAT THE AIRLOCK WAS PRIED OPEN, WHICH MEANS CLARKE MAY HAVE DESERTED HIS POST!

THE SHAFT WAS APPROXIMATELY 200 FEET LONG, WHICH PLACED ITS BASE 75 FEET BELOW THE LAKE BED. VAN DYKE WRAPPED A WET TOWEL AROUND HIS FACE TO HELP PROTECT HIM FROM THE METHANE GAS, BUT NO TOWEL OR MASK COULD EVER FILTER OUT THE ***HORRIFIC*** SIGHTS AND SMELLS THAT AWAITED HIM IN THE TUNNEL.

WHO?...WHO GOES DERE?...

HELP US... COUGH, COUGH... PLEASE... HELP US.

WE THOUGHT YOU'D NEVER RETURN...

PLEASE...PLEASE SAVE US...

WHO IS IT?? WHO ARE YA?? VOT'S YOUR NAME?

CLARKE...MY NAME IS CLARKE...AND THIS IS...JOHNNY... JOHNNY GALLAGHER.

ISS HE DEAD?

HE HAS EVERY RIGHT TO BE...BUT HE'S NOT. HE HAD A HEART ATTACK AND A STROKE, HE CAN'T SPEAK OR MOVE HIS ONE SIDE.

UND YOU CLARKE— VOT OF YOU? VOT HAPPENED TO YOUR LEG?

RUN OVER BY A MUCK CART! 'TWAS JOHNNY...JOHNNY WHO SAVED ME. I BEEN BANGIN' ON THE PIPE FOR A WEEK. WHAT THE HELL KEPT YE?

HOW DID YOU GEDT DIS FAR ON A BROKEN LEG VITH HIM?

I TIED A ROPE AROUND HIM AND CRAWLED TO THE SHAFT AND THEN DRAGGED HIM TOWARD ME. HE WAS ABLE TO HELP WITH HIS GOOD LEG.
...UND THE UDDERS? VERE ARE THE UDDERS?

DEAD ...ALL DEAD. THE COMPARTMENT LOOKS LIKE A MORGUE.

I TELL YA THEY'RE ALL DEAD! DON'T LEAVE US—YA GOTTA GET JOHNNY TO THE SURFACE! HE NEEDS A DOCTOR!!

OH! OH MIJN GOTT!

MOMENTARILY STUNNED BY WHAT HE FOUND IN THE AIRLOCK, WILLY QUICKLY REGAINED HIS SENSES AND DEVISED A DECEITFUL PLAN...

I HAFF TO VORK FAST–THEY'LL BE DOWN HERE SOON!

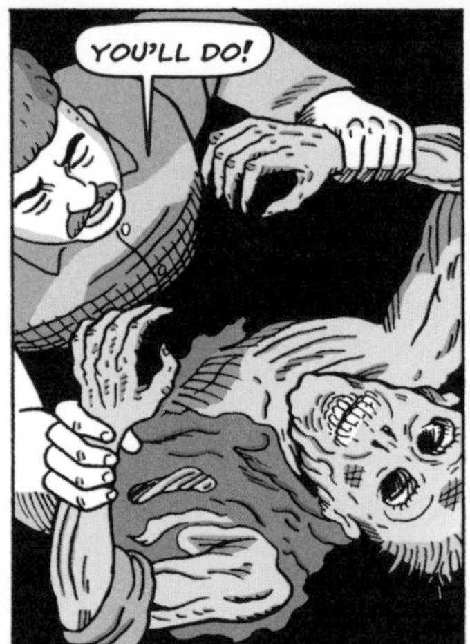
YOU'LL DO!

YA...YOU'LL DO ALRIGHT...

I SAW YA! I SEE WHAT YER UP TA... DUTCHMAN!

IT'S VAT YOU DON'T SEE DOT COUNTS HERE, SONNY!

JOHNNY WAS RIGHT ABOUT YOU! NO GOOD STINKIN' BASTARD. YOU DESERTED US!!

EVERYBODY KNOWS YE WERE ON THE AIRLOCK!
"EVERYBODY" IS DEAD! I TOLD 'EM IT VAS YOU MANNING THE AIRLOCK DOT DAY!

NO ONE WILL BELIEVE YE!
EVERYONE VILL BELIEVE ME—NOW LOOK, CLARKE, AS I SEES IT YOU HAFF A CHOICE.

GIMME DOT SPANNER!!

HMMFF! NOT SUCH A BIG MAN NOW, EH, GALLAGHER!?

I CAN BURY YOU SO DEEP THEY'LL NEFFER FIND YOU! THEY'LL SAY YOU DESERTED THE AIR LOCK!...AND YOUR VIFE WILL LIVE VITH YOUR SHAME!
I'LL TELL 'EM IT VAS THIS DUMB MICK HERE WHO POUNDED ON DER PIPE ...RIGHT BEFORE I SMOTHERED HIM!
OR YOU CAN TELL 'EM THE DEAD SANDHOG VATCHED THE AIRLOCK VILE YOU WENT TO VARN THE UDDERS!
IT VON'T BE YOUR FAULT HE DIED! EVERYBODY GOES HOME A HERO UND NO VON IS DA VISER!
IT'S BECAUSE OF YE THAT ALL THESE MEN ARE DEAD! I WON'T DO YER LYIN' FOR YE!
SO IT'S A DEAD LOSER YOU'LL BE-EH?
NO! MY WIFE IS ABOUT TA HAVE A BABY! LET ME GO!!!

NO!! DON'T KILL ME!!
ARRRGG!!
UGH!
GOTT! ERRGH!... CAN'T BREATHE!!
AACCCH!

GAAHH!
UHHH...
GALLAGHER!... GALLAGHER! HE'S GONE!...DEAD!
HE WAS A BIGGER MAN THAN ALL O' US SANDHOGS PUT TOGETHER!
GASP! AAGG!! COUGH!!... COUGH!
OK, VAN DYKE! I'D SELL ME OWN SOUL TA GET OUTA DIS STINKIN' HOLE! I'LL KEEP YER DURTY SECRET... JUS' LET ME LIVE! I WANT TA LIVE!!
UGH!...COUGH... LOUSY MICK BASTARDS!..

AUGHH! DAMN! DAMN!!
WHAT'RE YE DOIN'? I SWEAR I'LL KEEP YER SECRET!
GODDAM YOU!!
NO! NO!
BANG!
BANG!

YOU CHUST REMEMBER OUR BARGAIN! I CAN KILL YOU IN DAYLIGHT CHUST AS EASILY AS I CAN IN DARKNESS.

JUST THEN...
CLUNK!

YOU CHUST REMEMBER...
HOW CAN I EVER FORGET?

AN HOUR LATER ON IRISHTOWN BEND A GRIEVING MARY CLARKE SAT READING HER BIBLE, UNAWARE THAT WONDERFUL NEWS WAS RUSHING TO HER DOORSTEP...
"OUR SOUL WAITS FOR THE LORD. MAY YOUR KINDNESS BE UPON US WHO HAVE PUT OUR HOPE IN YOU."

MRS. CLARKE! MRS. CLARKE!!
YES? IS THAT YOU MRS. GATONS?

MARY!! ...A MIRACLE HAS HAPPENED!! IT'S A MIRACLE!!...

...IT'S RODGER! THEY FOUND HIM! MARY!...HE'S ALIVE!!
IT'S A MIRACLE!

IT'S A MIRACLE!

IT'S A MIRACLE!
3

CRIB 5 A
3

CHAPTER 5: "A BROTHER OF INVENTION"
THE Cleveland News Gazette
OVER 30,000 READERS
MR. BELTRAN, I'VE TOLD YOU A THOUSAND TIMES!...
CHARLIE, YOU COULD TELL ME A MILLION TIMES AND IT STILL WON'T MAKE ANY SENSE!

MR. BELTRAN, FOR THE LAST TIME...THE NEWS GAZETTE DOES NOT RUN ADS FOR COLORED BUSINESSES!

IS THAT SO?...TELL ME AGAIN... 'ZACTLY WHICH COLORS DOES THIS PAPER OBJECT TO?
CLASSIFIED ADS DEPT.

IS IT THE COLOR BLUE THAT BOTHERS THEM? MEBBE IT'S THE COLOR RED??!
MR. BELTRAN, I...
UH-OH!

CLA
ADS
...'CUZ THE ONE COLOR **EVERY** NEWSPAPER ON EARTH ACCEPTS IS **GREEN!...** AN' MY MONEY IS AS GREEN AS A **DRUNKARD'S LIVER!**

MR. BELTRAN, PLEEEZE...!!
UH...PERHAPS I CAN BE OF ASSISTANCE HERE...

TOM HARGAN AT YOUR SERVICE.
I'M BEN...

YOU, SIR, ARE BENJAMIN BELTRAN, **THE INVENTOR!...** REMEMBER ME? I DID A STORY ABOUT YOUR CONCOCTION THAT STRAIGHTENS OUT CURLY HAIR.
YOU? –WAS YOU THAT WROTE THAT PACK O' LIES?

CHARLIE–WHY DON'T YOU GO GET YOURSELF A CUP OF COFFEE? I'LL KEEP AN EYE ON THINGS HERE FOR YOU.
CLASSIFI AD DEPT
WITH PLEASURE!

NOT LIES, BEN. NOT LIES...MY EDITOR... HE ADDED A FEW EMBELLISHMENTS TO THE STORY–THAT'S ALL.
YOU WROTE THAT COLORED FOLKS WITH **STRAIGHT** HAIR WOULD HAVE TO REGISTER THEIR **NEW HEADS** WITH THE **POLICE.**

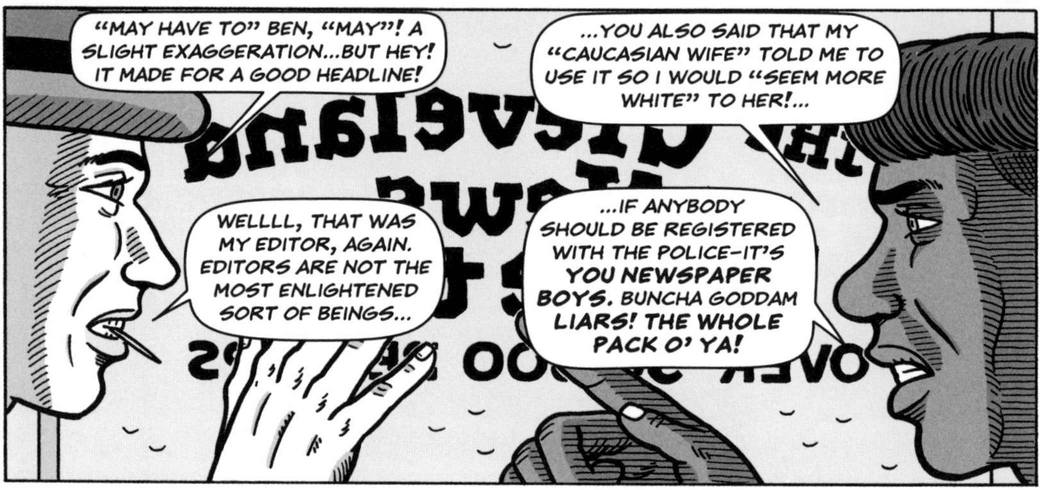
"MAY HAVE TO" BEN, "MAY"! A SLIGHT EXAGGERATION...BUT HEY! IT MADE FOR A GOOD HEADLINE!
...YOU ALSO SAID THAT MY "CAUCASIAN WIFE" TOLD ME TO USE IT SO I WOULD "SEEM MORE WHITE" TO HER!...
WELLLL, THAT WAS MY EDITOR, AGAIN. EDITORS ARE NOT THE MOST ENLIGHTENED SORT OF BEINGS...
...IF ANYBODY SHOULD BE REGISTERED WITH THE POLICE–IT'S **YOU NEWSPAPER BOYS.** BUNCHA GODDAM **LIARS! THE WHOLE PACK O' YA!**

I CAN MAKE IT UP TO YOU. LET'S SEE THOSE AD SLICKS. MAYBE I CAN DO ANOTHER ARTICLE ABOUT ONE OF YOUR LATEST DEVICES?
HUH! NOT LIKELY, SIR!... NOT LIKELY!

AWWW, NO NEED TO BE SORE! THE NEWSPAPERS IS A GREAT WAY TO SHOW OFF YOUR INVENTIONS... NOT TO MENTION THE ONLY WAY!

THE BELTRAN SMOKE HELMET
The Beltran Safety Co.
WHAT'S IT LOOK LIKE?!
HEY! WHAT THE...? WHAT THE HECK IS THIS CONTRAPTION?

IT LOOKS LIKE SOMETHING FROM THE LOWER REGIONS!... ...WHAT'S IT FOR?
IT ENABLES FIREMEN TO BREATHE INSIDE SMOKE-FILLED BUILDINGS.

...ENABLES FIREMEN TO BREATHE IN SMOKE? DOES IT WORK?
'COURSE IT WORKS! I INVENTED IT DIDN'T I?

BEN, I'VE COVERED MY SHARE OF FIRES. ONCE THAT SMOKE TAKES OVER THERE ISN'T MUCH THAT CAN BE DONE.
YEA? WELL, FIREMEN EQUIPPED WITH MY SMOKE HELMETS CAN DO PLENTY! THEY CAN SAVE LIVES! PRINT THAT!

BUT, HOW DID YOU GO FROM HAIR CREMES TO SMOKE HELMETS?
I CREATE THINGS THAT HELP PEOPLE. THAT'S THE COMMON THREAD RUNNIN' THRU ALL MY INVENTIONS. YOU CAN PRINT THAT, TOO!

I MEAN, WHAT INSPIRED IT? EDISON WANTED LIGHT AND SO HE MADE A LIGHT BULB...WHAT DID YOU WANT?
A COW.

A COW?...OH, I GET IT! MRS. O'LEARY'S COW!...RIGHT? ...THE CHICAGO FIRE?
NOPE. JUST A PLAIN AND SUNDRY COW. I NEEDED A COW.

I CAN SEE YOU WON'T BE HAPPY WITH THAT EXPLANATION.
OK...TELL ME MORE. I'M ALL EARS.
CLAS
AD
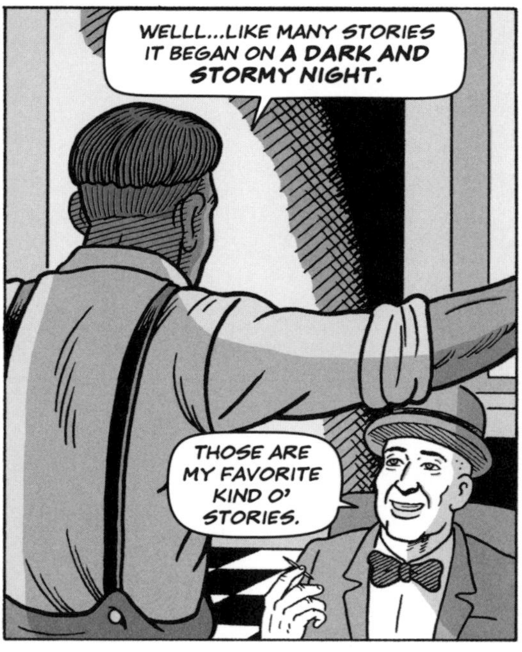
WELLL...LIKE MANY STORIES IT BEGAN ON A DARK AND STORMY NIGHT.
THOSE ARE MY FAVORITE KIND O' STORIES.

RUMMBLE!
KRAK!
THE YEAR WAS 1892 AND I WAS A YOUNG MAN GROWING UP ON OUR KENTUCKY FARM. IT WAS A HARDSCRABBLE KIND O' PLACE.

I WAS SLEEPING TIGHT AFTER A DAY MY OL' PAP HAD WORKED ME SO HARD–NOTHING SHORT OF A FREIGHT TRAIN CRASHING DOWN OUR HOLLOW COULD WAKE ME UP!
CRASH!

WHAT ON EARTH IS THAT NOISE?
BANG!
SCREEE!

SHREEEEK!

C'MON, BOY! GET YO' ASS OUTA THAT BED! I THINK THE 49 TRAIN JUS' CAME **CRASHIN' DOWN** THE HOLLA'!
BOOM!

OL' PAP DRAGGED ME AND MY BROTHER, LOUIS, OUT OF BED AND WE RAN UP TO THE TRESTLE IN THE POURIN' RAIN! WE DARED NOT ARGUE WITH HIM. IF OL' PAP SAID "DO IT"– YOU DID IT!
HURRY UP! YOU TWO ARE SLOWER THAN SLUDGE! MOVE IT!

THE 49 TRAIN HAULED COAL TO THE STEEL MILLS UP NORTH AND CAME SOUTH CARRYIN' ALL MANNER OF THINGS. THE TRAIN DERAILED WHEN IT HIT A SECTION OF TRACK WASHED AWAY BY THE STORM. IT WAS A MIRACLE NOBODY GOT HURT, BUT...

...ONE OF ITS CARS PACKED WITH LOADED CRATES SPILLED OFF THE RIDGE...RIGHT DOWN INTO FOX HOLLOW!
BOYS, WE GOT OUR WORK CUT OUT FOR US TONIGHT! GET BACK TO THE FARM. WE NEED THE WAGON!

MY OL' PAP LIVED BY THE RULE, "WHAT LANDS IN THE HOLLOW STAYS IN THE HOLLOW." HE RODE THAT WAGON LIKE A DEMON DETERMINED TO GET FIRST PICKINS'.

ALL NIGHT WE WORKED LIKE DOGS IN THE MIDST OF THAT STORM–LOADING UP OUR WAGON AND HAULING THAT CONTRABAND BACK TO OUR FARM!
C'MON YOU FOOLS–MOVE!! WE AIN'T GOT ALL NIGHT!

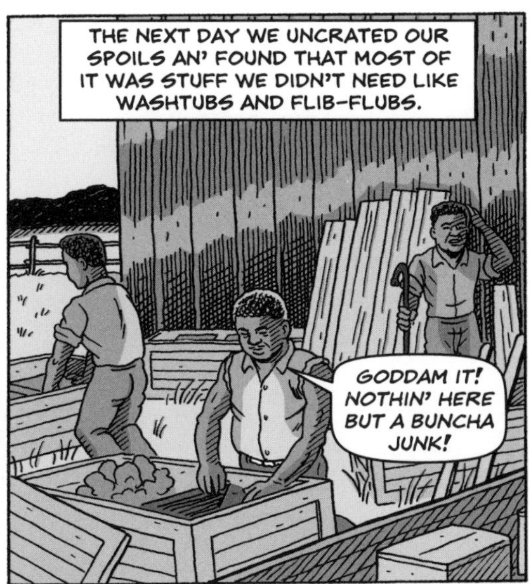
THE NEXT DAY WE UNCRATED OUR SPOILS AN' FOUND THAT MOST OF IT WAS STUFF WE DIDN'T NEED LIKE WASHTUBS AND FLIB–FLUBS.
GODDAM IT! NOTHIN' HERE BUT A BUNCHA JUNK!

AS FOR ME, I OPENED CRATES FULL O' PARTS MEANT FOR A CLOCK TOWER O'ER IN LEXINGTON. THEY GAVE ME THE BIG IDEA THAT STARTED ALL THE FUSS 'N' TROUBLE.

Y'SEE, I WAS A NATURAL WITH ANYTHING MADE O' GEARS AND SUCH. WHEN I SAW ALL THOSE GIANT CLOCK PARTS I KNEW I COULD PUT THEM TO GOOD USE...BUT HOW?

THAT'S WHEN I DREAMED UP A PLAN TO BUILD A "WINDLESS" WINDMILL. IF I COULD MAKE OUR WINDMILL WORK IN CALM WEATHER AND WITHOUT ELECTRICITY, I WAS CONVINCED THAT GOOD FORTUNE WOULD SURELY FOLLOW!

THE JOB OF OUR WINDMILL WAS TO PUMP WATER FROM THE WELL. IF MY IDEA WORKED, THE FARM WOULD ALWAYS HAVE WATER AND NOT JUST WHEN GOD FELT LIKE IT.

SO, EVERYDAY FOR A WEEK AFTER MY FARM CHORES WERE DONE, I ASSEMBLED ALL THOSE CLOCK PARTS JUST LIKE A BIG OLD WATCH! MY OL' PAP WASN'T HAPPY, BUT MA PLEADED WITH HIM TO GIVE ME A CHANCE.

HMMPH! WHAT FOOLISHNESS!
ALL I WANTED WAS MY FATHER TO BE PROUD OF ME...FOR ONCE.

WHEN THE TIME CAME, I GATHERED MY FAMILY 'ROUND ME AND PULLED A LEVER THAT SET THE GEARS AND—I GUESS YOU COULD SAY—THE STORY OF MY LIFE IN MOTION.

I CANNOT PUT INTO WORDS THE SHEER EXHILARATION I FELT WHEN THAT FIRST INVENTION O' MINE SPRANG TO LIFE!

BUT MY JOY WAS SHORT-LIVED 'CUZ I HAD LEFT OUT ONE IMPORTANT DETAIL FROM THE DESIGN.
SLOW IT DOWN, YOU FOOL! IT AIN'T BUILT TO SPIN THAT FAST!

IT SEEMS I HAD SPENT ALL O' MY INVENTIVE ENERGIES ON HOW TO MAKE IT GO...BUT NONE AT ALL ON HOW TO MAKE IT STOP!
WHOA! ...WHOA!!!!!

KRIK!
STOP IT, BOY! STOP IT!! IT'S COMIN' APART!!

KRAK!
I CAN'T STOP IT, PAP! IT'S GOT A MIND OF ITS OWN!!!

KRISH!

WHIIZZZ!
THWIP!
HONK!
HONK!

ZIP!
KRAK!

WHAM!
AWK!

WHIZ!

GOOD GOD ALMIGHTY!!

MUNCH-MUNCH-MUNCH

WHIP!
WHIP!
WHIP!
OH NO! NO! WATCH-IT!! STOP!!

MY OL' PAP WAS BESIDE HIMSELF SEEING OUR ONLY COW LAYIN' THERE–DEADER THAN DEAD. HE YANKED THAT WINDMILL BLADE FROM CLARABELLE'S LIFELESS BACKSIDE AND USED IT TO LEAVE A LIVING IMPRESSION ON MINE.

THE WIND NEVER BLEW COLDER THAN IT DID THAT FIRST NIGHT ON THE ROAD. WE CAMPED IN A FOREST AN' LOUIS WAS SCARED TO DEATH. I ACTED BRAVE FOR HIS SAKE BUT, TRUTH BE TOLD, I WAS EVERY BIT AFRAID AS HE WAS.

TO KEEP OUR SPIRITS UP WE ATE EVERY SCRAP O' FOOD MA HAD PACKED FOR US. IT WAS FOOLISH, BUT WE WERE SO HOMESICK. I TURNED THAT FOOD SACK INSIDE OUT LOOKING FOR ANY MORSELS THAT WERE LEFT BEHIND.

WHEN I TURNED O'ER THE SACK AN OL' HAND-CARVED WHISTLE CAME TUMBLING OUT. THE WORD "BIRDY" WAS SCRAWLED ON IT'S SIDE. I KNEW THEN IT BELONGED TO MY MOTHER. PEOPLE CALLED HER..."BIRDY."
BIRDY

MA WAS BORN A SLAVE AND WAS A MERE CHILD WHEN SHE ESCAPED WITH THE HELP OF ABOLITIONISTS. I HEARD TELL THEY USED WHISTLES AN' SUCH TO SIGNAL EACH OTHER ON THE UNDERGROUND RAILWAY TO FREEDOM.
RRRR

THE SOUND IT MADE WAS PECULIAR, LIKE LEAVES RUSTLING. NO DOUBT MA GAVE IT TO US FOR GOOD LUCK. IT SURE WAS COMFORTING TO HOLD THAT SMALL PIECE O' HOME.

RRRRR!

WHOOOOOO!

THAT FIRST NIGHT ON THE ROAD WAS THE LONGEST NIGHT O' MY LIFE.
GRRR!
WHOOOO!
GRICK-GRICK-GRICK!

THEY SAY THAT EVERYTHING LOOKS BETTER IN THE MORNING, BUT THAT WASN'T SO IN OUR CASE. WE ASKED FOR WORK AT THE FIRST PLACE WE STOPPED, BUT THAT FARMER TOLD US TO KEEP ON MOVING.

AFTER A COUPLE MORE STOPS WE FINALLY FOUND SOME DAY WORK HAULING WATER, CHOPPING WOOD, AN' OTHER CHORES. THAT FARMER PAID US WITH FOOD, WHICH WAS ALRIGHT WITH US.

WE'D BEEN ON THE ROAD FOR SEVERAL DAYS AND WEREN'T ANY CLOSER TO STEADY WORK OR FINDIN' A NEW COW. I BEGAN TO FEEL REAL BAD FOR LOUIS WHEN SUDDENLY...

...A WONDROUS SIGHT STOPPED US DEAD IN OUR TRACKS!
LOUIS—DO YOU SEE WHAT I SEE?

IT WAS A FIELD FULL OF COWS—HUNDREDS O' COWS—AS FAR AS OUR EYES COULD SEE!

THE THOUGHT OF PUTTING AN END TO OUR MISERY BY STEALING A COW DID CROSS MY MIND, BUT SO DID THE THOUGHT OF ME AN' LOUIS SWINGING FROM A TREE. INSTEAD WE DID THE RIGHT THING...

WE SWUNG OUR WAGON DOWN THE FARM ROAD AND ASKED THOSE PEOPLE FOR A JOB!
KORN'S COBB
DAIRY FARM

LUCKY FOR US A FARMHAND HAD JUST QUIT! I TOLD 'EM THEY COULD HIRE THE BOTH OF US FOR THE PRICE OF ONE!
I DUNNO–WE NEVER HAVE MUCH LUCK WITH NIG'RAZ!
THEY LOOK LIKE SUCH NICE BOYS.
YA JES' GOTTA WHIP 'EM NOW AN A'GIN!

AFTER SOME DISCUSSION THEY TOLD US WE HAD JOBS! WE WERE SO HAPPY WE FELL TO OUR KNEES AND THANKED GOD!
AWRIGHT... WE'LL GIVE Y'ALL A TRY!
Y'ALL LOOK LIKE SUCH NICE BOYS.
BEST WORK YER FANNIES OFF OR WE'LL WHIP YA!

WE WEREN'T SO THANKFUL ONCE WE GOT TO WORK! THEY RAN US AS HARD AS OL' PAP. IT DIDN'T TAKE LONG BEFORE I KNEW EVERYTHING THERE WAS ABOUT THE BUSINESS END O' A COW.

THE MAN RUNNING THINGS WAS JOE COBB. HE WAS MARRIED TO THE OL' MAN'S GRANDDAUGHTER. THEY HAD A BABY BOY THAT EVERYBODY CALLED "GOOCH"...A MORE SPOILED CHILD I NEVER SAW IN MY LIFE!
THEM BOYS'RE GOOD WORKERS, HUH?

THE MAN THAT OWNED THE FARM WAS A TETCHED OL' BUZZARD NAMED EZRA KORN. HE WOULDN'T ACCEPT THE CIVIL WAR HAD ENDED AN' HE'D TAUNT ME AN' LOUIS ALL DAY WITH HIS STUPID WHISKEY SONGS FROM THE TIME OF SLAVERY.
OHHH, WHEN THE SUN GO DOWN AND THE TIDE GO OUT THE DARKIES COME 'ROUND AND BEGIN TO SHOUT, "HEY-HEY UNCLE FUDD!, HEY-HEY UNCLE FUDD!, IT A TREAT TO BEAT FEET ON THE MISSISSIPI MUD!" HEE-YAH!

THAT BEING SAID, LIFE ON THEIR FARM WAS VERY TOL'RABLE. I WAS SO RELIEVED TO HAVE A ROOF O'ER OUR HEADS AND FOOD IN OUR BELLIES.
I STARTED TO BELIEVE IN MYSELF AGAIN.

NOW, EVERY FEW DAYS JOE COBB WOULD TAKE US INTO COVINGTON FOR SUPPLIES. A BIG TOWN LIKE THAT WAS SOMETHING NEW FOR US AN' I LOVED IT! IT WAS ON ONE SUCH TRIP WE WERE LOADING UP THE WAGON WHEN ALL OF A SUDDEN...
OODS
GROCERY
BANG!
CLANG
CLUNK!
WHAT THE...?
FLOUR

I SAW A CRAZY MAN THROWING BROKEN SEWING MACHINES OUT OF HIS SEAMSTRESS SWEATSHOP. IT WAS SUCH A WASTE ! BUT, IT GAVE ME AN IDEA...

GODDAM PIECES O' JUNK!!

I TOLD THAT MAN I WAS GOOD AT FIXING THINGS AN' OFFERED TO REPAIR HIS SEWIN' MACHINES FOR POCKET MONEY. HE SAID THAT IF I COULD REPAIR EVEN ONE MACHINE, HE'D GIVE ME A JOB IN HIS SHOP!

SO, I ASKED JOE COBB IF I COULD TAKE THE BROKEN MACHINES BACK TO THE FARM TO WORK ON THEM. HE SAID "OK," AS LONG AS I KEPT UP WITH MY FARM CHORES.

WORKING NIGHTS I WAS ABLE TO FIX THREE SEWING MACHINES FROM PARTS I SCAVENGED FROM TWO OTHERS. I HAD TO TEST THEM BACK AT THE SWEATSHOP, BUT I KNEW THEY'D WORK AGAIN.

SURE ENOUGH, WHEN ME AND LOUIS BROUGHT THEM BACK AND HOOKED THEM UP, THEY PURRED LIKE KITTENS. THAT MAN OFFERED ME A JOB ON THE SPOT AT $2 PER WEEK AN' I ACCEPTED WITHOUT BATTIN' AN EYE!!

WE LEFT COVINGTON AND HEADED BACK TO THE FARM. WE WERE JUST A HALF MILE AWAY WHEN TROUBLE APPEARED ON THE HORIZON!
LOUIS! THE FARMHOUSE!! IT'S ON FIRE!

ONE THING I KNOW...THE TROUBLE WITH TROUBLE IS THAT IT USUALLY SHOWS UP WEARIN' A FAMILIAR FACE.

I HEARD MRS. AVIS SAY MANY TIMES, "GRAMPA, SMOKIN' WILL BE YOUR DEATH!" BUT HE NEVER LISTENED. I GUESS HE WAS TOO BUSY BEING HIMSELF.
Z-Z-Z-Z-Z-Z

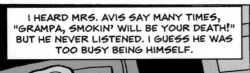

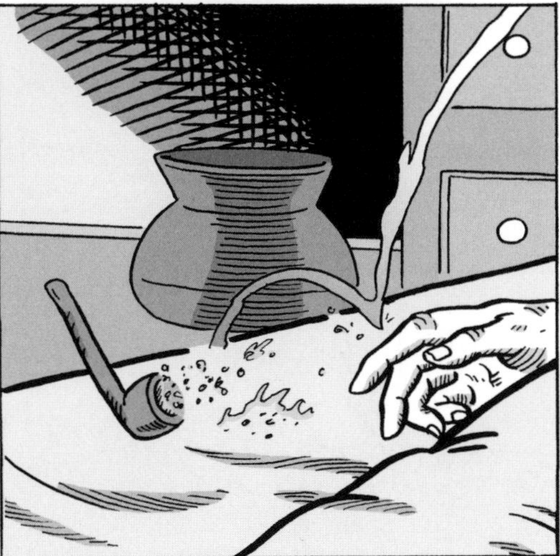

IN THE END, SHE WAS RIGHT! THE OL' GEEZER HAD MADE HIS PLAY FOR THE AFTERLIFE, AND IT APPEARED HE WOULD TAKE SOMEBODY WITH HIM!

LOUIS AND I ARRIVED UPON A SCENE OF TOTAL CHAOS! WE DIDN'T UNDERSTAND HOW BAD IT WAS UNTIL SOMEBODY SAID...
THERE'S A BABY IN THERE!!

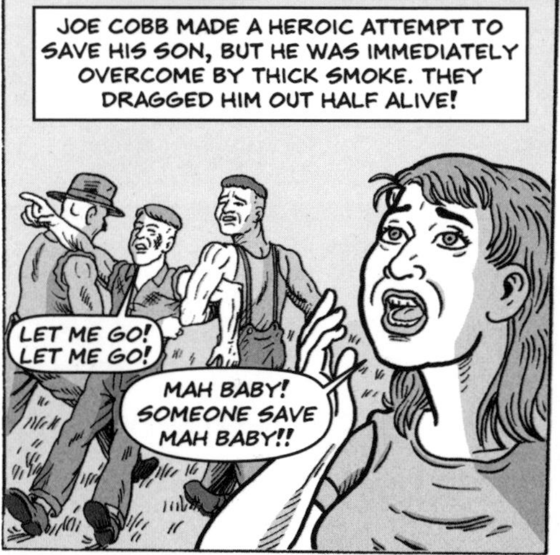
JOE COBB MADE A HEROIC ATTEMPT TO SAVE HIS SON, BUT HE WAS IMMEDIATELY OVERCOME BY THICK SMOKE. THEY DRAGGED HIM OUT HALF ALIVE!
LET ME GO! LET ME GO!
MAH BABY! SOMEONE SAVE MAH BABY!!

IT WAS FORTUNATE THE CHILD HAD THE INSTINCTS TO SAVE HIS OWN SELF. SOMETHIN' HE MUSTA SEEN HAD INSPIRED HIS FIRST GOOD IDEA...

...'CUZ 'OL BABY GOOCH CLIMBED RIGHT OUT O' THAT CRIB AN' DROPPED HIS LITTLE FANNY ONTO THE FLOOR!

AND FROM THERE HE FOUND THE PLACE WHERE CHILDREN, DOGS, AND DRUNKS HIDE OUT WHEN TROUBLE IS IN THE HOUSE!

WELL, I COULDN'T JUST STAND THERE AND DO NOTHING! THAT'S WHEN MY INVENTOR'S BRAIN STARTED TO PERCOLATE!

SUGA

OLD MILL FLOUR XXXX

FIRST, I PICKED UP A WHOLE SACK OF FLOUR AND EMPTIED IT OUT ON THE GROUND...

OLD MILL FLOUR XXXX

WHILE CUTTING EYE HOLES IN THE FLOUR SACK, I SPOTTED SOMETHING THAT GAVE ME ANOTHER IDEA!

QUICK, BROTHER! GRAB ME THAT HOSE!

LOUIS–TAKE YOUR BELT AND TIE THIS SACK AROUND MY NECK!

I LOOKED LIKE A GRAND WIZARD, BUT THE SACK PROTECTED MY HEAD FROM HOT EMBERS, AND THE GARDEN HOSE WOULD SUPPLY FRESH AIR FROM THE OUTSIDE!
SAY A PRAYER FOR ME, LOUIS–I'M GONNA GET THAT BABY OUTA THERE!
BEN, DON'T GO DYIN' ON ME!

THE FIRE WAS WORSE THAN I THOUGHT, AN' THE SMOKE MADE MY EYES BURN LIKE HELL. I WANTED TO TURN AROUND BUT INSTEAD...

...I DROPPED TO THE FLOOR AND GOT BELOW THE SMOKE!

THANKFULLY, IT WAS CLEAR ENOUGH DOWN LOW TO STAY IN THE HUNT. I DIDN'T REALIZE IT AT THE TIME, BUT I HAD INVENTED THE BASIC ELEMENTS O' MY SMOKE HELMET!

DAMNATION! THERE GOES THE LAST O' THE HOSE!

GOD, PLEASE
DON'T LET MY
BROTHER DIE!

I REACHED THE TOP OF THE STAIRS IN TIME TO WITNESS THE FATE OF EZRA KORN. NO SLAVE SONGS WERE COMING OUTA OF HIM ANYMORE...EXCEPT MAYBE "SWING LOW, SWEET CHARIOT"!

I TURNED MY EYES AWAY FROM EZRA IN FLAMES AND FOCUSED ALL O' MY EFFORTS ON FINDIN' THAT CHILD!

I MADE A BEELINE FOR THE BABY'S ROOM AS THE FIRE ENGULFED THE STAIRCASE BEHIND ME!

...JUST THEN I INHALED A LUNGFUL OF HOT SMOKE! THE FIRE HAD EATEN THROUGH MY BREATHING HOSE! NOW, I WAS IN REAL TROUBLE!
HACK!
KOF!
KOF!
KOF!

WITH THE FIRE HOT ON MY HEELS AND MY AIR RUNNING OUT, I LEAPT INTO THE BABY'S ROOM AN' SHUT THE DOOR BEHIND ME!

I WAS FEARING GOD PRETTY GOOD AT THAT POINT AND HAVING SOME TROUBLE FINDING THAT DAMN BABY!
GOOCH! COUGH! ... BABY GOOCH! WHERE THE HELL ARE YA?

I LOOKED EVERYWHERE! WITH NO TIME TO SPARE, I TURNED MY EYES TO THE ONE PLACE I HADN'T CHECKED YET...
BABY GOOCH! SHOW YO' DAMN SELF!

AN' THERE HE WAS–SNUG AS A BUG. HUNKERED DOWN IN THE ONE PLACE THE SMOKE HADN'T REACHED. HE'D BEEN PROTECTED BY THE ANGELS, NO DOUBT ABOUT IT!
HI!!!

I HAD FOUND THE BABY, BUT THE FIRE HAD FOUND US! THE WHOLE ROOM WAS GOING UP IN FLAMES.

HOT CINDERS WERE FLYING EVERYWHERE. SO I PUT MY SACK OVER THE BABE AND CARRIED HIM TO THE WINDOW–IT WAS OUR ONLY WAY OUT.

I TRIED TO OPEN THE WINDOW, BUT IT WAS STUCK AND WOULD ONLY RAISE A FEW INCHES...HIGH ENOUGH, THANK GOD, TO SQUEEZE THAT CHILD OUT ONTO THE ROOF!
OHHH! MAH BABY! MAH BABY!

...BUT ALL THAT FRESH AIR MADE THE FIRE MUCH, MUCH WORSE–I WAS RUNNING OUTA TIME!

AND THEN I LOOKED OUT THE WINDOW AND SAW THAT FOOL BABY ABOUT TO DANCE HIMSELF RIGHT OFF THE DAMN ROOF!
BAH-LE-LAH BOM! BOM! BOM!

CATCH HIM, LOUIS! CATCH HIM!!

BOM...BOM... WOOOOOOOOO!
OH NO!! HE'S FALLING!!

CATCH HIM, LOUIS! CATCH HIM!!

WEEEEEEEEEEEEEE!

GOTCHA!!!

IS HE OK?

WAAAAAAAAAA!

THAT KID HAD MORE LIVES THAN CARTER HAS PILLS! NOW I HAD TO GET MYSELF OUTA THERE BEFORE I ENDED UP LIKE EZRA KORN!

AS I BURST THROUGH THAT WINDOW I KNEW THEN MY LIFE WOULD NEVER BE THE SAME. BY SHEER DETERMINATION I HAD SOMEHOW CREATED MY GREATEST INVENTION...MYSELF!

A YOUNG LIFE HAD BEEN SAVED BUT THE FARMHOUSE WAS A TOTAL LOSS. THE ONLY THING LEFT OF EZRA KORN WAS A PILE OF ASHES AND ONE OF HIS STINKY OL' FEET. THE NEXT DAY THEY HONORED THAT FOOT WITH A FULL CHRISTIAN BURIAL AND A CHICKEN LUNCH.

MRS. COBB ATTEMPTED TO SCATTER HER GRAMPA'S ASHES, BUT A GUST O' WIND CARRIED THEM ACROSS THE BARNYARD AND INTO THE PIG PEN. 'TWAS POETIC JUSTICE FOR THAT OL' SLAVE-RUNNING SONOVABITCH!

I STILL HADN'T TOLD JOE AND AVIS COBB ABOUT MY JOB OFFER IN COVINGTON. WE WERE WAITING FOR THE RIGHT MOMENT WHEN, TO OUR SURPRISE, THEY WALKED OVER AND TALKED TO US!
ME AN' THE MISSUS WOULD LIKE TO HAVE A WORD WITH YOU BOYS.

EZRA KORN IS DEAD—NO ONE SHOULD DIE LIKE THAT, BUT SOMETHIN' WOULDA GOT HIM SOONER OR LATER. AN' MAYBE WE'VE LOST OUR HOME...BUT, SHOOT! WE CAN ALWAYS BUILD A NEW AND EVEN BETTER HOUSE!...

BUT, A FAMILY CANNOT BE REPLACED... AND IF OUR DARLIN' BOY HAD DIED...WELL... MRS. COBB AND I WOULD HAVE DIED RIGHT ALONG WITH HIM!

THANKS TO YOU BOYS, AND THE SPECIAL COURAGE OF BEN, OUR FAMILY LIVES ON... AND MRS. COBB AND I WILL HOLD YOU IN OUR HEARTS UNTIL WE ARE DUST.

UP TO THEN, JOE COBB HAD ALWAYS BEEN A MAN WITH TWO OR THREE WORDS IN HIS MOUTH BUT THAT WASN'T THE END OF IT...
AND NOW WE'RE GONNA DO SOMETHIN' FOR YOU BOYS...

WE KNOW YOUR WHOLE STORY. YOUR PA WON'T LET YOU GO HOME EMPTY-HANDED. WELL, I DON'T THINK I LIKE YOUR PA, BUT WE'RE GONNA HELP SAVE YOUR FAMILY SAME AS YOU SAVED OURS. **OK, PEDRO, BRING HER ON OUT!**

PEDRO CAME WALKING OUT OF THAT BARN WITH THE MOST BEAUTIFUL COW WE EVER SAW! YOU COULDA KNOCKED US BOTH DEAD AND STUCK US IN THE PIG PEN WITH EZRA.
SHE'S ALL YOURS, BOYS. THE BEST HEIFER OF THE LOT!

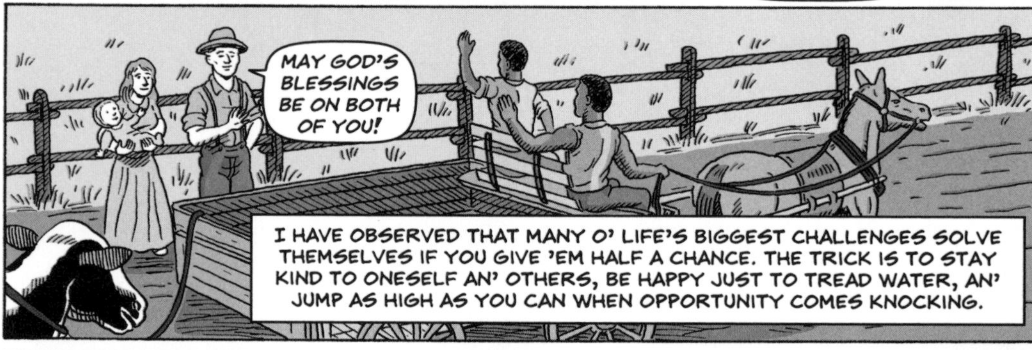
MAY GOD'S BLESSINGS BE ON BOTH OF YOU!
I HAVE OBSERVED THAT MANY O' LIFE'S BIGGEST CHALLENGES SOLVE THEMSELVES IF YOU GIVE 'EM HALF A CHANCE. THE TRICK IS TO STAY KIND TO ONESELF AN' OTHERS, BE HAPPY JUST TO TREAD WATER, AN' JUMP AS HIGH AS YOU CAN WHEN OPPORTUNITY COMES KNOCKING.

LOUIS WAS SO HAPPY TO BE GOING HOME, BUT I DID NOT SHARE IN HIS DELIGHT. I HAD TO MAKE A DIFFICULT CHOICE BETWEEN TAKING THE JOB UP IN COVINGTON OR LIVING UNDER THE THUMB OF MY OL' PAP AGAIN.
FWEE
KORN
DAIRY

GROWING UP A NEGRO WAS HARD ENOUGH! LIVIN' WITH A FATHER SO ANGRY AT LIFE MADE IT ALL THE MORE PURGATORIAL FOR ME. HE WAS THE "DARK AND STORMY NIGHT" THAT I HAD TO WAKE UP FROM!
BEN!...WAKE UP! WAKE UP, BEN!

LOOK, BEN! WE'S HOME! THERE'S MA AND PAP!

HERE YA GO, BROTHER. SHOW 'EM YOU CAN TAKE IT IN THE REST O' THE WAY.

LOUIS, I HAVE A CHANCE FOR A BETTER LIFE THAN WHAT OL' PAP HAS IN STORE FOR ME DOWN THERE. IF I DON'T TAKE IT NOW, I MAY NEVER GET OUTA HERE.

I KNOW YOUR MIND, BEN. I FIGGERED THIS MIGHT HAPPEN. DON'T WORRY, I'LL FIX THINGS WITH MA. SHE'LL UNDERSTAND.
YOU'RE A GOOD BROTHER, LOUIS... AN' THE BEST FRIEND I'LL EVER HAVE.

SO, I MADE MY CHOICE TO JOURNEY DOWN THE UNCERTAIN ROADS IN SEARCH OF A BETTER FUTURE.

UPON REACHING THE CREST O' THE HILL ABOVE THE FARM, I REMEMBERED SOMETHING I'D BEEN CARRYING AROUND MY NECK FOR WEEKS.

IT WAS THE CARVED WHISTLE MA USED DURING HER ESCAPE FROM SLAVERY.
BIRDY

I WAVED AN' SAID "FARE THEE WELL" TO MY FAMILY AND GAVE THAT WHISTLE A GOOD BLOW.
RRRR

IT MADE THE STRANGE, PITIFUL SOUND THAT SEEMED FITTING FOR THE UNJUST WORLD IT CAME FROM...

...AN' OFF I WENT. WITH THE MONEY EARNED IN COVINGTON AN' OTHER PLACES, I PAID MY WAY THROUGH SCHOOL. EVENTUALLY, MY JOURNEY BROUGHT ME HERE, TO CLEVELAND, WHERE I CHOSE TO LAY DOWN MY ROOTS.

AN' THAT, SIR, IS HOW A LOWLY COW INSPIRED ONE O' MY FINEST INVENTIONS–THE BELTRAN SMOKE HELMET.
azette

WELL, THAT'S QUITE A STORY, BELTRAN, QUITE A STORY, BUT...
...BUT WHAT?

BUT...MY EDITOR WILL NEVER PRINT IT. HE AND OUR READERS WOULD FIND IT...WELL..., "UNACCEPTABLE."
WHAT WON'T THEY ACCEPT? THAT A NEGRO HAS THE INTELLIGENCE TO INVENT SUCH A DEVICE?
CL
AD

NO, IT'S NOT THAT. IT'S JUST THAT OUR READERS WILL NEVER ACCEPT A NEGRO AS THE "HERO" OF A STORY.
HMMPH! SPOKEN LIKE A TRUE GATEKEEPER OF THE EVERLASTING LIE!

GODDAM IT! JUST WHO ARE THESE "READERS" ANYWAYS? AREN'T I A "READER," TOO?
HE Clevel
News
Gazett
OVER 30,000 REAL

MA—THERE'S STILL PEOPLE IN THE WORLD THAT CAN HEAR THE CALL OF YOUR OL' WHISTLE...

BIRDY
...(SIGH)...AN' I GUESS I'M ONE OF 'EM.

CHAPTER 6: "TOO BEAUTIFUL FOR TRAGEDY"

LOOK AT 'ER, CLARKE! **CHUST LOOK AT HER!** SHE'S FINEST, SAFEST CRIB EVER BUILT!

8 PM–JULY 24, 1916
WATERWORKS
CRIB #5

AS A CHASTENED BENJAMIN BELTRAN MADE HIS WAY HOME, THE TRAGEDY THAT CHANGED HIS LIFE FOREVER WAS UNFOLDING 4 MILES OFF THE COAST OF CLEVELAND.

AYE, THE SUN SETS COLORFULLY HERE!

YEA–IT'S 'CUZZA ALL THE SOOT IN TH' AIR

TOOOT!
ALL TUNNEL MEN REPORT TO THE FOREDECK!

THERE'S THE CALL, LAD! LET'S GO!
THEY BEST 'AVE GOOD NEWS WIT' 'EM

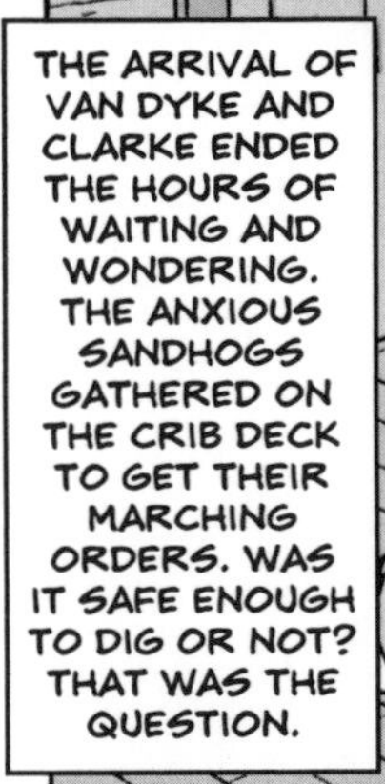
THE ARRIVAL OF VAN DYKE AND CLARKE ENDED THE HOURS OF WAITING AND WONDERING. THE ANXIOUS SANDHOGS GATHERED ON THE CRIB DECK TO GET THEIR MARCHING ORDERS. WAS IT SAFE ENOUGH TO DIG OR NOT? THAT WAS THE QUESTION.

OK, BOYS, GATHER 'ROUND, VE HAFF NEWS!

WE'RE DIGGIN' TONITE!
GOOD!
OH, YEAH?! AN' WHAT ABOUT DA GAS?

PIPE DOWN!! THE GAS HAS VENTED OUDT! WE GOTTA GET THIS PROJECT BACK ON SCHEDULE OR ELSE!

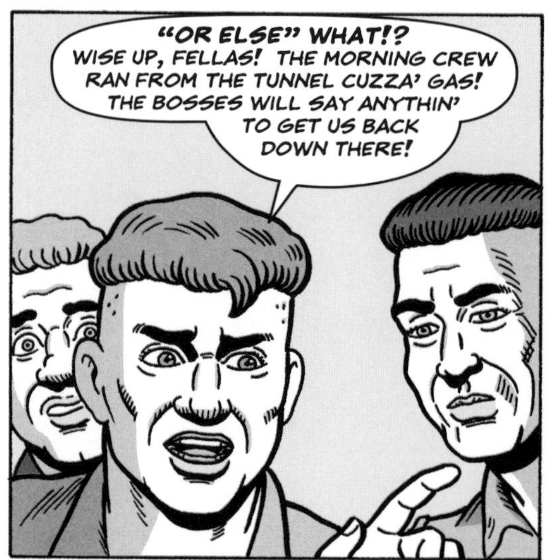
"OR ELSE" WHAT!? WISE UP, FELLAS! THE MORNING CREW RAN FROM THE TUNNEL CUZZA' GAS! THE BOSSES WILL SAY ANYTHIN' TO GET US BACK DOWN THERE!

RODGER, WE'LL TRUST IN WHATEVER YOU SAY–IS IT SAFE TO DIG TONIGHT OR NOT?

D'YA THINK I'D BE GOIN' DOWN ME'SELF IF IT WASN'T SAFE?

B'SIDES, THE GAS COMIN' OUTA O'MALLEY'S ARSE IS YER GREATEST DANGER! YE CAN'T OUTRUN IT!

HA! HA! HA!
HA! HA! HA!
GOOD ONE, RODGER!

LADS, IF YE WORK TONITE, YE'LL END UP WIT' AN EXTRA FIVER IN YER POCKET!

HMMPH! MAKE IT A SAWBUCK AND WE'LL THINK ABOUT IT!

HOW ABOUT "NO BUCKS" UND YOU GO DOWN ANYVAYS–EH?
YEAH! NOW YER SHOWIN' US YER TRUE COLORS!

OK–WE'LL PAY YEZ TEN DOLLARS PER MAN! BUT ONLY IF WE HIT OUR MARK!
SHUT IT, CLARKE!!

AHH! I WOULDN'T GO INTO THAT TUNNEL FOR ALL THE TEA IN CHINA!...I QUIT!

SUIT YERSELF! PACK UP YER GEAR AN' GET ON THE TUG WITH SUPERINTENDENT VAN DYKE. ANYONE ELSE WANNA GO WIT' HIM?

NOT ME! TEN BUCKS IS A LOT O' MONEY!
YER SHEEP! THE WHOLE LOT OF YEZ—JUST SHEEP!

ENUF! GO PACK YER BAGS OR YE'LL MISS THE TUG!

THE REST OF YEZ... GEAR UP!... MEET ME HERE ON DIS FOREDECK IN 30 MINUTES!

MR. CLARKE! I'D LIKE A VORD WITH YOU, PLEASE!

YOU STUPID MICK! I'M NODT PAYING NO GODDAM $10 APIECE.
QUIET, WILLY! SHUT YOUR BLESSED PIE-HOLE!

YOU CAN PAY DEM IF YOU WANT, BUT IT COMES OUT OF YOUR SHARE–NOT MINE!
YOU HEARD 'EM! FIVE BUCKS WOULDN'T DO IT! I HAD TA RAISE IT TO $10.
AHHH! YOU LET DOT BIG-MOUTHED SANDHOG PUSH YOU AROUND!
YER PAYIN', DUTCHMAN! WHEN THE TIME COMES–YER PAYIN'!!

I'LL PAY DEM $5 OR I'LL PAY THEM NOTHING!
TURN AROUND! YE FECKIN' EEDJIT!

WHAT YOU CALL ME!?
YER A FECKING EEDJIT! AS STUPID AS YE ARE UGLY. THAT FACE COULD FRIGHTEN THE BLIND!
WHAT?
I SEEN COWPLOP WIT' BETTER CHEEK.

WHY GALLAGHER'S WIDOW MARRIED YEZ, I'LL NEVER FIGGER OUT!

ME?...UGLY?

THE SANDHOG WHO QUIT LEFT CLARKE HAUNTED WITH A SENSE OF DOUBT AND DREAD. "WHAT GOOD IS MONEY," CLARKE PONDERED, "IF YOU'RE TOO **DEAD** TO SPEND IT?"

"...AND WHAT OF MY OWN FAMILY-WHO WILL PROVIDE FOR THEM?"

"AWW, STOP YER WORRYIN'. THEY'RE TOO BEAUTIFUL FER TRAGEDY..."

"...THIS NIGHT WILL BE LIKE A THOUSAND OTHER NIGHTS IN THE TUNNEL **NO BETTER-NO WORSE!**"

HEY! **CLARKE!!**

YEAH?

DON'T BE A SAP, CLARKE! THERE'S ENOUGH GAS DOWN THERE TO LIGHT UP THE ENTIRE CITY OF CLEVELAND!!!

I'LL TAKE IT UNDER ADVISEMENT!
THEN MAY GOD BE WIT' YEZ ALL TONIGHT!

DON'T LISTEN TO HIM! HE'LL BE SORRY VEN HE REACHES SHORE VIT NO DOUGH IN HIS POCKETS!

ACHH! GO FECK YERSELVES! DA' BOTH O' YEZ!

NIGHT CREW! PREPARE TO DESCEND!

MEANWHILE, INSIDE THE CLARKE HOME ON IRISHTOWN BEND...

INRI

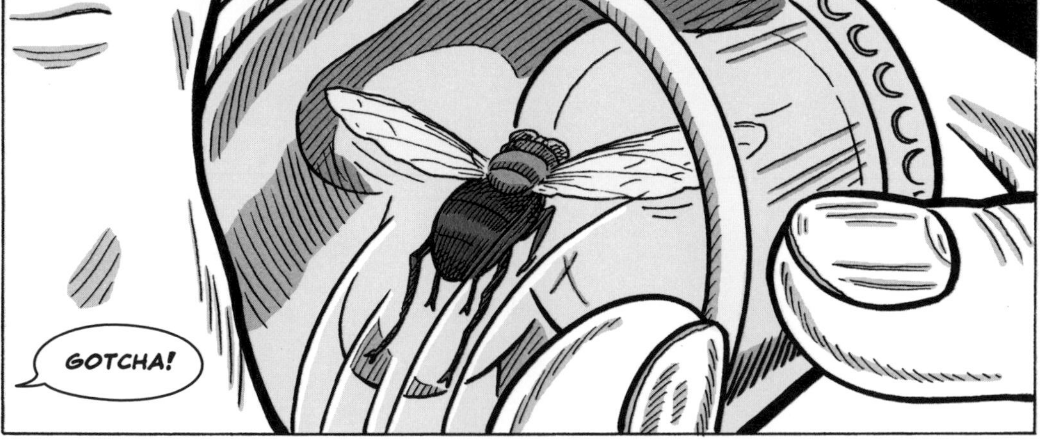
GOTCHA!

OOH! HE'S A BIG ONE!
OFT WIT' YER NOW, OL' MISTER FLY!
MA, YE SHOULDA KILLED THE FLY!
REMEMBER OUR POEM "...ALL CREATURES GREAT AND SMALL?"
"THE LORD GOD MADE THEM ALL!"

EVEN A WEE FLY DESERVES A FIGHTIN' CHANCE IN THIS WORLD.

I'LL KNIT AWHILE AND THEN IT'S OFF TA BED WITH YA!

WHAT'S 'DIS, NOW?

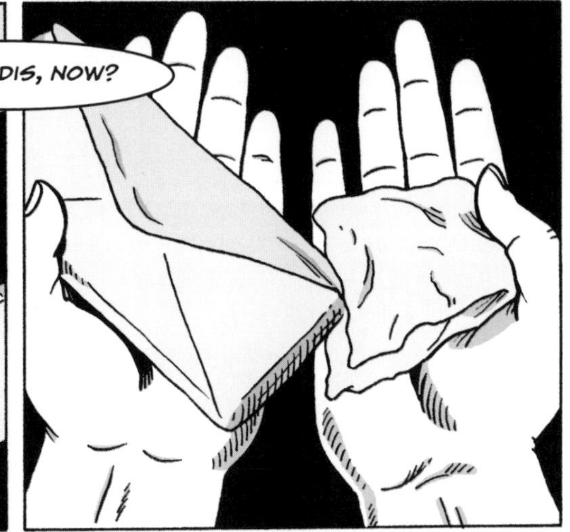

SWEENEY!!

I'LL BE BACK IN A JIFF, SWEET GIRL!...I HAVE TO TALK TO MRS. SWEENEY.
ALRIGHT!

AT THE SWEENEY HOME...
KNOCK KNOCK KNOCK

WHY?...HELLO, MRS. CLARKE?

BEFORE TH' SHIFT YER SON COMES BY AN' HANDS RODGER 'DIS NOTE.

MY SON? P.J.? HE CANNO' READ NOR WRITE!...SO? WELL, ...WAZZIT SAY?
IT SAYS: "WE DIG TONITE-WET RAGS"!

"WET RAGS" IS IT? ... OH DEAR.
TELL ME WHA' IT MEANS!

Y'MEAN AFTER ALL THESE YEARS IN TH' TUNNELS, RODGER NEVER TOLD YE 'BOUT "WET RAGS"?
HE DID NOT.

'TIS ABOUT THE GAS! MEN WRAP WET KERCHIEFS AROUND THEIR FACES...SO THEY CAN BREATHE BETTER!

YE SAY YER SON CANNO' READ NOR WRITE? THEN WHO DID THE FANCY SCRAWL?
SHOW IT TO ME!

NOR CAN I READ, BUT I KNOW THE HAND WHAT DID THIS! I SEEN OTHER NOTES LIKE IT IN ME BOY'S POCKETS!

WHO THEN?!
WHO ELSE? THE DUTCHMAN!

GOBSHITE!!

OH, BUT YER NEEDN'T WORRY, LASS! ME BOY SEZ THERE'S ALWAYS GAS IN THE TUNNELS!

OH, RODGER! WHAT HAVE YE GOTTEN YERSELF INTA?

HEY, MA! LOOK!

LOOKS LIKE WE GOT 'NUTHER FLY IN HERE!

SPLAT!

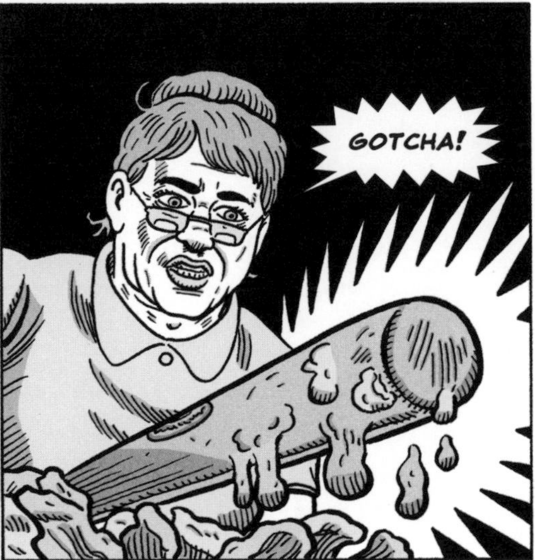
GOTCHA!

GODT IT?!! GODT ME, Y'MEAN?

WELLL...LET'S JUST SAY I GOT BOTH OF YEZ, AND WE'LL LEAVE IT LIKE THAT.

WELL..GEEEZ, CHUST LOOK AT THIS MESS!
FLIES ARE FILTH!...AN' MR. GALLAGHER WOULD NOT TOLERATE FILTH IN HIS HOUSE! WE STILL LIVE BY HIS RULES.

NOW CLEAN THIS MESS UP!!!... AND THEN TIDY YERSELF—YE ARE A WRETCHED SIGHT BEFORE THE LORD!

MOMENTS LATER...
...LIEFJE?
WHAT IS IT?

AM I...AN UGLY MAN??

JAYSUS, MARY, AN' JOSEPH...WHAT A THING TO ASK YER OWN WIFE!

VELL...?
WELL, WHAT? IF YE HAVE GROWED ANXIOUS O'ER YER LOOKS THEN I SAY YER A WEE LATE, BUCKO!

AN' WHAT MAY I ASK HAS INSPIRED THIS LATEST FIT O' MADNESS?

AWWW...ZUMTHINK CLARKE SAID TO GET MY GOATS...

AN' SUCCEEDED, I SEE!...AHH, MY JOHNNY THOUGHT CLARKE THE BEST SANDHOG HE EVER HAD.

ZO YOU AGREE!!! YOU AGREE... YOU MARRIED AN UGLY MAN!!!

AYE, IT'S TRUE, BUT A WOMAN IN MY POSITION CANNO' BE TOO PARTICULAR!!
WHEN JOHNNY DIED I NEEDED THE SECURITY OF A STEADY MAN...AND YE HAVE BROUGHT ME THAT, WILLY.

OOH...SOB... SOB...SOB!

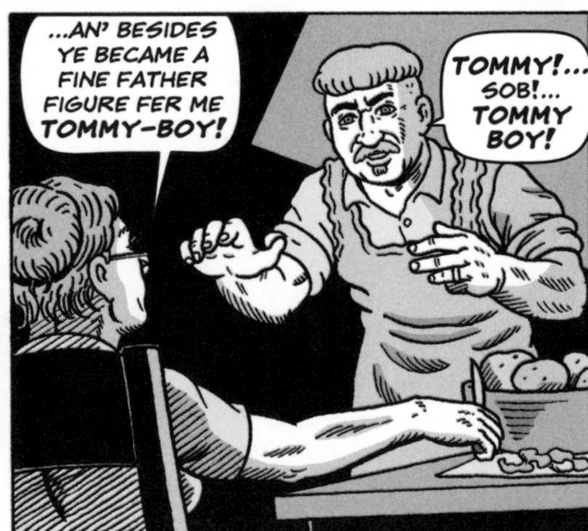
...AN' BESIDES YE BECAME A FINE FATHER FIGURE FER ME TOMMY-BOY!
TOMMY!... SOB!... TOMMY BOY!

LORD KNOWS WHAT THE BOY WOULDA' BECOME WITHOUT A MAN IN HIS LIFE!
I LUFF DOT BOY LIKE MY OWN SON! VERE THE HELL IS HE?!

HE'S WORKIN' A DOUBLE SHIFT AT THE TAXI STAND- WORKIN' LIKE A SLAVE!
I TAUGHT HIM TO BE CHUST LIKE ME!

IN AN ALLEYWAY ACROSS FROM THE E. 9TH STREET TAXI STAND.
POST NO BILLS
GEEZIZ, TOMMY! IF YER MA COULD SEE YEZ NOW!
BLARRGGG!

WAZZIT THE WHISKEY OR THE GIN?...GEEZ, I TOLD YA NOT TO DRINK ALL THAT BEER!
AAAGGH!...SCHNAPPS!

WHA...?
UGH!...THE SCHNAPPS...IT WAS THE DAMN SCHNAPPS! UGHHHHH!

I PINCHED A BOTTLE OF WILLY'S BOYSENBERRY SCHNAPPS! THEY SHOULD MAKE THAT CRAP ILLEGAL...AGGH!

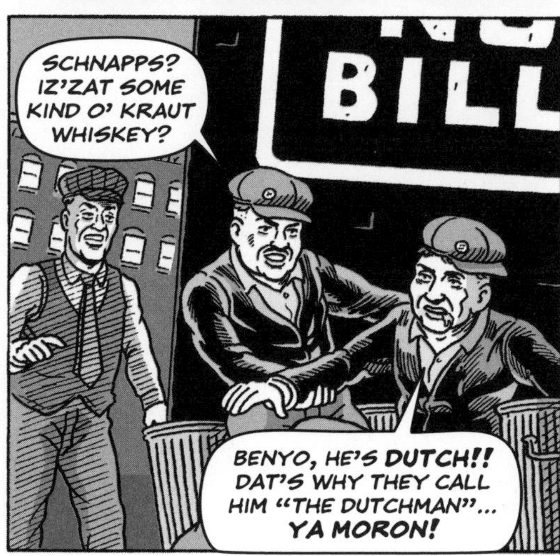
BILL
SCHNAPPS? IZ'ZAT SOME KIND O' KRAUT WHISKEY?
BENYO, HE'S DUTCH!! DAT'S WHY THEY CALL HIM "THE DUTCHMAN"... YA MORON!

HEY! EITHER O' YOU DUMB KLUCKS WORKIN' TONIGHT? I GOT FARES WAITIN'!!
WHO YOU CALLIN' A DUMB KLUCK?!
WHOO-WHOAAA!
CLEVELAND
JOHNNY
VS.
KID
PATRICK'S

YOU! YA DUMB KLUCK!!
AAAGH!

AGGG! HALP!!

KNUCKLEHEADS!
YOU REST UP, TOMMY-BOY! I GOTTA TAKE THIS FARE!

IT'S GONE!!
NOW WHAT?!

MY BOYSENBERRY SCHNAPPS! I HAD A FULL BOTTLE IN THIS VERY CUPBOARD!
YE COULDN'T EMBALM ME WITH THAT FRUITY SWILL, PRAISE GOD!

VELL, SOMEBODY TOOK IT, I TELL YA!
MAYBE THE FAIRIES TOOK IT! TRY THE BUTTERMILK AN' STOP YER BLATHERIN'!
OLD FER

A FEW MOMENTS LATER...
HERE'S THE BUTTERMILK. GOOD AND COLD.

HMMM...I THOUGHT THE ICEMAN COMES ON FRIDAYS?

THE ICEMAN DOES COME ON FRIDAYS, BEN.

HOW'YA KEEPIN' THE BUTTERMILK COLD IN THIS HEAT?
A HANDSOME INVENTOR I KNOW FIGURED A WAY TO KEEP ICE FROZEN TWICE AS LONG!

IF I WAS YOU I'D MARRY THAT FELLA RIGHT QUICK!
HEE-HEE! I WOULD, BUT HE'S NOT MY TYPE!

SIGH...

WAS IT ANOTHER DIFFICULT DAY, DEAR?

EVERY DAY BRINGS A DIFFERENT SHADE O' "DIFFICULT."

I CAN'T KEEP DOIN' THIS!
CAN I HELP?

BEN...?

I'M SERIOUS, FRIEDA! I AM AT THE END OF MY...
BEN!

REMEMBER WHO YOU ARE!...A GREAT MAN!

I AM **NOT** A GREAT MAN...
WELL...I'LL LEAVE YOU TO WALLOW IN YOUR BUTTERMILK...

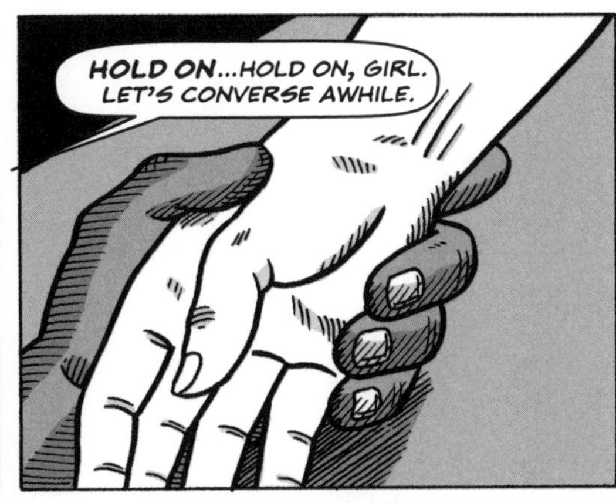
HOLD ON...HOLD ON, GIRL. LET'S CONVERSE AWHILE.

WHAT I MEAN IS I'M NOT "GREAT" LIKE **TOM EDISON** IS GREAT... NO SIR, I'M NO EDISON!

TOM EDISON IS A STINKY OLD MAN WHO PUTS HIS NAME ON THE SWEAT AND TOIL OF OTHERS...AND LOOK AT WHAT HE DID TO **TESLA!**

TESLA? THAT MAN IS AS MAD AS A MARCH HARE. I'LL TAKE STINKY O'ER CRAZY ANY OL' DAY!

I'M JUST SAYING THAT THE SMOKE HELMET IS GOING TO SAVE LIVES AND SOON THE WORLD WILL KNOW THAT YOU ARE A GREAT MAN, TOO!

I'M A GREAT MAN WHO DRAGS HIMSELF ALL O'ER CREATION DRESSED LIKE AN INDIAN. IT'S NUTHIN' BUT PURE HUMILIATION...!

IT'S CALLED PROVIDING AND PUTTING A ROOF OVER OUR HEADS! YOU'RE A GREAT MAN, BEN–IT'S NOT YOUR FAULT!

WELL...I MAY BE THIS AND I MAY BE THAT...IN THE LARGER SCHEME O' THINGS I'M JUS'...AN ORDINARY MAN.

JUS' A SIMPLE...

ORDINARY...

...MAN.

9 PM–CRIB #5 SHAFT ELEVATOR...
TAKE 'ER DOWN, MR. JESSUP.

130 FT
LAKE BED
...HOLD TIGHT, LADS. A FEW MORE SECONDS TO THE BOTTOM...

THE VENTING WORKED! WE HAVE GOOD AIR! HEAD FOR THE AIRLOCK!
FOOM!

TUNNEL PRESSURE, MR. JESSUP?

HOLDING FAST AT 22 PSI, MR. CLARKE!

BY SOME MIRACLE IS THE CRIB PHONE WORKIN'?
NO SMO
NOPE... DEAD AS MY MOTHER!

BLESS HER MEMORY. CIRCLE 'ROUND LADS AND LISTEN TO WHAT HAS TO BE SAID!

WE MAY BE SIMPLE MEN, BUT WE HAVE THE SAME FIVE SENSES GOD GAVE MR. ROCKEFELLER. YOU'LL BE NEEDIN' EVERY ONE O' EM T'NIGHT!

THE CRIB PHONE IS OUT AS USUAL. MR. JESSUP WILL REMAIN AT THE AIRLOCK IN CASE O' TROUBLE.

AIRLOCK
TUNN
MR. JESSUP, PRESSURIZE THE CHAMBER TO 22 PSI.

UP ON THE CRIB DECK THE GAUGES OF A POWERFUL AIR COMPRESSOR SPRANG TO LIFE AS THE SANDHOGS BELOW PRESSURIZED THE AIRLOCK CHAMBER.
CHUG-A-CHUG-A-CHUG!
HEY! THE CHAMBER IS BEING PRESSURIZED MARK THE TIME!

SEAN, EAMONN- TAKE THE BIRDS AND PROCEED WITH CAUTION TO 100 FEET. IF ALL IS WELL, GIVE US THE SIGNAL.
BE CAREFUL, LADS. YE KNOW THE DRILL.

EAMONN, D'YA BELIEVE WHAT THEY SAY 'BOUT THE PIGEONS O' CLEVELAND?

WHAZZIT THEY SAY?

AHHH! NUTTIN' BAD 'BOUT DEM BIRDS! LET'S WAVE IN THE CREW!

IF THE BIRDS ARE AS TOUGH AS YE SAY-MEBBE WE SHOULD GIVE 'EM MORE TIME.

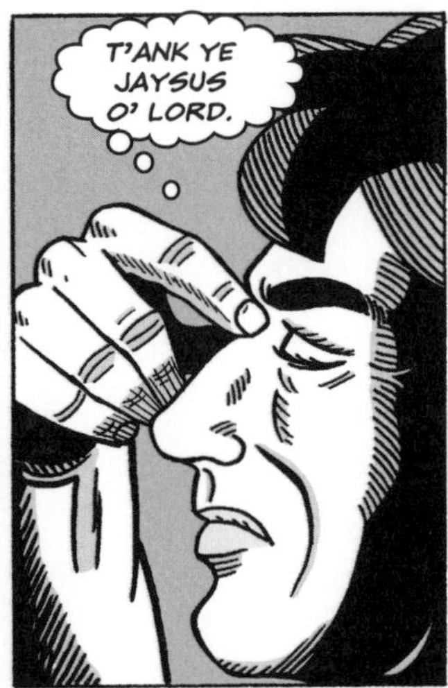

THE SANDHOG'S FATEFUL DESCENT INTO THE BOWELS OF CRIB #5 HAD TAKEN PLACE ON A HOT JULY NIGHT IN 1916 FOLLOWING A DAY WHERE LITTLE HAD GONE RIGHT IN CLEVELAND. THE CITY WAS COPING WITH A KILLER HEAT WAVE AND A LARGE WAREHOUSE FIRE IN BIG ITALY. THE LATTER REQUIRED ALL OF THE FIREFIGHTING AND RESCUE RESOURCES THAT THE CITY COULD MUSTER. IRONICALLY, WHILE PEOPLE SLEPT OUTSIDE OF THEIR STIFLING TENEMENTS AND FIREMEN LABORED IN HELLISH CONDITIONS, THE COOLEST PLACE IN TOWN WAS A TUNNEL 200 FEET BELOW THE SURFACE OF LAKE ERIE.

GAMBLING WITH LIFE IN ORDER TO REMAIN EMPLOYED WAS AN UNSPOKEN JOB REQUIREMENT FOR THE SANDHOGS. THE SIZE OF EACH MAN'S GAMBLE WAS ROUGHLY EQUAL TO HIS OWN PERSONAL LEVEL OF DESPERATION. HAD IT NOT BEEN FOR THE MISADVENTURES OF POVERTY, PERHAPS THESE TUNNEL MEN WOULD HAVE SWEATED OUT THE SUMMER HEAT WITH MUGS OF BEER IN THE DIVE BARS OF WHISKEY ISLAND AND IRISHTOWN BEND. SADLY, THE MERE PROMISE OF A FEW EXTRA DOLLARS WAS ENOUGH TO TEMPT RATIONAL MEN DOWN A SHAFT AND INTO A TUNNEL WHERE THE SPECTERS OF CATASTROPHE AND DEATH LAY IN WAIT FOR THEM.

Y'KNOW EAMONN, I BEEN T'INKIN' A LOT.
'TIS NOT POSSIBLE.

NOT POSSIBLE? Y'MEAN THA' I'M GOIN' HOME?
NO...THA' YER CAPABLE OF "T'INKIN' A LOT."

I'M WORRIED 'BOUT ME OL' MA NOW THA' IRELAND IS GOIN' UP IN FLAMES.
YER JES' A'NUTTER IRISH BOY JOINED AT THE TIT WIT' HIS MA!

OH! AN' I 'SPOSE YE NEVER 'AD A MUTTER OF YER OWN, EH?! ...HATCHED WERE YE?!

I HAD A MUTTER. HER NAME WAS ANNIE O'DONNELL. SHE WERE A RAVEN-HAIRED BEAUTY FROM THE ROSSES.

'AN DID YE LOVE 'ER, EAMONN? WERE YE "JOINED AT THE TIT" LIKE A GOOD IRISH BOY?

AH,...WELL, I NEVER KNEW HER, Y'SEE...SHE WAS SHOT DEAD BY MILITIA WHEN I WAS...WELL...TOO YOUNG TO HOLD 'ER MEMORY.

IRELAND IS A GRAVE, EAMONN. YOU MUST MISS HER TARRIBLE.
SEAN, BOY, I CANNO' MISS SOMETHIN' I NEVER HAD.

T'WAS A COLD, WINDY WORLD FOR THAT BOY WITH NO MUTT'ER.
...WELL, I SHARE ME MA WITH YA, IF YE LIKE?

EAMONN, LET'S GO BACK T' IRELAND TOGETHER–YOU AND ME!

CAREFUL THAT I MAY MARRY YER MA AN' BECOME YOUR DA! T'INK O' DAT WOULD'YA!
HMMPH! YER THE CLOSEST T'ING TO A DA I GOT IN DIS WORLD, ANYWAYS.

I BE PROUD TO 'AVE YE AS A SON, BOYO.

AS THE TUNNEL BORERS AND MUCKERS PREPARED TO START DIGGING, RODGER CLARKE MAINTAINED A SAFE POSITION NEAR THE AIRLOCK PORING OVER TUNNEL SCHEMATICS WITH HIS DIG FOREMAN, TOM SKALSKI.

BUT...THE GAS IS ALL CLEARED OUT–THANKS TO THE VENTILATORS.

FER NOW, MEBBE. HERE, LAD, LEMME SHOW YE SOMETHIN'...

CUZ' O' GAS WE BUILT BULKHEADS HERE. AN' SEE MORE POCKETS 'AVE OPENED HERE AND –HERE!

YEA, BUT IT'S NOTHIN' WE CAN'T HANDLE!
I DON'T LIKE THE PATTERN O' DESE BREACHES.

THEY AREN'T RANDOM. THEY'RE TOO CLOSE TOGETHER. THE GEOLOGY IS WORKIN' AGAINST US!

GEOLOGY?!
IT'S THE STUDY O' ROCKS, BUCKO!
...LIKE THE ONES ROLLIN' 'ROUND IN OUR HEADS!

HA! HA! HA!

UGH!
LEG FLARING UP? GO ON UPTOP, MR. CLARKE? I CAN COVER IT HERE.

I PAY ME OWN WAY IN 'DIS LIFE. CARRY ON 'BOUT YER BUSINESS.

THERE WOULD BE NO REST FOR CLARKE ON THIS NIGHT. NO REST FROM THE PAIN IN HIS RUINED LEG, OR FROM THE RELENTLESS PRESENCE OF HIS SOUL'S TORMENTORS. HE HAD DONE ALL HE COULD FOR HIS FAMILY, BUT IT WOULD NEVER BE ENOUGH AND HE KNEW IT. LEFT ALONE AND BARELY ABLE TO COPE WITH HIS CONSUMING DESPERATION, HIS MIND RETREATED INTO A FITFUL DREAM.

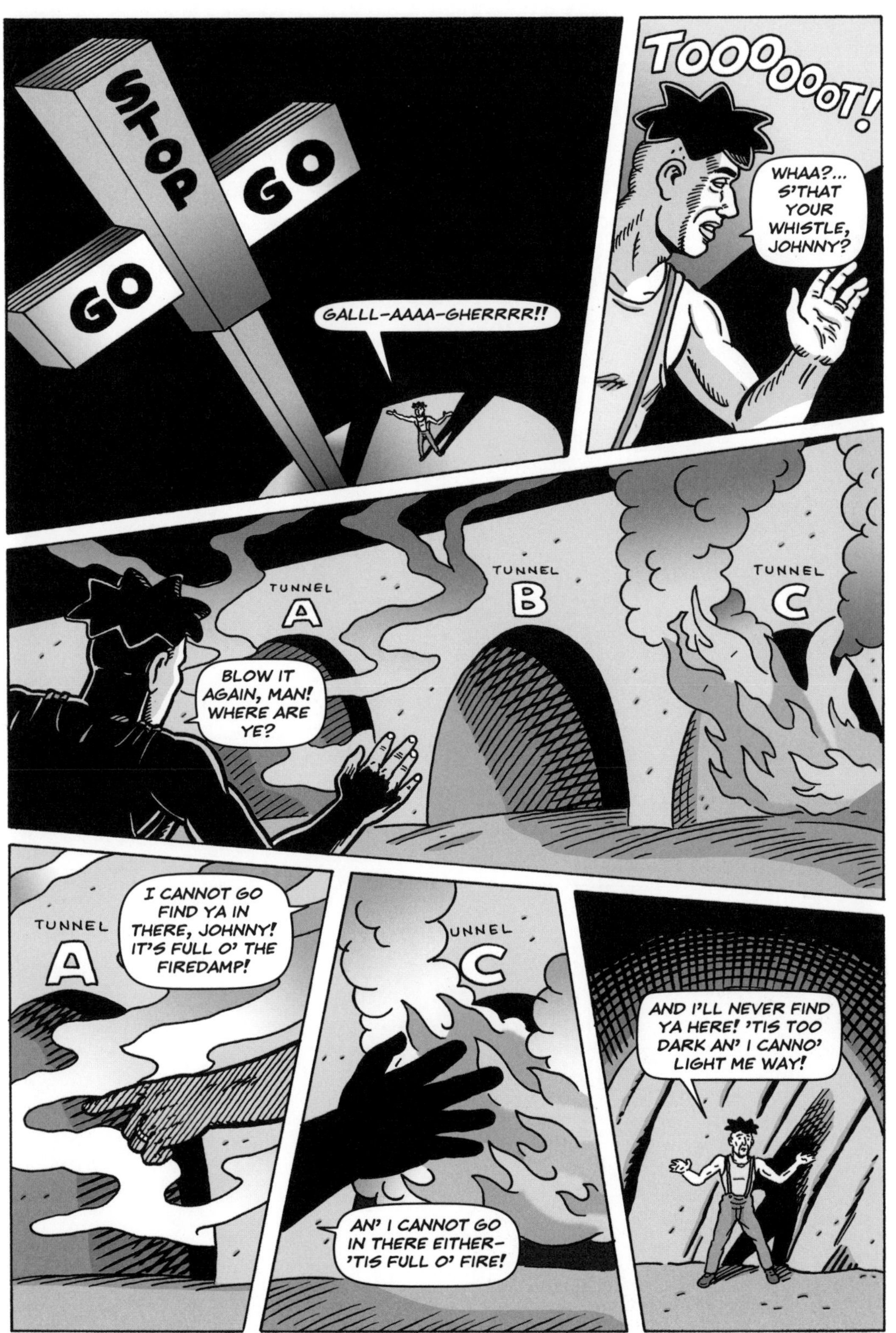
STOP
GO
GO
GALLL-AAAA-GHERRRR!!
TOOOOOOOT!
WHAA?... S'THAT YOUR WHISTLE, JOHNNY?
TUNNEL A
TUNNEL B
TUNNEL C
BLOW IT AGAIN, MAN! WHERE ARE YE?
TUNNEL A
I CANNOT GO FIND YA IN THERE, JOHNNY! IT'S FULL O' THE FIREDAMP!
UNNEL C
AN' I CANNOT GO IN THERE EITHER- 'TIS FULL O' FIRE!
AND I'LL NEVER FIND YA HERE! 'TIS TOO DARK AN' I CANNO' LIGHT ME WAY!

'TIS USELESS, JOHNNY!... I CANNO' SAVE WHAT I CANNO' SEE!
TOOOOOOOT!
...I GIVE YE A SIGNAL, JOHNNY...WITH ME OWN WHISTLE!
WHA...? WHAT'S THIS, NOW?
BIRDY
SSSSSHH!
BIRDY
...'TIS JUST A STICK...AN' NOTHING MORE!

I HEAR YER FOOTSTEPS! WHO GOES THERE?!
OH!...OH NO...!
SPLISH-SPLASH! SPLISH!

I CANNOT LOOK AT YE! HAVE MERCY ON ME! FORGIVE ME!

CLARKE... LOOK AT ME!

CLARKE!!
HUH?!! MY GOD!... SWEET JESUS!

BEN?...
WHAT IS IT?
POPULAR MECHANICS MAGAZINE

WHOA!...I HAD A BAD DREAM IS ALL...A **REAL BAD DREAM.**

IT'S THIS TERRIBLE HEAT...IT CAUSES UNQUIET DREAMS.

WHO THE HELL IS **"CLARKE"**?

BACK AT THE #5 TUNNEL...
BLEEEEEETT!

FIRE UP THE MOLE! LET'S START DIGGING!

THE MOLE IS FIRED UP AND READY, SEAN! WHAT YER SAY WE DRIVE 'ER ALL THE WAY TA' IRELAND!
YEAH-YEAH... SETTLE DOWN.
THOSE TWO MICKS CRACK ME UP!
THICK AS THIEVES THEY ARE!

RAISE THE SHIELD!

SHIELD IS RAISED!

GO AHEAD AN' EASE 'ER IN SLOWLY, EAMONN!
HEE-HEE! THA' T'WERE THE FIRST THING THE PRETTY GIRL SAID!
EAMONN!! FER THE SAKE O' JAYSUS AN' THE SAINTS DRILL THE DAMN HOLE!!
AN' THA', ME LAD, T'WERE THE SECOND THING THE PRETTY GIRL SAID!
FWEEEEEEE!
VRRRRRRR!
HERE WE GO, SEAN! WE'RE TAKIN' THE ROCKY ROAD TO DUBLIN!!

...BACK ON IRISHTOWN BEND...
TIME FER BED, ME FINE YOUNG LADY!

MA–CAN I LIGHT THE CANDLE NOW?

YES...WE MUSN'T FORGET THAT TONIGHT.
I'LL GET THE MATCHES!

WHY DO WE LIGHT THE CANDLE, MA?
AHH, YE KNOW WHY...I'VE TOLD YEZ MANY TIMES.

WE PUT A LIGHT IN THE WINDOW SO YER DA CAN FIND HIS WAY BACK TO US.
THROUGH THE "FEARSOME DARKNESS"?

WHA...?? WHAT D'YA MEAN?
DA TOLD ME...

HE SAYS,...EVEN IN FEARSOME DARKNESS, HE "WILL FIND THE ROAD HOME AN' WE WILL MEET ATOP...A RISEN PATH..."

"...WHERE A CARELESS SUN TURNS DEW TO LIGHT."

WORDS THAT CAME BY WAY O' A POEM HE WROTE TO ME WHEN YER DA WAS RECOVERING FROM HIS ACCIDENT.
WHAZZIT MEAN, MA?

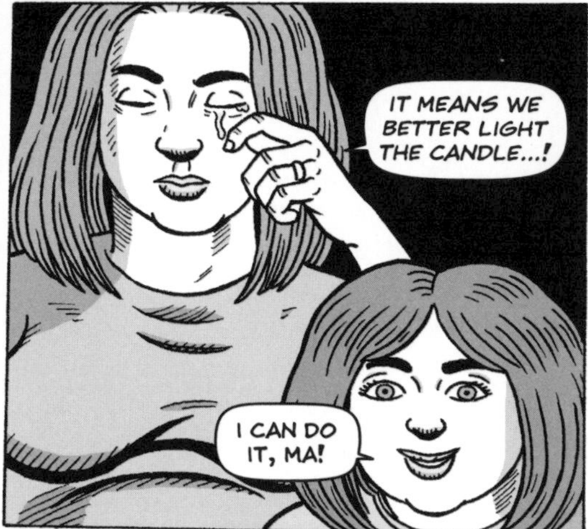
IT MEANS WE BETTER LIGHT THE CANDLE...!
I CAN DO IT, MA!

SKRITCH!
SAFETY

NOW THEN, DARLIN', BLOW IT OUT.

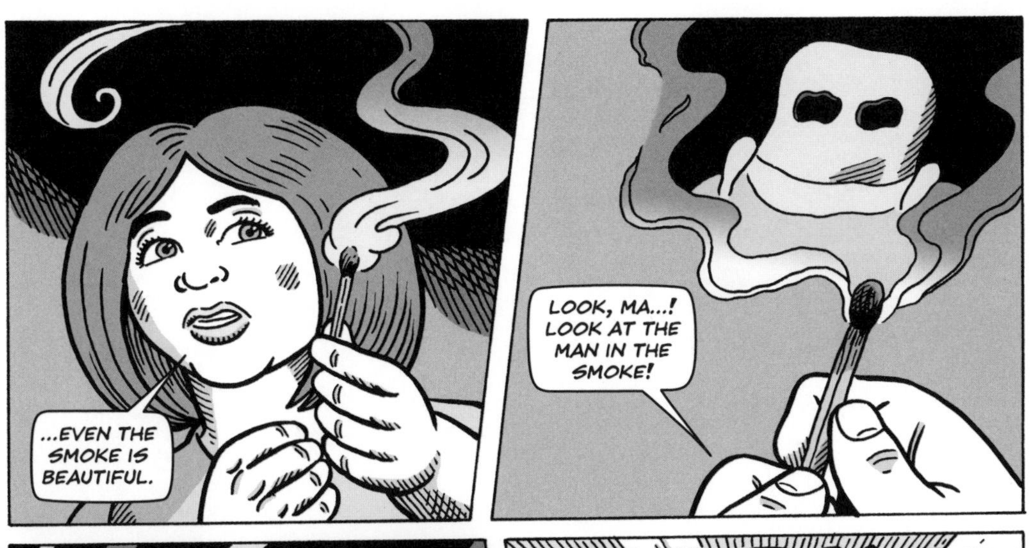
...EVEN THE SMOKE IS BEAUTIFUL.
LOOK, MA...! LOOK AT THE MAN IN THE SMOKE!
CLARKE!!
CLARKE!
MR. CLARKE!
MR. CLARKE!! WAKE UP! MR. CLARKE!
HUH?!... WHA?!...WHA' WHAT IS IT?
WHO ERE YE?!

IT'S BORELLI!... MR. CLARKE!...ME! JOE BORELLI!

BORELLI! UGH... SORRY! I MUSTA DOZED OFF FER A SECOND!
MR. CLARKE!... SERVICE TUNNEL! COME QUICK!

YEA, I'M WIT' YA...HELP ME UP WILL'YA? WE'LL TAKE THE HANDCAR.

TUNNEL FACE
CLARKE WONDERED IF THE HOODED MAN IN HIS DREAM WAS AN OMEN, BUT WHAT HE SAW NEXT SHOOK HIM STRAIGHT TO HIS BONES!

AH...I SEES YA, OL' FRIEND. YER WIT' ME TONIGHT, AREN'T YE?
WHEN BORELLI DIDN'T SHARE THE SPECTRAL VISION, CLARKE REALIZED THAT IT WAS ONLY MEANT FOR HIM...

...AND HE KNEW THAT HIS NIGHT WOULD NOT BE LIKE A THOUSAND OTHER NIGHTS' IN THE TUNNEL!
WE GOTTA PROBLEM IN THE SERVICE TUNNEL. IT'S CLOSED UNTIL CLARKE CHECKS IT OUT!
WHAT?! GODDAMIT, SKALSKI, YER PUTTIN' ME BEHIND SCHEDULE!
STOP-START STOP-START! IT'S NO WONDER WE'RE BEHIND ON THIS DIG!
SEE THERE, MR. CLARKE! THE TRACK IS LOOSE WHERE THE SHIELD CAR DERAILED!

LOOK! IT-ZA CRACK ONNA DA EARTH!
sniff!...YEA- IT'S A BREACH! YE CAN STILL SMELL THE METHANE!
DA SAME BREACH THAT DRIVE OUT DA MORNING CREW?
FOLLOW ME, MR. BORELLI!
BREACHES CAN COME IN GROUPS-LOOK FER MORE O' 'EM.
THERE'S MORE OUT THERE, I TELL YA.
WE GOTTA FIND 'EM, ...B'FORE THEY FIND US!

CHAPTER 7: "GONE...THEN GONE AGAIN"
MEANWHILE, AT THE HOME OF WILHELM AND AGNES VAN DYKE...
SNORE!

ZZZZZZ
TOM SWIFT AND HIS BIG TUNNEL
BY VICTOR APPLETON

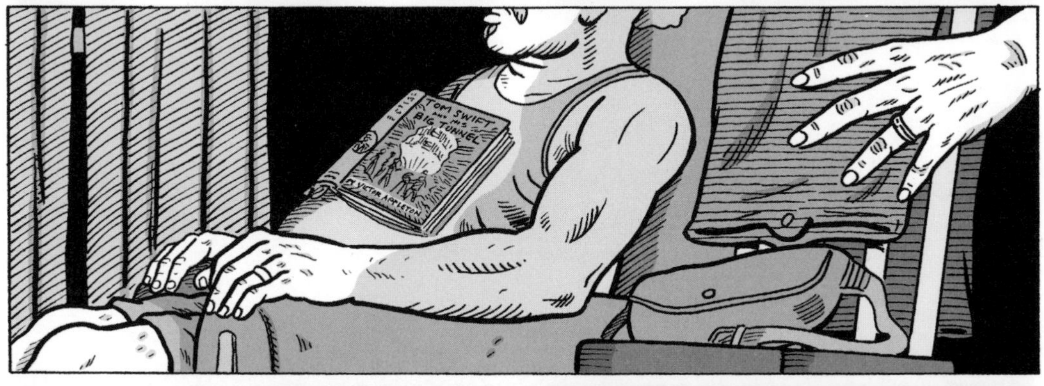
TOM SWIFT AND HIS BIG TUNNEL
BY VICTOR APPLETON

ZZZZZZZ
AN' NOW WE SEE WHAT THE GOBSHITE IS HOLDIN' BACK ON US...

JAYSUS, MARY AND JOSEPH!!

YOU! GIMME MY MONEY!!

DIS IS MONEY TO PAY THE SANDHOGS!!
WADD'YA MEAN? 'TIS THE JOB O' THE WATERWORKS TO PAY 'EM!

SOMETHIN' SMELLS HERE, WILLY...AN' IT'S NOT JUST YER STOCKINGS!
DIS IS BONUS MONEY!! BONUS MONEY!!

"BONUS MONEY" ME EYES! 'TIS BLOOD MONEY MORE LIKE IT!!!
YAH! CALL IT VAT YOU LIKE BUT IT STAYS VITH ME, YOU THIEF!!
CALL ME A THIEF, WILL'YA? WE'LL SEE ABOUT THAT, NOW...

AAAAGGGG!
WHACK!

MR. GALLAGHER WARNED ME ABOUT YA!! HE ALWAYS SAID YE WERE A GOBSHITE!!!
HELP!!! AIEEEE!! YE'VE LOST YOUR MYNDT!!!

AAIEEEEEEE!
THWACK!

LEGGO, YOU DURTY CREATURE!!
EEERRSHH!! YOU GIMME DOT BELT!!

EEEEEEE!

BUMP!
MY BEST CHINA!! NOOOOOOO!
KRISH!

YOU KEEP YOUR CLOVEN HOOVES OFF MY MONEY!!
I'LL KILL YA ...DURTY ROTTEN GOBSHITE!!

I SEE YA! YA DUTCH DIVIL!!

WELL, ME FINE GENTLEMAN! WE WILL JUST SEE ABOUT THIS!

UGH! pant! pant! IT'S GOOD YE LIKE P'TATERS, 'CUZ pant! I'M ABOUT TA BAKE YE INTA ONE!

HMMM...AND WHAT HAVE WE HERE?!

WHAT ON EARTH IS IN ALL THIS WRITIN'?!
CLEVEL

WILLY! WHAT DOES ALL THIS SCRIBBLE MEAN?! WHAT HAVE YE DONE?!!

MEANWHILE, BACK IN THE TUNNELS OF WATERWORKS CRIB #5...
BORELLI–SHINE YER LIGHT AGAINST THE WALL–IS DAT WHAT I THINK IT IS?!
CRACKS AN'NA MORE CRACKS!!
JAYSUS! DIS WHOLE AREA COULD BLOW ANY MOMENT!
FIREDAMP! BUBBLIN' RIGHT OUTA DA CLAY!
GET OUTA THERE, BORELLI, ON THE QUICK!
HEY! WHAT'S HOLDIN' UP THE SHOW?! WE GOT LOADED MUCK CARTS STACKING UP IN THE MAIN TUNNEL!
SHUT YER GOB, JACKSON! WE HAVE A BREACH!
LISTEN BOYS!...I'M ORDERIN' EVERYONE OUT! WE GOT US ONE CHANCE TO DO THIS RIGHT–WE DON'T WANT MASS PANIC!
BORELLI! TAKE THE HANDCAR TO THE AIRLOCK AND INFORM JESSUP. THEN GET YER ASS UPTOP AND TELL'EM WHAT'S HAPPENING!
I DO IT, MR. CLARKE!

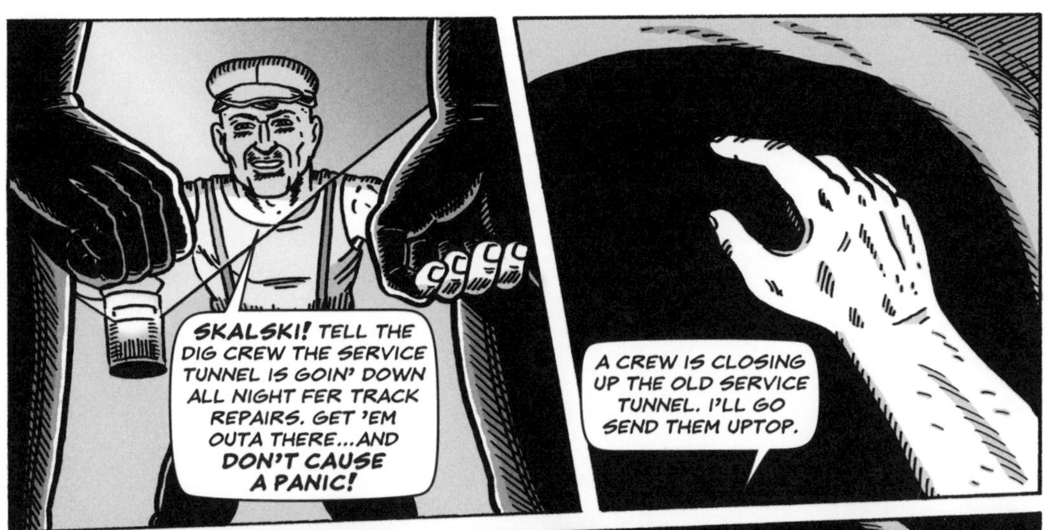
SKALSKI! TELL THE DIG CREW THE SERVICE TUNNEL IS GOIN' DOWN ALL NIGHT FER TRACK REPAIRS. GET 'EM OUTA THERE...AND DON'T CAUSE A PANIC!
A CREW IS CLOSING UP THE OLD SERVICE TUNNEL. I'LL GO SEND THEM UPTOP.

BUT...MR. CLARKE! WHAT ABOUT'A YOR LEG?
LEG?...AN' WHAT LEG WOULD THAT BE?

PLEASE BE CAREFUL, MR. CLARKE.
SKALSKI, YOU AN'NA JACKSON, PLEEZE TAKE'A CARE OF MR. CLARKE. HE NOT'A WELL MAN.

WHEN SKALSKI AND JACKSON ARRIVED AT THE DIG SITE, THEIR NEWS TO EVACUATE WAS MET WITH ANGER AND FRUSTRATION...
THE BOSS SAYS WE GO UPTOP NOW! WE GOT BUSTED TRACK IN THE SERVICE TUNNEL!
LET'S GO! EVERYBODY TO THE AIRLOCK!
YER KIDDIN' ME!
TA HELL YE SAY!! WE JUST STARTED OUR SHIFT!
IT'S CLARKE'S ORDERS- SNAP TO IT!
AAAAGGGGG!
GET OFFA' ME MACHINE, SKALSKI!
OOF!

V-R-R-R-R-R-R-R-R-R!

WHAT THE HELL'S GOIN' ON, JACKSON?! WE'RE IN THE MIDDLE OF A DIG!

SHUT'ER DOWN, IRISH! THAT'S AN ORDER!

FWEEEEEE!

STOW YOUR GEAR AND ASSEMBLE HERE!! WE'RE HEADED FOR THE AIRLOCK!!!

EAMONN! LOOK WHAT WE HIT!!
WE HAVE TA WIND 'ER DOWN EASY!

HEY! I TOLD YOU TO SHUT IT DOWN!!
THE BLADES'RE MIRED IN SANDY CLAY! WE HAVE TO SPIN 'ER CLEAN!

YOW!!

LOOKS LIKE AN ICE CREAM SODA!!
GET OFF ME MACHINE, YE FECKIN' DIVIL!!

LOOKS JUST LIKE AN ICE CREAM SODA!!!

AT 10 PM JACKSON'S "ICE CREAM SODA" EXPLODED INTO A DEADLY **METHANE MILKSHAKE!**
AUGHHH!!
VROOOOOSSH!
OH GOD! **GAS!!**

UNHH!

NO! OH NO!!
AIEEEEEEEE!

WITH TERRIBLE SUDDENNESS THE TUNNEL BORER HAD UNLEASHED THE LARGEST GAS DEPOSIT **EVER** ENCOUNTERED IN ALL THE YEARS OF TUNNEL DIGGING!

AND WITH THE GAS CAME **THE DEATH ANGELS!**
OOOOH
HOOOO

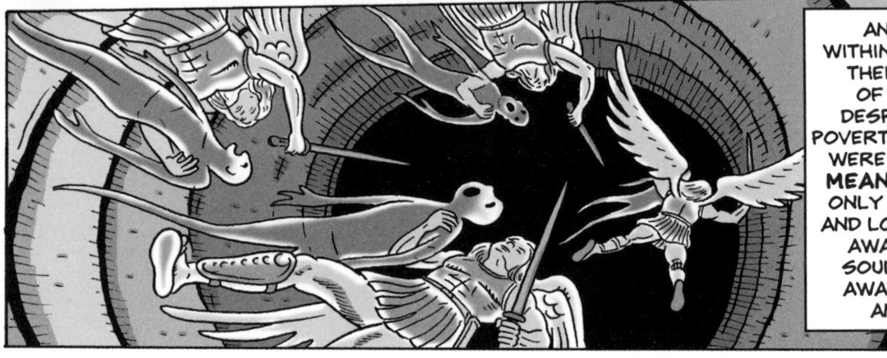
AND THEN WITHIN SECONDS, THEIR YEARS OF SHARED DESPERATION, POVERTY, AND FEAR WERE RENDERED **MEANINGLESS.** ONLY DARKNESS AND LONELY CALM AWAITED THE SOULS SWEPT AWAY BY THE ANGELS.

SEAN... COUGH!...EYR' YE STILL WIT' ME, SON?

OH, ME POOR BOY...

COUGH...COUGH! FIRST ONES IN- LAST ONES OUT... WHAT A JOB!

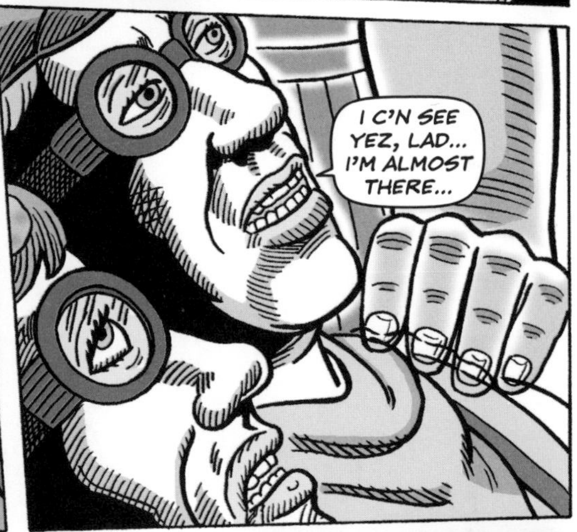
I C'N SEE YEZ, LAD... I'M ALMOST THERE...

AH!...COUGH! SO IT'S YOU, EH? I DO HOPE YE ARE A DONEGAL MAN?

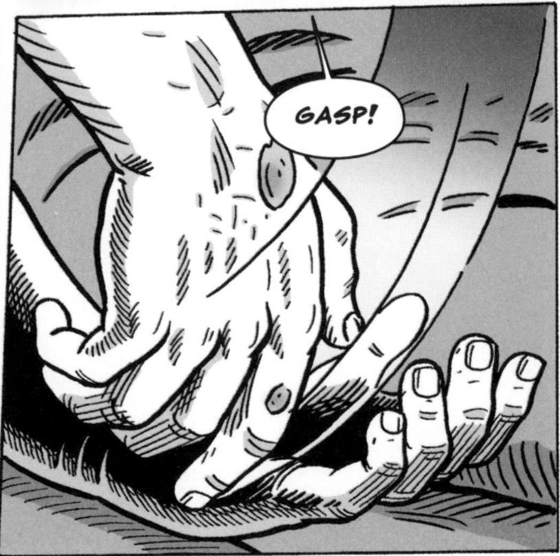
GASP!

SECONDS **BEFORE** THE CATASTROPHIC BREACH, CLARKE HAD JOINED UP WITH A TEAM OF SANDHOGS TASKED WITH SEALING A PASSAGE TO THE OLD SERVICE TUNNEL.
GET THAT FECKIN' LIGHT OUTA ME EYES!

I'M ORDERING EVERY MAN UPTOP! WE GOT A BUSTED TRESTLE NEAR THE TUNNEL FACE.

WUZ THAT GOT TO DO WIT' US?! WE'RE BUILDIN' UP A BULKHEAD HERE!
NEVER YE MIND! DO WHAT I SEZ AND GET YER ASSES UPTOP!

THIS MAKES NO SENSE! C'MON, BOYS. WE'LL LEAVE THIS **GIMPY-LEGGED** MICK TO HIS TUNNEL!
HEY!! YOU!!

YE GOT A BONE TO PICK WIT' ME? YE EVER BEEN **THUMPED** BY A "GIMPY-LEGGED MICK"?

AWW FORGET IT! THAT'S ONE ON ME, CLARKE! C'MON, BOYS, **HEAD FOR THE AIRLOCK!**

WHAT IN THE NAME OF JESUS AND THE APOSTLES **WAS THAT?!**

GALLAGHER USED TO CALL IT "THE MOAN O' THE SERPENT"

THE WHAT?!

WE'RE TOO LATE! GET INTO THE PASSAGE AND BURY YER FACES INTO THE GROUND!

AT THE TIME OF THE BREACH, BORELLI WAS ON THE CRIB PLATFORM BRIEFING THE DECK FOREMEN

WE FINDA DA CRACKS ALL OVER DIS SECTION OF DA SERVICE TUNNEL!

EDDIE! COME LOOK AT THIS!!

LOOK, THIRTY SECONDS AGO TUNNEL PSI SHOT TO THE END OF THE DIAL. IT'S STILL NOT BACK TO NORMAL!
KEEP YOUR EYES ON THEM DIALS!

WE NEED TO GET CLARKE AND HIS TEAM OUTA THERE!

IN THE TUNNEL, CLARKE MOUNTED A HAND CAR AND HEADED STRAIGHT INTO THE "SERPENT'S MOUTH." HE COULD'VE ESCAPED TO SAFETY AND NO ONE WOULD'VE HELD IT AGAINST HIM...

TWEEEEETT!
...INSTEAD, HE WENT IN SEARCH OF THE SOUL HE'D LOST TEN YEARS EARLIER.

LOOKING FOR SURVIVORS, CLARKE HAD LOCATED TWO MEN NEAR DEATH AND PUT THEM INTO A MUCK CART. WOOZY AND WEAKENED BY THE GAS HE BEGAN TO FALTER ON HIS WAY BACK TO THE AIR LOCK.
ARRRGH!... COUGH!...COUGH! AUGGHH!

COUGH!...I'M NOT GOIN' TA MAKE IT...HELP ME, GOD, HELP ME!

WHA'?... WHAT'S HAPPENIN'?

WELL, I BE DAMNED!

GALLAGHER! WHERE YA BEEN?

GOOD TO SEE YA, JOHNNY! FER A SECOND...COUGH!...I WAS WORRYIN' MY SITUATION MIGHTA' GONE HOPELESS!

MR. CLARKE! THANK GOD— YOU'RE ALIVE!
COUGH!... JESSUP! GIVE US A HAND!
MR. CLARKE— HOW BAD IS THE BREACH?
IT'S ONE FER THE AGES, JESSUP! GET THESE MEN UPTOP... I'M GOIN' BACK IN!
SHAFT ELEVAT
WHAT?!...NO! YOU CAN'T GO BACK IN THERE!
I'M THE ONLY ONE THA'S BEEN THROUGH ONE O' DESE. I CAN SAVE MORE MEN!
CLARKE! I CAN'T STAND BY AND LET YOU COMMIT SUICIDE!
JESSUP, YOU STOOD YER GROUND WHEN OTHERS WOULDA RUN. ME AND GALLAGHER ARE PROUD OF YE!
I'M NOT GOING TO LET YOU DO THIS, CLARKE! THINK OF YOUR WIFE AND LITTLE GIRL!
LEGGO O' ME!!
SORRY, JESSUP! DON'T SPEAK ILL O' ME WHEN I'M GONE!
SMAK
OOOF!

"...AND THAT WAS THE LAST I SAW OF HIM...HE HAD HIS CAP ON AND WAS BLOWIN' HIS WHISTLE UNTIL HE DISAPPEARED INTO THE DARKNESS..."

I TRIED TO STOP HIM. I THINK THE GAS AFFECTED HIS MIND...HE WAS GOING ON ABOUT JOHNNY GALLAGHER...LIKE HE WAS **STILL ALIVE!**

I TRIED TO STOP HIM! HONESTLY, I DID! sob!
IT'S OK, JESSUP. YA DID ALL A BODY COULD DO.

MEN! LISTEN 'N' LEARN SOMETHIN'...

"...WE NEED TO FORM A RESCUE PARTY, BUT WE DON'T NEED ANY MORE **"HEROES"!** MEN LIKE CLARKE... WELL, THEY'S THEIR OWN DYIN' BREED...
FWEEEETT!

"...CLARKE AND THE OTHERS GREW OLD BEFORE THEIR TIME THINKING THE TUNNELS COULDN'T BE BUILT WITHOUT THEM...
FWEEEEETT!

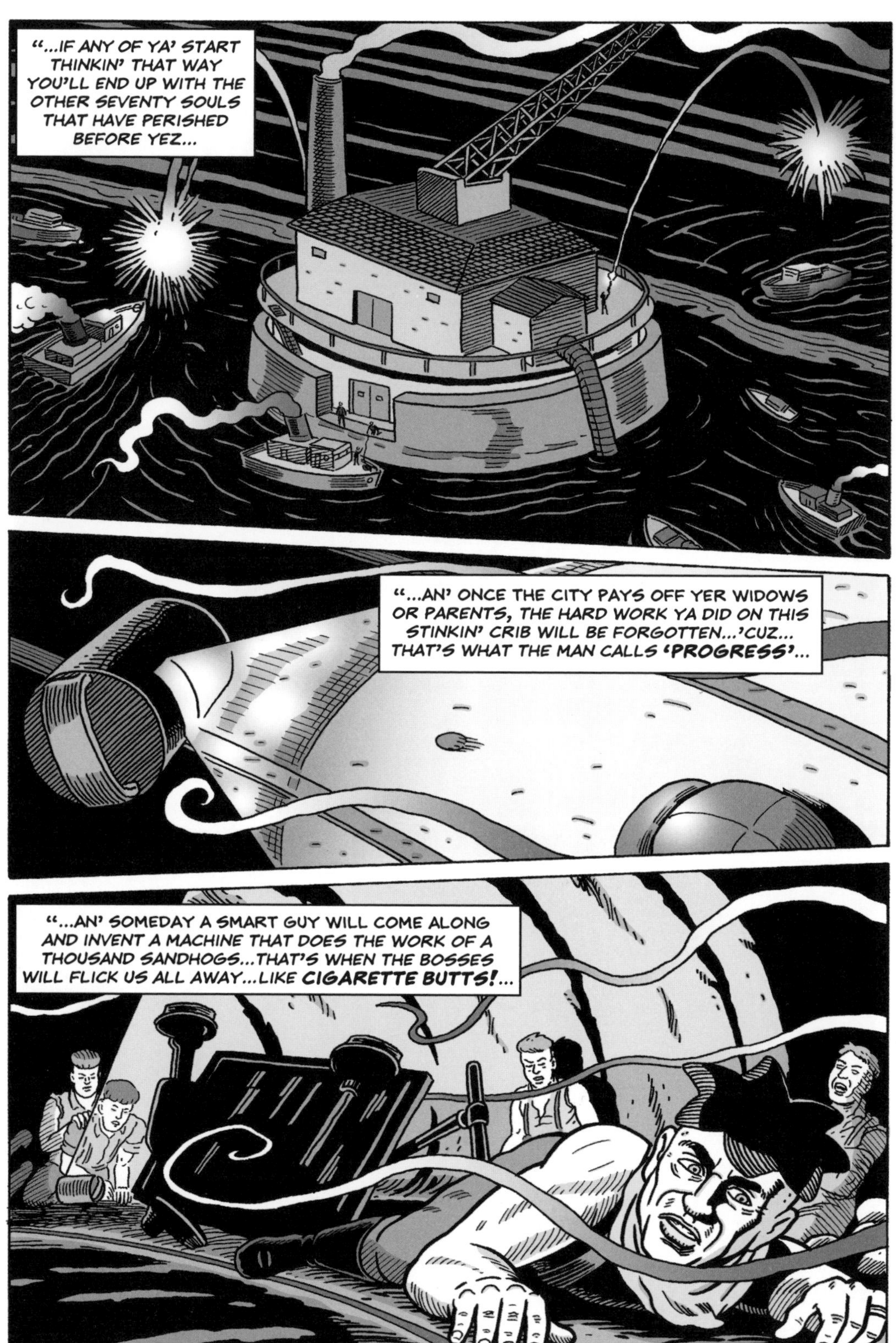
"...IF ANY OF YA' START THINKIN' THAT WAY YOU'LL END UP WITH THE OTHER SEVENTY SOULS THAT HAVE PERISHED BEFORE YEZ...
"...AN' ONCE THE CITY PAYS OFF YER WIDOWS OR PARENTS, THE HARD WORK YA DID ON THIS STINKIN' CRIB WILL BE FORGOTTEN...'CUZ... THAT'S WHAT THE MAN CALLS 'PROGRESS'...
"...AN' SOMEDAY A SMART GUY WILL COME ALONG AND INVENT A MACHINE THAT DOES THE WORK OF A THOUSAND SANDHOGS...THAT'S WHEN THE BOSSES WILL FLICK US ALL AWAY...LIKE CIGARETTE BUTTS!...

"...SO, WATCH AFTER YOUR OWN ASSES, MEN...'CUZ I GUARANTEE YEZ THE BOSSES ARE ONLY WORRIED ABOUT THEIR OWN!"
COUGH! MOVE BOYS! KEEP MOVIN' AND STAY LOW TO THE GROUND!
FORGIVE ME, DEAR LORD...COUGH!...FER THE SINS I COMMITTED. PLEASE WATCH OVER ME FAMILY...COUGH!
SAY THE PRAYER WIT' ME DARLIN', "OUR FATHER, WHO ART IN HEAVEN..."
"HALLOWED BE THY NAME. THY KINGDOM COME..."COUGH!...
"...THY WILL BE DONE..." COUGH!..."ON EARTH AS IT IS IN HEAVEN..."
"GIVE US THIS DAY OUR DAILY BREAD AND FORGIVE US OUR TRESPASSES..."

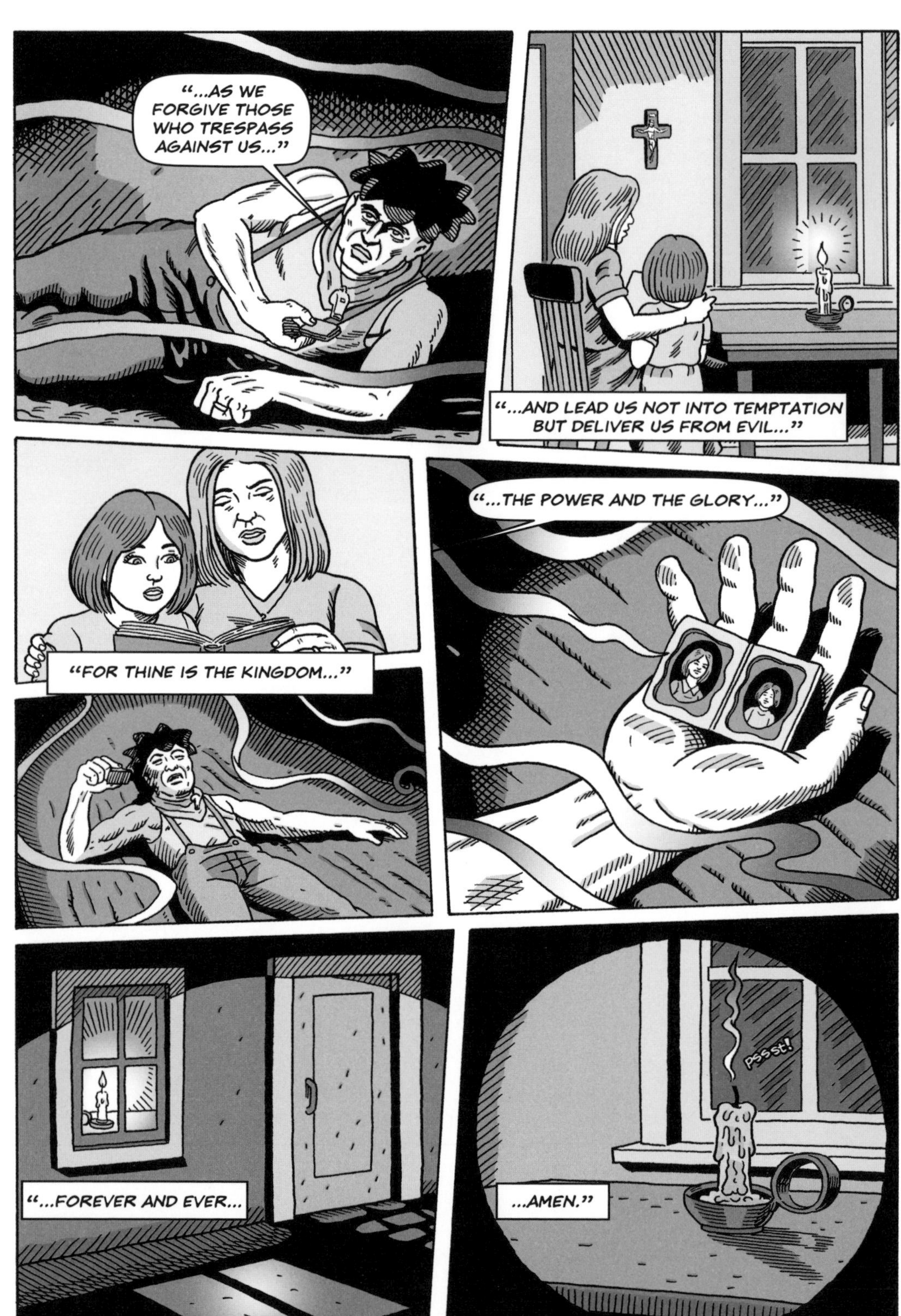
"...AS WE FORGIVE THOSE WHO TRESPASS AGAINST US..."
"...AND LEAD US NOT INTO TEMPTATION BUT DELIVER US FROM EVIL..."
"FOR THINE IS THE KINGDOM..."
"...THE POWER AND THE GLORY..."
"...FOREVER AND EVER...
PSSST!
...AMEN."

MA? WHAT 'TIS IT, MA?

RODGER!!

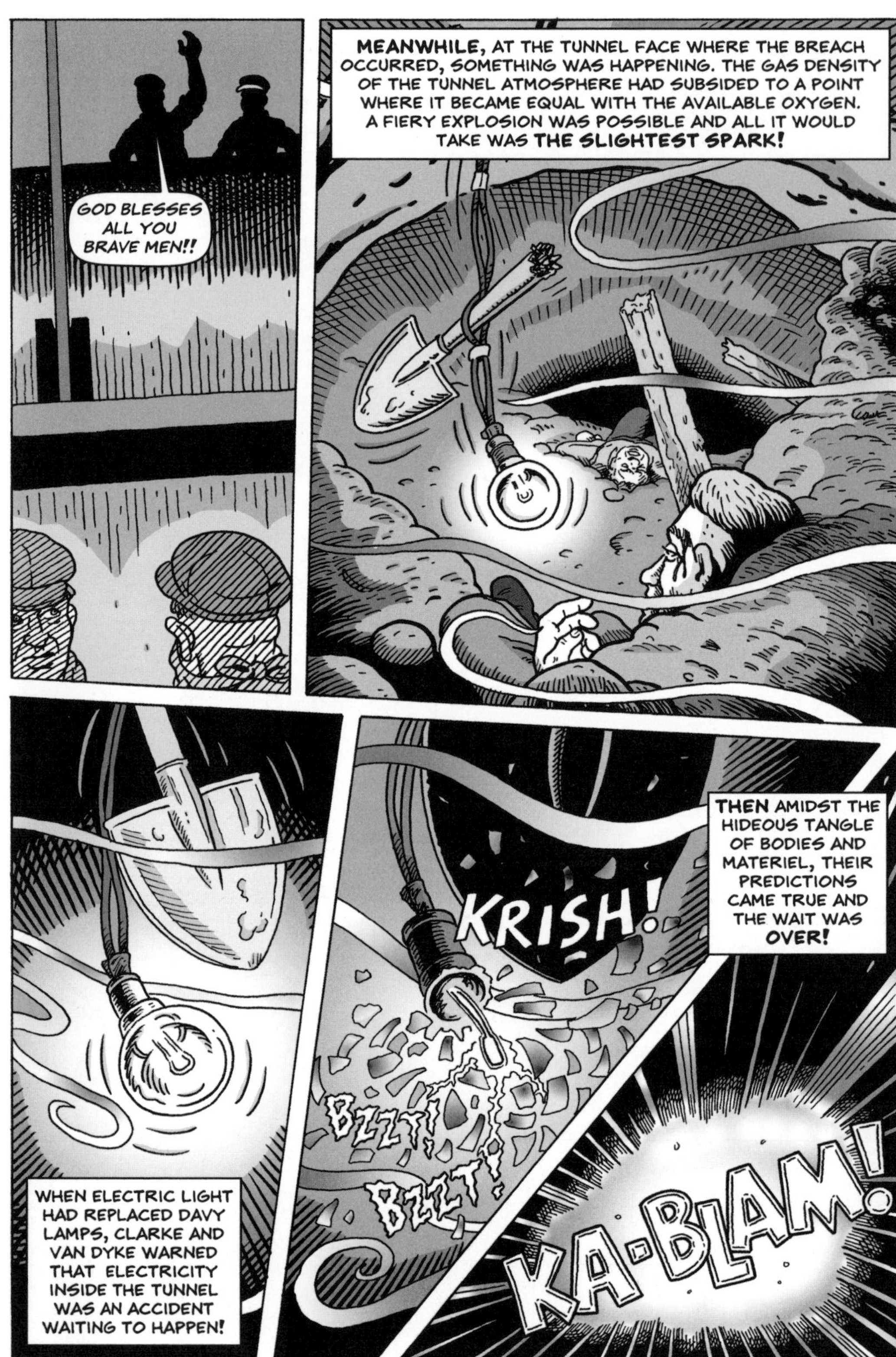
GOD BLESSES ALL YOU BRAVE MEN!!
MEANWHILE, AT THE TUNNEL FACE WHERE THE BREACH OCCURRED, SOMETHING WAS HAPPENING. THE GAS DENSITY OF THE TUNNEL ATMOSPHERE HAD SUBSIDED TO A POINT WHERE IT BECAME EQUAL WITH THE AVAILABLE OXYGEN. A FIERY EXPLOSION WAS POSSIBLE AND ALL IT WOULD TAKE WAS THE SLIGHTEST SPARK!
WHEN ELECTRIC LIGHT HAD REPLACED DAVY LAMPS, CLARKE AND VAN DYKE WARNED THAT ELECTRICITY INSIDE THE TUNNEL WAS AN ACCIDENT WAITING TO HAPPEN!
THEN AMIDST THE HIDEOUS TANGLE OF BODIES AND MATERIEL, THEIR PREDICTIONS CAME TRUE AND THE WAIT WAS OVER!
KRISH!
BZZT!
BZZT!
KA-BLAM!

LOOK! LOOK, WILL'YA! OUT THERE ON THE WATER!!

I CAN'T BELIEVE ME EYES! IT'S THE LAKE CREATURE!
HEY! THE DECK IS SHAKIN'!

THE CRIB! IT'S COMIN' APART!!
WHOA!
RRUMBLE!

GOOD GOD! LOOK AT THESE GAUGES! WHAT'S GOING ON DOWN THERE?

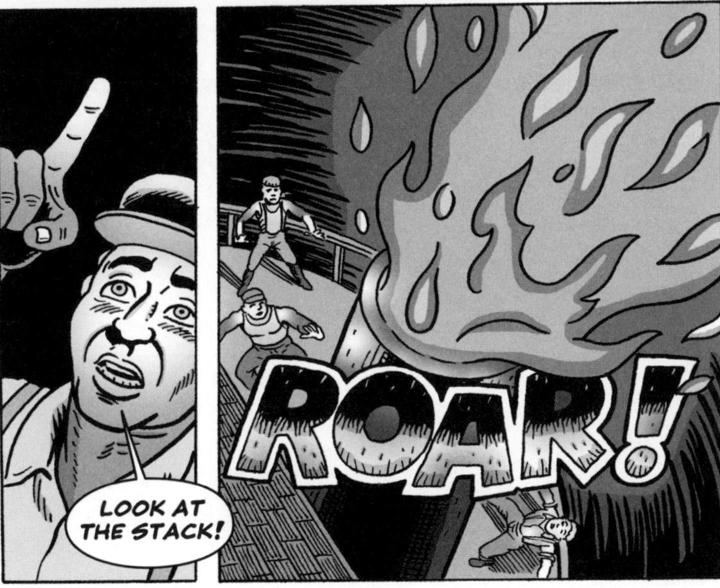
LOOK AT THE STACK!
ROAR!

ROAR!

AWWW... THIS IS NUTS!

WITH BURNING DEATH BEHIND THEM THE ANGELS RACED TO REAP THE AWAITING SOULS!

OH NO!! THE RESCUE TEAM!!!
HEY?! WHAT IS ALL THAT LIGHT HEADED THIS...
OOOH!
OOH!
AGGG! HELP ME!
AUGHH!!
NO!NO! AIEEEEEEEE!!
EDDIE! SUPT. NORTON AND THE MAYOR ARE ON DECK!
THAT'S GREAT. LET THE MONKEY SHOW BEGIN!

MAKE WAY YOU MEN! WHO'S IN CHARGE?

I'M IN CHARGE, BUT IT'S YOU TWO THAT'S RESPONSIBLE!

SAYYYYY! WHAT'S YOUR NAME?
EDWARD JOSEPH JOYCE! SHALL I SPELL IT FOR YA, YER LORDSHIP?

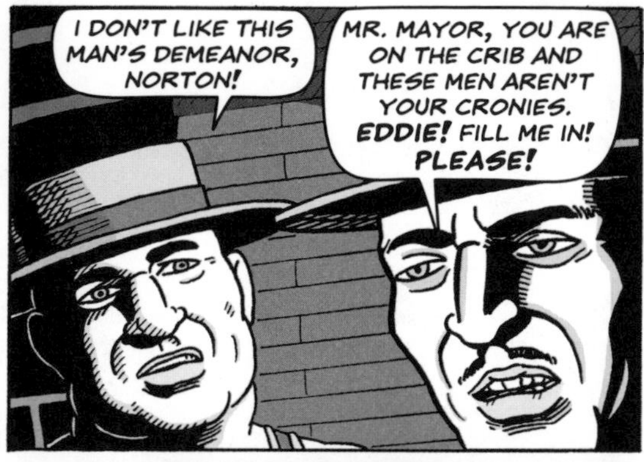
I DON'T LIKE THIS MAN'S DEMEANOR, NORTON!
MR. MAYOR, YOU ARE ON THE CRIB AND THESE MEN AREN'T YOUR CRONIES. EDDIE! FILL ME IN! PLEASE!

A CREW OF SIXTEEN LED BY CLARKE DESCENDED AT NINE PM. AROUND TEN PM THE BORER STRUCK A MOTHER LODE AND FILLED THE TUNNEL WITH GAS.

HOW MANY MADE IT OUT?
FOUR!

GASP!...AND WHAT OF THE OTHER TWELVE?
MISSING AND PRESUMED DEAD... INCLUDING CLARKE.

WELL, WHY DON'T YOU SEND DOWN A RESCUE PARTY BEFORE ASSUMING THEY'RE ALL DEAD!
A RESCUE PARTY OF SIX ENTERED THE TUNNEL AT 10:30, RIGHT BEFORE THE EXPLOSION!

WHA'?!... EXPLOSION?!!
...AND THE FATE OF THE RESCUERS?

MISSING!...SOB! ...AND PRESUMED DEAD!

HOW COULD YOU SEND PEOPLE DOWN THERE WHEN AN EXPLOSION WAS IMMINENT?!

BOYS! THE MAYOR IS GOIN' FOR A SWIM! GRAB 'IM!
MR. JOYCE!! UNHAND HIM AT ONCE!

MR. MAYOR... A WORD PLEASE?
WHAT SORT OF SHOW ARE YOU RUNNING HERE? I'M THE MAYOR FOR CHRISSAKES!

YOU SLIP UP AGAIN AND THEY'LL THROW YOU DOWN THE SHAFT! LET ME HANDLE THIS!
OK, BUT I'M ORDERING IN MY POLICE GUARD!

NO ONE COULD SURVIVE DOWN THERE! IT'S HOPELESS!
THAT'S WHAT WE SAID TEN YEARS AGO ON CRIB #3! WE WON'T MAKE THAT MISTAKE AGAIN!

LOOK! THE FIRE IS SUBSIDING!
YEP! GET A TEAM TOGETHER! WE'RE GOING BACK DOWN!

AND...I KNOW JUST THE MAN WHO'S GONNA LEAD THEM!

GIMME THAT MONEY, YE LEAPING TOAD! AN' I'LL LET YE OUTA DERE!
NEFFER!!

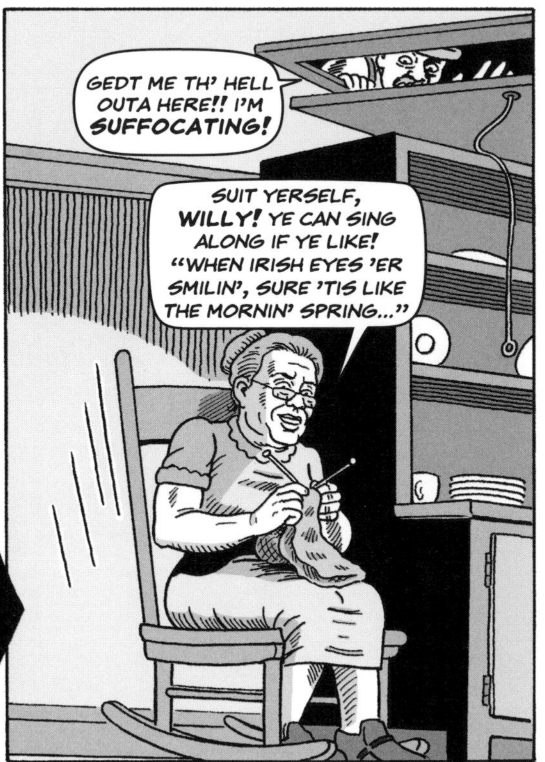
GEDT ME TH' HELL OUTA HERE!! I'M SUFFOCATING!
SUIT YERSELF, WILLY! YE CAN SING ALONG IF YE LIKE! "WHEN IRISH EYES 'ER SMILIN', SURE 'TIS LIKE THE MORNIN' SPRING..."

GOD BLESS THIS HOUSE
THUMP! THUMP! THUMP!
OPEN UP! POLICE!

GOD BLESS THIS HOUSE
NOW WHO COMES THUMPIN' AT DIS HOUR?
THUMP! THUMP! THUMP!

IS THIS THE HOME OF WILHELM VAN DYKE?
NOW, WATCHA BOYS WANT WIT' WILLY?

HE'S TO COME WITH US BY ORDER OF THE MAYOR!
HEY NOW! IS HE IN TROUBLE?

WHERE THE HELL IS HE?!
EEEEEEEEE!
HE'S IN DA CEILIN' WATCHA T'INK?!

AAAGG! HELP ME!
GEEZIZ, LADY! HE'S GOTTA BE ROASTIN' UP THERE!

WHOOAAAA!

AN' THERE YE HAVE IT! ONE DUTCHMAN HALF BAKED!

GOEDE HEMEL! SHE TRIED TO KILL ME!
I WILL HOLD THE MONEY, IF YE PLEASE!

C'MON VAN DYKE...WE'VE NO TIME TO LOSE!
VERE ARE YOU TAKING ME?
45, 50, 60, 65, 75, 95

CRIB ACCIDENT! NORTON SAYS YOU WILL BE LEADING THE RESCUE TEAM!
VOT?!

VOT KIND OF ACCIDENT?
THEY HIT A GAS POCKET. A DOZEN MEN ARE DEAD!

WHOA! LOOK AT ME. I CAN'T LEAD A RESCUE!
THAT'S NOT MY DEPARTMENT!

THE WATERWORKS KILT ME FIRST HUSBAND, DEAR GOD—NOW THEY WANT TO KILL THE SECOND! ...110, 120, 140, 145...
THAT'S NOT MY DEPARTMENT NEITHER. I GOT MY ORDERS!

THAT'S MY MONEY! DON'T CHUST STAND THERE! FIND TOMMY!!!
POLI

UHNN...
UHHH!
BACK AT THE TAXI STAND, TOMMY GALLAGHER HAD A WATERWORKS CRISIS OF HIS OWN...

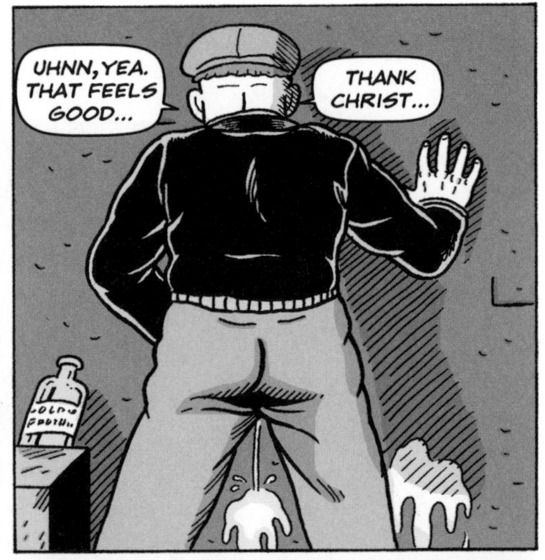
UHNN, YEA. THAT FEELS GOOD...
THANK CHRIST...

TAXI
WHO?...OH, YEAH! YEAH, HE'S HERE, ALRIGHT! WHO WANTS HIM? WHO??

HEY! GALLAGHER! QUIT MILKIN' YER SNAKE AND GET OVER HERE! YER MA WANTS YA!
TAXI
CALL SPEEDY TAXI

YEA? MA? WATCHA WANT?
TAXI
TAXI
CALL SPEEDY TAXI

TOMMY! YOU GET DOWN TO WHISKEY ISLAND NOW! THE COPPERS DRAGGED WILLY OUT TO THE CRIB! THERE'S BEEN AN EXPLOSION!

DID'YA HEAR ME?! THEY TOOK WILLY TO THAT CRIB O' DEATH! THEY'RE GONNA KILL 'IM!!
WHA'? CRIB O' DEATH? WHO'S KILLIN' WILLY?

FIRST THEY KILT YER DA AN' NOW THEY WANNA KILL WILLY!
AIN'T NOBODY GONNA KILL WILLY! AIN'T NOBODY!!

IT'S UP TO YEZ, TOMMY! ONLY YE CAN SAVE 'IM AN' BRING 'IM BACK TO OUR LOVIN' HOME!
I'LL SAVE HIM, MA!!
AIN'T NOBODY GONNA KILL WILLY!!
HEY, YOU IDIOT! LEGGO O' THAT PHONE!
WHACK!
WHAP!

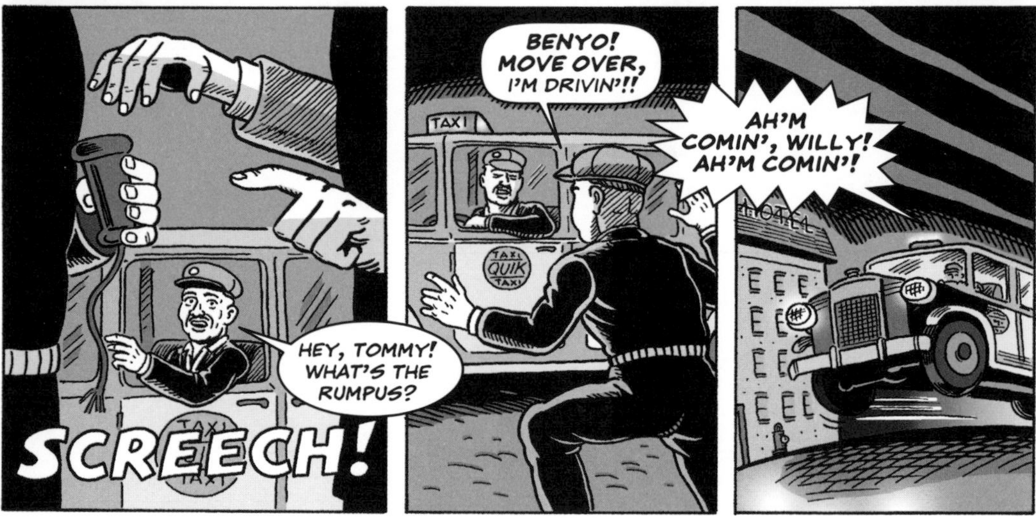
HEY, TOMMY! WHAT'S THE RUMPUS?
SCREECH!
TAXI
BENYO! MOVE OVER, I'M DRIVIN'!!
TAXI
QUIK
TAXI
AH'M COMIN', WILLY! AH'M COMIN'!
HOTEL

MEANWHILE, RUMORS OF A CRIB ACCIDENT HAD DRIFTED UPRIVER TO THE INHABITANTS OF IRISHTOWN BEND.
TOOOOT!
TOOOOOT!

ALWAYS THE LAST TO KNOW, CRIB FAMILIES DEPENDED ON TUGBOATS AND BARGES TO BRING NEWS AND MESSAGES FROM THEIR MEN WORKING ON THE LAKE PLATFORMS...
WHAT NEWS DO YE BRING US?!

BIG ACCIDENT ON THE CRIB! GAS EXPLOSION!!
OH GOD! THIS BE BAD... I CAN FEEL IT!

ANYBODY WAS KILT, SIR?
ERE ANY BE HURT BADLY?

TWELVE DEAD AND MANY OTHERS ARE TRAPPED OR MISSIN' IN THE TUNNELS!!

GASP!

MERCIFUL JESUS!
FINN! DEAR GOD NO! NO!
MY PADDY! NOOOO!!
JIMMY!!

NOOOOOOO!!
EEEEE!!
HAIL MARY, FULL OF GRACE, THE LORD IS WITH THEE...

ALL A BODY CAN DO NOW, DARLIN', IS WAIT... AND PRAY.

12 AM–CRIB #5.
"...WELL, LOOKSEE WHAT THE CAT DRAGGED IN!"

HMMMPH!...IF IT AIN'T THE PRODIGAL DUTCHMAN!

LOOK! IT'S VAN DYKE! GET HIM!!!

BREAK HIS STINKIN' NECK!
AAAGGGGGH!!
LET 'IM GO!!
PITCH 'IM INTA THE DRINK!

WE'RE FEEDIN' YOU TO THE SERPENT, DUTCHMAN!

BANG!
BANG!

BANG! BANG!

LET HIM GO OR BY GOD I WILL SHOOT ALL OF YOU!
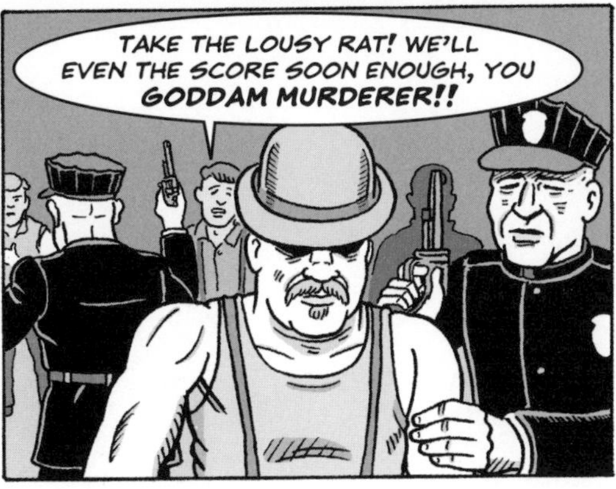
TAKE THE LOUSY RAT! WE'LL EVEN THE SCORE SOON ENOUGH, YOU GODDAM MURDERER!!

I VON'T GO INTO DOT HOLE! IT'S PURE SUICIDE!
YER GOING, WILLY!

AN' VERE IN HELL IS THE FIRE DEPARTMENT? DIS BE DERE JOB, BY GOD!

...WON'T BE HERE FOR HOURS. THERE'S A HUGE WAREHOUSE FIRE IN BIG ITALY!

KILLING ME VON'T FIX DIS. THE TRUTH VILL COME OUT ABOUT YOU TWO...
...VETHER I'M DEAD... OR ALIVE!

THAT BEIN' THE CASE, I CHOOSE DEAD! FEED HIM TO THE MOB!

NO!! STOP! VAIT! VAIT!
LET 'IM GO!

LET 'IM GO! OR I'LL SHOVE DIS WRENCH UP THE ASS O' THE NEXT MAN THAT TOUCHES 'IM!

DUTCH–YER SCUM, BUT YER OUR SCUM. SO STOP MOANIN' 'CUZ YER GOIN' DOWN WIT' US!

GODSPEED, YE BRAVE MEN! YOU GO WITH THE PRAYERS OF A GRATEFUL...

AWWW! SHUT YER TRAP, YE FECKIN' CROOK! YE JUS' BETTER TAKE CARE OF OUR FAMILIES IF WE DON'T COME BACK!

YEAH! OR I'LL 'AVE ME IRA COUSINS BLOW YER HOUSE TA KINGDOM COME!

HOORAY!
HOORAY!
GIVE 'EM A CHEER, LADS!

NORTON! THESE SANDHOGS OF YOURS ARE CRAZY!
THEY MUST BE. THEY ALL VOTED FOR YOU!

MEANWHILE–AT THE WHISKEY ISLAND PIER.
LOOKS LIKE WE MISSED THE BOAT, TOMMY-BOY!
GODDAM IT!!

...UH-OH!

UH...BEG YER PARDON, LADIES, FOR TAKIN' THE **LORD'S NAME** IN VAIN.
AN' WHAT ELSE WOULD WE EXPECT FROM A **PIG** BUT A **GRUNT**?

CAPT. FRANK'S
FISHING EXCURSIONS
HEY, TOMMY! WHAT ABOUT THIS BOAT?
HMMM...C'MON WITH ME!

YEA! THIS'LL DO! **CAST OFF** THEM LINES, BENYO, ME BOY!

DO'YA THINK CAPT. FRANK WILL MIND THAT WE TOOK HIS BOAT?
FROM THE LOOKS OF IT...CAPT. FRANK ISN'T MINDIN' MUCH RIGHT NOW!
WRRRRRRRRR!
ZZZ...ZZZ...SNORT!

HANG ON, BENYO! HERE WE GO!

MR. VAN DYKE, WE ARE READY TO ENTER THE TUNNEL... OPENING THE AIRLOCK NOW!

...BACK ON IRISHTOWN BEND...
Rodger & Mary Clarke
Married 19

The Road Home

"HIDE IN MY HEART... YOUR FINE, LOW MOURNINGS, WHERE A CARELESS SUN TURNS DEW TO LIGHT..."

"...YOU ARE GONE NOW, GONE...THEN GONE AGAIN,"
COUGH! VE MUST HURRY!
"...INTO THE SOFT MISTS OF DREAMT BACKROADS,"
UGH! I CAN'T BREATHE!
"...BIND EACH TATTER HIDE THEM IN YOUR HEART,"
COUGH!
HELP ME!
"...FIND THE ROAD HOME THAT WAITS FOR YOU,"
WE'RE DYING!
EFF'RYVON OUDT!

"...AND WE WILL MEET AGAIN ATOP A RISEN PATH,"

COUGH! OH-NO! NO!!!

"...WHERE A CARELESS SUN TURNS DEW TO LIGHT."

YES, EDDIE, WHAT IS IT?

VAN DYKE AND HIS TEAM SHOULD HAVE BEEN BACK BY NOW.
YES...I KNOW.

WE NEED TO PUT ANOTHER TEAM TOGETHER NOW!
NO. WE CAN'T RISK IT.

WE'RE NOT LOSING ANY MORE MEN TONITE!
WELL, WE JUST CAN'T GIVE UP!

WE'VE RECEIVED WORD THAT CHIEF CASEY AND A CONTINGENT OF FIREMEN WILL BE HERE WITHIN THE HOUR. LET'S HAVE THEM TAKE A STAB AT IT!

WHAT?! WE HAVEN'T GOT AN HOUR! THOSE MEN ARE DYING NOW!
DAMMIT, EDDIE!

THAT'S ENOUGH! WE WAIT FOR THE FIRE DEPARTMENT!!
LEGGO O' ME!! LET GO, DAMN'YA!!

HEY! MR. NORTON!!
GEEZIZ! WHAT'S HE DOING HERE?!

WHERE'S WILLY? MY MA SAYS YOU GUYS ARE TRYIN' TO KILL HIM!
HE'S IN THE TUNNEL.

HE LED A RESCUE TEAM DOWN AN HOUR AGO.
WHAT?!

TOMMY, I'M GOING TO LEVEL WITH YOU BUT YOU MUST STAY CALM! CAN YOU DO THAT?
SURE, I S'POSE.

BECAUSE I HAVE NEWS THAT YOU'LL HAVE TO TAKE LIKE A MAN.
C'MON 'N' SPILL IT ALREADY!

TOMMY—IT ISN'T CONFIRMED, BUT WILLY AND HIS TEAM MAY HAVE PERISHED IN THE TUNNEL.
WHAT??!! WHAT DID YOU SAY!!

WE THINK THEY WERE OVERCOME BY THE GAS. IF TRUE, THEN HE DIED A HERO!
NO!! NO!!

WILLY! NOOOOOOO!!

WILLY!! WILLY!!
SWI SH!
ROPE THE SONOVABITCH!!

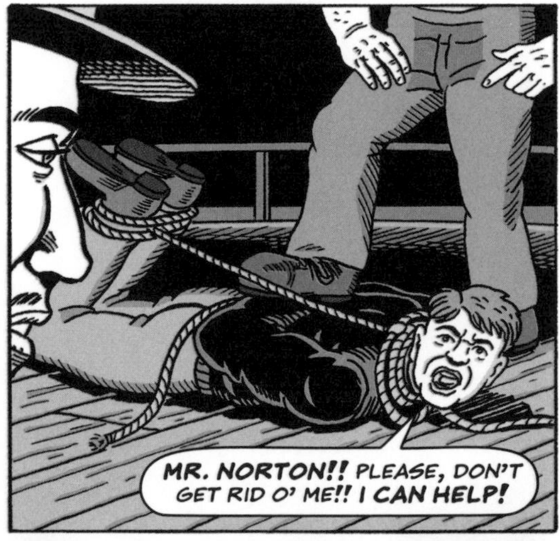
MR. NORTON!! PLEASE, DON'T GET RID O' ME!! I CAN HELP!

YA GOTTA LET ME GO DOWN THERE! I HAVE TO SAVE WILLY!

THE ANSWER IS "NO." IT WOULD BE SUICIDE.
OH YEA? IF MY MA HEARS YA HELD ME BACK THEN GOD HELP EVERY ONE O' YEZ!

THE BOY MAKES A POINT. D'YA REMEMBER WHAT SHE DID AFTER CRIB #3?
DO I REMEMBER? IT STILL HURTS TO PISS!

WILLY! sob! WILLY! DEAR GOD... PLEASE DON'T DIE!
IT'S HARD TO BELIEVE HE IS THE SON OF JOHNNY GALLAGHER!

TOMMY! YOU AND BENYO STAY DOWN FOR TEN MINUTES TOPS! THEN COME UP FOR AIR!

TEN MINUTES! YA GOT IT?
STOP WORRYIN'! I GOT TUNNELIN' IN MY BLOOD!

2 MINUTES LATER...
HEY, BOSS! THEY'RE ON THEIR WAY UP ALREADY!
WHAT?!

COUGH! ...A LITTLE HELP.
UNNHHH!

HOW'D YOU AND TOMMY GET BACK TO THE SHAFT?
WE... COUGH! WE NEVER LEFT THE SHAFT!

MR. NORTON! COME OVER HERE IF YOU PLEASE!
NOW WHAT?!

GODDAMMIT! WHAT HAPPENED HERE, MR. MUNIAK?
AIR COMPRESSOR! SHE IS KAPUT!

I CAN SEE SHE'S "KAPUT," MR. MUNIAK! HOW BAD IS IT?!
BURNED-UP CYLINDER I GUESS!

NO AIR COMPRESSION? THAT MEANS NO FRESH AIR!
IT SEEMS LIKE ALL THE STARS ARE LINED UP AGAINST US THIS NIGHT.

AFTER AWHILE, THE FLOODING AND CAVE-INS START.
WE JUST CAN'T GIVE UP ON THOSE POOR LADS!

CHIEF CASEY! YOU FINALLY MADE IT! WHERE'S THE REST OF THE FIRE DEPARTMENT?
I BRING...erp! BAD NEWS!

WE GOT US A FIVE-ALARM FIRE IN BIG ITALY. I WON'T HAVE...erp! A TEAM HERE FER TWO-THREE HOURS!

BLUHHHAAAGGG!!!

GREAT... THAT'S JUST GREAT! DAMMIT!

hic!..I'M FINE...JUST A WEE SEASICK FROM THE TUG RIDE...erp!
...JUST GREAT.
YEA-YEA... JES' GIMME A FECKIN' REPORT!

MOMENTS LATER...
...VAN DYKE'S TEAM WENT DOWN OVER AN HOUR AGO AND ARE PRESUMED LOST. WE TRIED AGAIN, BUT THERE'S TOO MUCH GAS IN THE SHAFT!

BRAVE MEN ALL, FER SURE... BUT HOW COULD YE KEEP SENDIN' 'EM DOWN WHEN YE KNEW THERE WAS GAS?
I HAVE WONDERED THE SAME THING!

IT'S IN THE NATURE OF OUR BUSINESS!!
YOU RUN A RECKLESS BUSINESS, NORTON!

WE NEED PROPER PROTECTION FROM THE GAS. MASKS! WE NEED BREATHIN' MASKS!
ISN'T THE FIRE DEPARTMENT EQUIPPED WITH MASKS?

NOPE! HIS HONOR HERE STRUCK OUR REQUESTS FOR MASKS FROM HIS BUDGET!
THAT DEVICE WAS OF DUBIOUS QUALITY AND DESIGN! I WAS RIGHT TO...

DUBIOUS QUALITY?! IT WAS TURNED DOWN 'CUZ THE MAYOR FOUND OUT IT WERE INVENTED BY A NEGRO!!
IT WAS THE PRODUCT OF A SHADY LOCAL BUSINESS!

WELL, THERE'S PLENTY O' SHADE TO SIT UNDER AT CITY HALL, TOO! **WAIT!... WHAT DID YOU SAY?!**
CHIEF CASEY! YOU WILL NOT TALK TO YOUR MAYOR LIKE THAT!

YEA, YEA, NOW **PLEEZE** REPEAT WHAT YER SAID BEFORE!
I SAID THE CITY WILL NOT BUY PRODUCTS FROM A SHADY **LOCAL** BUSINESS!

LOCAL!! OF COURSE! **HE'S RIGHT HERE IN CLEVELAND!!**

JAYSUS CHRIST! THERE'S NO TIME TO **WASTE!!**

BELTRAN!!

CHAPTER 8: "A SIMPLE, ORDINARY MAN"
RRIING! RRRIING!
2 AM: THE HOME OF BENJAMIN BELTRAN

YEA...I'M BELTRAN... WHO'S CALLIN' ME AT THIS HOUR?... HMMM...WELL, I'M SORRY TO HEAR IT BUT...
...WHAT'S THAT GOTTA DO WITH ME?

5 MINUTES LATER.
BEN! STOP! EVERYONE KNOWS THOSE TUNNELS ARE DEATHTRAPS! YOU DON'T HAVE TO DO THIS!
FRIEDA... I'M GOIN'!!

BEN, THE CITY REFUSED TO BUY YOUR HELMETS... AND NOW THEY WANT **YOU** TO RISK **YOUR LIFE** FOR THEM?

LISTEN, FRIEDA...I GOTTA HELP THOSE MEN. THIS ISN'T A DANG FIREMEN'S CONVENTION–THIS IS OPPORTUNITY **KNOCKIN'** ON THE DAMN DOOR!

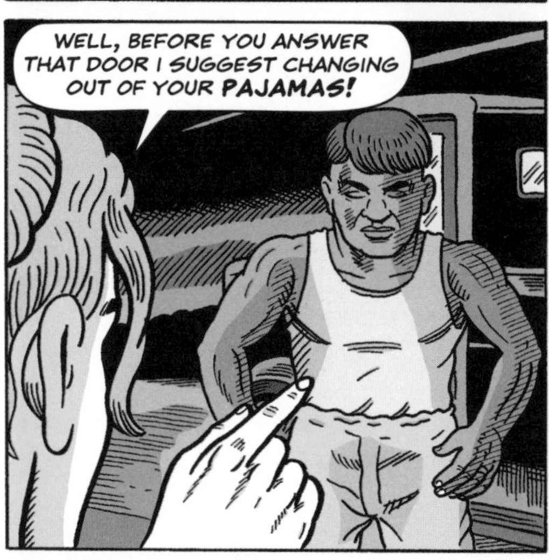
WELL, BEFORE YOU ANSWER THAT DOOR I SUGGEST CHANGING OUT OF YOUR **PAJAMAS!**

THERE'S NO TIME!–CALL MY BROTHER, LOUIS. TELL 'IM WE'RE **GOIN' TUNNELIN'!**
AND PUT SOME SHOES ON!!

A FEW MOMENTS LATER...
TUNNELIN'?... UNDER THE LAKE?
YEP...THEY'RE GOIN' AFTER WATER THAT'S FURTHER OUT INSTEAD O' FIXIN' THE WATER THAT'S FURTHER IN!

PHEW! IT SURE IS A **WHITE** MAN'S WORLD!
YEA, WELL... HEH, HEH! **WAIT** 'TIL THEY GET A LOAD O' US!

3 AM: WHISKEY ISLAND...
LOOK AT 'EM ALL, BEN! I BETCHA EVERY BOAT IN CLEVELAND IS ON THE LAKE TONIGHT!
THIS IS A BIG DEAL, LOUIS...MIGHT EVEN BE ONE OF THEM THINGS PEOPLE WILL REMEMBER.

PUSH 'EM BACK!
GO ON! MOVE BACK! GO BACK TO YER HOMES!
TELL US WHO WAS KILT OUT THERE!
WHY WON'T NOBODY TELL US NOTHIN'?
COMIN' THRU! MOVE ASIDE!
I TOLD YEZ, NOBODY KNOWS NOTHIN' YET!

MAKE WAY!! OFFICIAL BUSINESS COMING THROUGH!

WHAT IN BLAZES HAS YA BRUNG US NOW?!

MEANWHILE, THE CRIB HAD BECOME A SCENE OF VIOLENT CHAOS. FIGHTS HAD BROKEN OUT BETWEEN FACTIONS BOTH FOR AND AGAINST THE RESCUE EFFORTS. BELTRAN SENSED IMMEDIATELY THAT HE WAS THE LAST BEST HOPE FOR THE SOULS ABOVE AND BELOW THE CRIB PLATFORM...

HE'S HERE...
HEY!
BELTRAN!

PUT ALL YER EFFORTS HERE. IF THERE BE ANY SURVIVORS, YOU'LL FIND THEM CLOSE TO THE AIRLOCK.
WHO'S GOIN' DOWN WITH LOUIS AN' ME?

WE ARE CALLING FOR VOLUNTEERS! THIS TIME YOU WILL GO DOWN WEARING THESE PROTECTIVE HOODS!

C'MON, BOYS! THIS IS OUR LAST CHANCE! WE CAN STILL SAVE SOME LIVES!

YOU BUNCHA COWARDS! I'M NOT AFRAID!!

I'LL GO DOWN WITH THESE SHINERS AND WE'LL BE THE HEROES, AND Y'ALL BE LOUSY, STINKIN' COWARDS!

ONE O' YOU SHINERS GIMME A HAND WITH THIS GODDAM MONKEY SUIT!

THAT BOY AIN'T GOT THE GOOD SENSE GOD GAVE A PEANUT!
TEN YEARS AGO HIS STEPFATHER SAVED CLARKE'S LIFE ON THE #3 CRIB.

CLARKE? DID YOU SAY... CLARKE?
AYE, RODGER CLARKE. IT'S HIS CREW THAT STRUCK THE GAS POCKET. D'YA KNOW 'IM?

AND, THEN BELTRAN REMEMBERED HIS NIGHTMARE...

...I FEEL AS THOUGH I DO KNOW HIM.
C'MON ALREADY! LET'S GET THIS SHOW ON THE ROAD!

HEY, BELTRAN! THE MAYOR WANTS TO TALK TO YEZ!

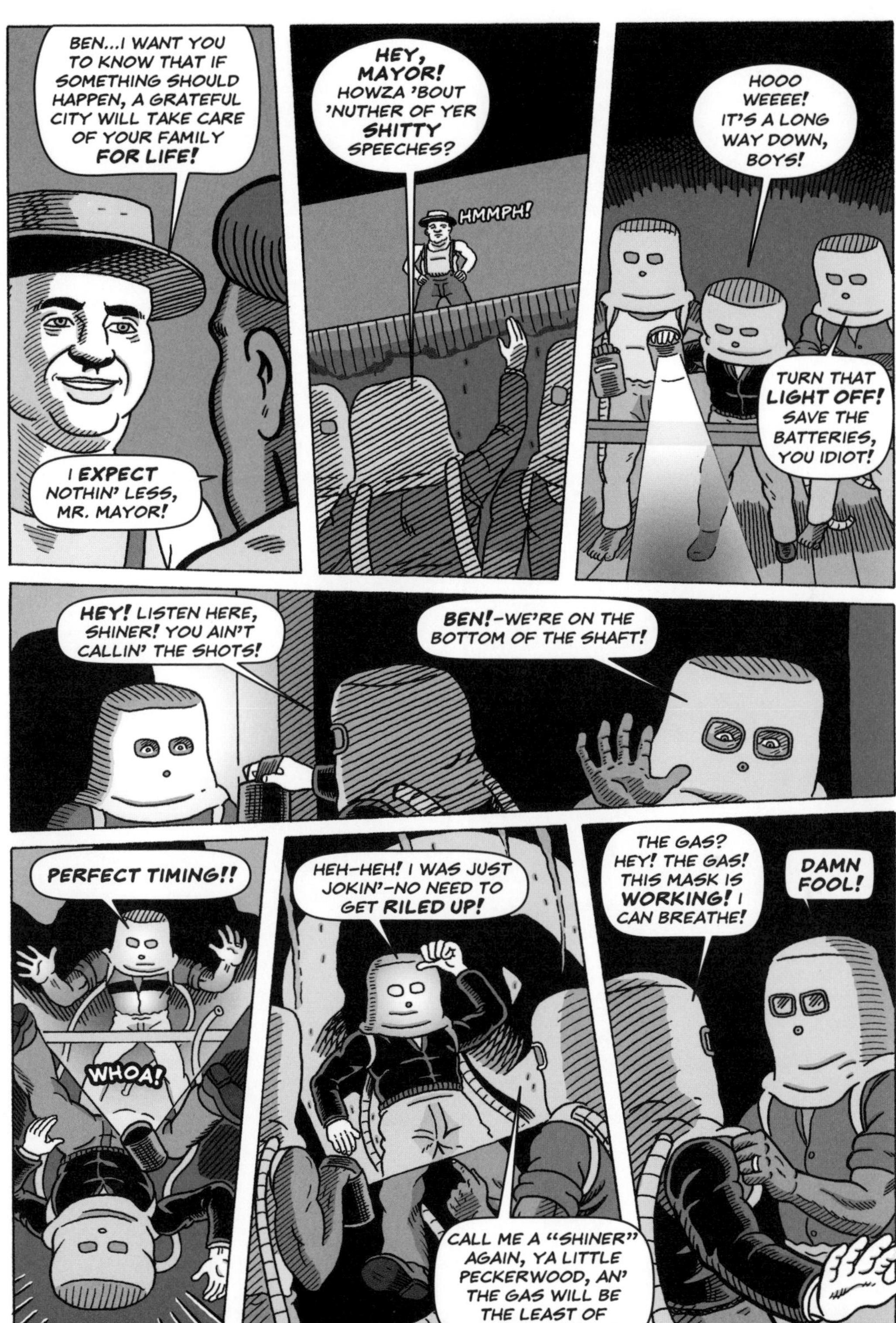
BEN...I WANT YOU TO KNOW THAT IF SOMETHING SHOULD HAPPEN, A GRATEFUL CITY WILL TAKE CARE OF YOUR FAMILY FOR LIFE!
I EXPECT NOTHIN' LESS, MR. MAYOR!
HEY, MAYOR! HOWZA 'BOUT 'NUTHER OF YER SHITTY SPEECHES?
HMMPH!
HOOO WEEEE! IT'S A LONG WAY DOWN, BOYS!
TURN THAT LIGHT OFF! SAVE THE BATTERIES, YOU IDIOT!
HEY! LISTEN HERE, SHINER! YOU AIN'T CALLIN' THE SHOTS!
BEN!–WE'RE ON THE BOTTOM OF THE SHAFT!
PERFECT TIMING!!
WHOA!
HEH-HEH! I WAS JUST JOKIN'–NO NEED TO GET RILED UP!
CALL ME A "SHINER" AGAIN, YA LITTLE PECKERWOOD, AN' THE GAS WILL BE THE LEAST OF YOUR WORRIES!
THE GAS? HEY! THE GAS! THIS MASK IS WORKING! I CAN BREATHE!
DAMN FOOL!

THOSE HOSES ARE PULLING IN OXYGEN FROM BELOW THE GAS LAYER. HELL, I'VE KNOW'D BABIES THAT COULD FIGURE THAT OUT!

THAT GODDAM BABY GOOCH!
OL' BABY GOOCH! EH, BEN?

WELL, IT'S LIKE THEY SAID. THERE'S VERY LITTLE AIR PRESSURE **LEFT.**
WHAT'S IT MEAN, BEN?

IT MEANS THAT WITHOUT AIR PRESSURE THE TUNNEL COULD COLLAPSE AND FLOOD IN ITS WEAKER SECTIONS.

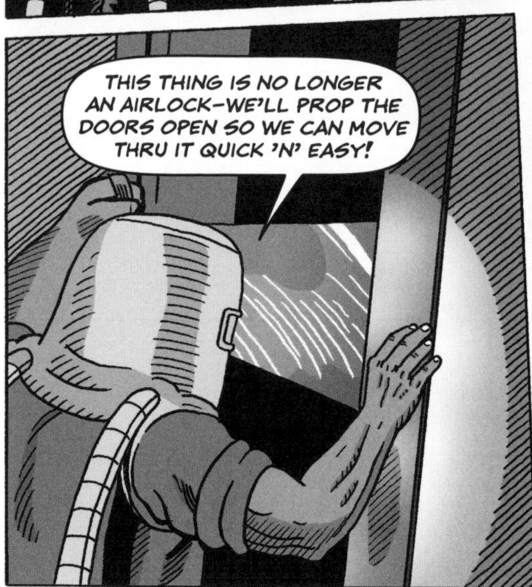
THIS THING IS NO LONGER AN AIRLOCK–WE'LL PROP THE DOORS OPEN SO WE CAN MOVE THRU IT QUICK 'N' EASY!

GASP!
NO! CAN'T BE!
OH MY GOD! LOOK AHEAD! ARE THOSE BODIES?

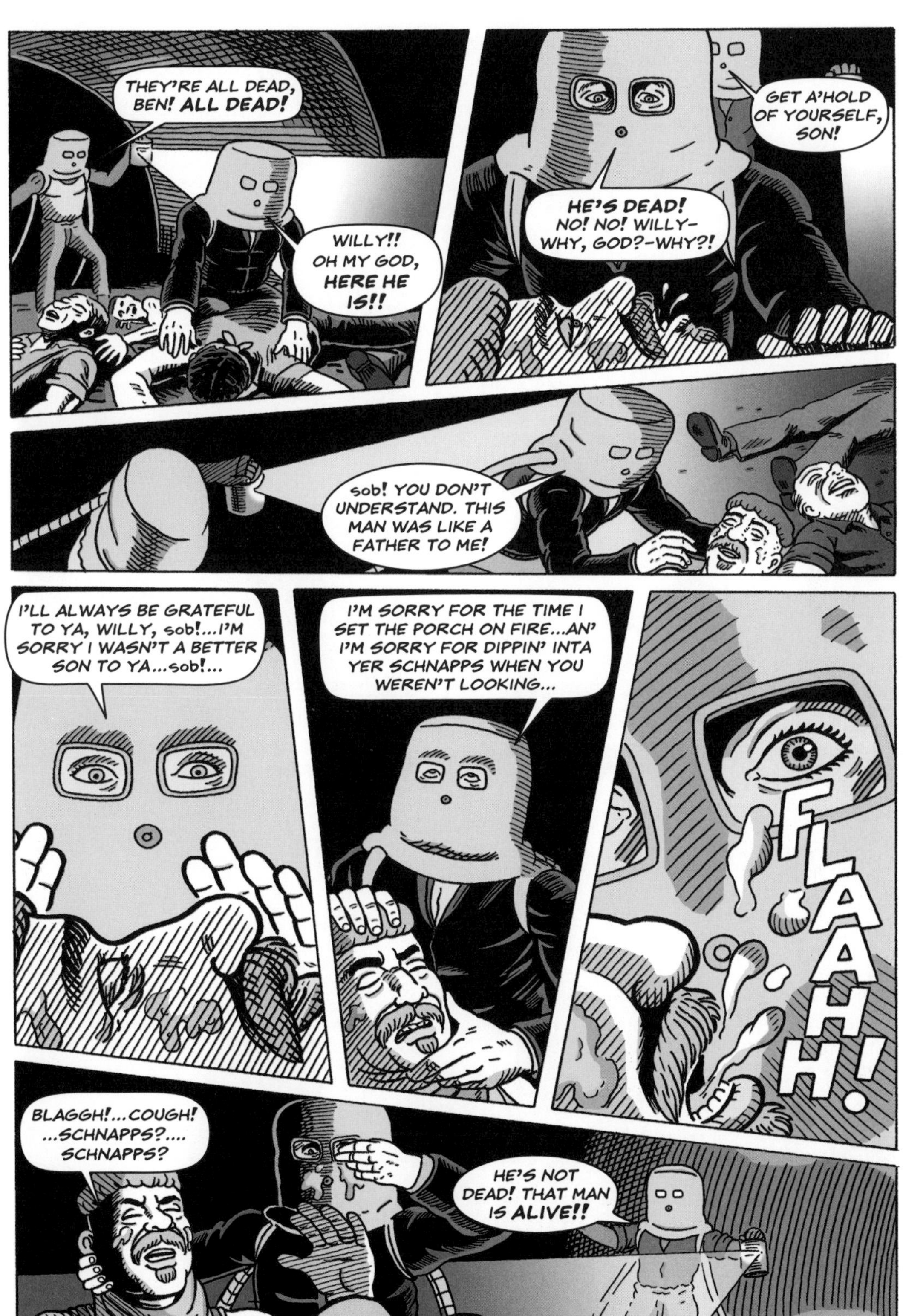
THEY'RE ALL DEAD, BEN! ALL DEAD!
WILLY!! OH MY GOD, HERE HE IS!!
HE'S DEAD! NO! NO! WILLY- WHY, GOD?-WHY?!
GET A'HOLD OF YOURSELF, SON!
sob! YOU DON'T UNDERSTAND. THIS MAN WAS LIKE A FATHER TO ME!
I'LL ALWAYS BE GRATEFUL TO YA, WILLY, sob!...I'M SORRY I WASN'T A BETTER SON TO YA...sob!...
I'M SORRY FOR THE TIME I SET THE PORCH ON FIRE...AN' I'M SORRY FOR DIPPIN' INTA YER SCHNAPPS WHEN YOU WEREN'T LOOKING...
FLAAHH!
BLAGGH!...COUGH! ...SCHNAPPS?.... SCHNAPPS?
HE'S NOT DEAD! THAT MAN IS ALIVE!!

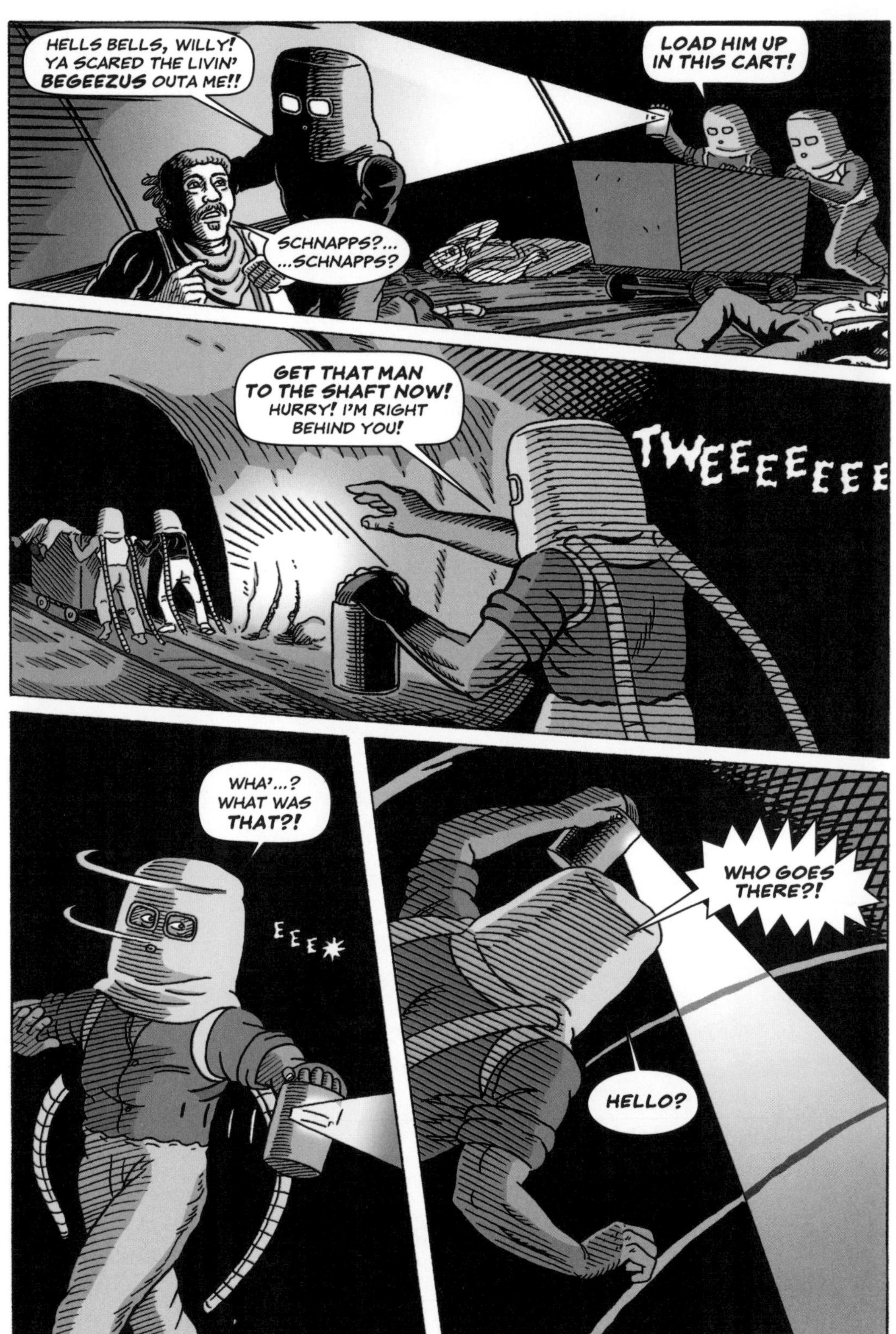
HELLS BELLS, WILLY! YA SCARED THE LIVIN' BEGEEZUS OUTA ME!!
LOAD HIM UP IN THIS CART!
SCHNAPPS?... ...SCHNAPPS?
GET THAT MAN TO THE SHAFT NOW! HURRY! I'M RIGHT BEHIND YOU!
TWEEEEEEE
WHA'...? WHAT WAS THAT?!
EEE
WHO GOES THERE?!
HELLO?

ON THE CRIB DECK...
WHIRR!
MR. NORTON! THEY'RE COMIN' BACK UP!!

WHIRR!
STAND BACK! DON'T CROWD THE SHAFT!

WE GOT US A LIVE ONE, BOYS!!

HOORAY!
HOORAY!
AND BY GOD'S GRACE WHO WAS SAVED?!

IT'S THE DUTCHMAN!!
BOOOOOOO!
ACHH! THROW 'IM BACK!

PRIMITIVE RESPIRATORS CALLED PULMOTORS WERE RUSHED TO THE SCENE TO PUMP GAS FROM THE LUNGS OF SURVIVORS
C'MON, GET THAT DOCTOR OVER HERE!
THIS MAN NEEDS A **PULMOTOR!**

IF HE MADE IT, THERE COULD BE OTHERS— LET'S GO!
I GOT WHAT I CAME FOR. I AIN'T GOIN' BACK DOWN THERE!

BELTRAN! GIVE ME YOUR REPORT!
THERE'S MORE **LIVE ONES** DOWN THERE. I'M SURE OF IT!

YOUR BROTHER SAYS THEY'RE ALL **DEAD!**
THEN LET'S HAVE A TEAM BRING UP THE DEAD WHILE I GO **DEEPER** DOWN THE TUNNEL!

OK, LADS...THE HELMET **WORKS!** BELTRAN AIN'T EVEN A SANDHOG AND HE'S WILLIN' TO GO BACK DOWN. WHO'S GONNA HELP HIM?!
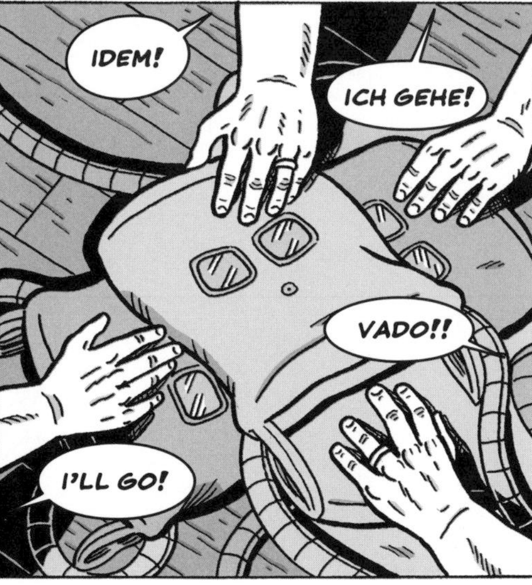
IDEM!
ICH GEHE!
VADO!!
I'LL GO!

ON BELTRAN'S SECOND DESCENT, HIS TEAM REMOVED SEVERAL DEAD BODIES BEFORE CLOUDS OF GAS FORCED THEM TO RETREAT. IT HAD BECOME CLEAR THAT THEIR ONLY HOPE OF FINDING MORE SURVIVORS REQUIRED THEM TO VENTURE FARTHER AND FASTER INTO THE CRIPPLED TUNNEL.
BEN...COUGH!... WE GOTTA GET OUTA HERE! THE GAS–IT'S TOO MUCH!
LOUIS–DID'YA HEAR THAT? SOUNDS LIKE A WHISTLE!
TWEEEEE
BEN! THERE AIN'T NO WHISTLE– LET'S GO!
GO ON UP INTO THE FRESH AIR. I'M RIGHT BEHIND YOU!
BEN?...COUGH!... DAMMIT, WHERE YA GOIN' NOW?...BEN!
20 MINUTES LATER.
THANK THE LORD! DON'T EVER SCARE ME LIKE THAT AG'IN!
I'M FINE...COUGH! I GOTTA LOOK AT THOSE TUNNEL SCHEMATICS!

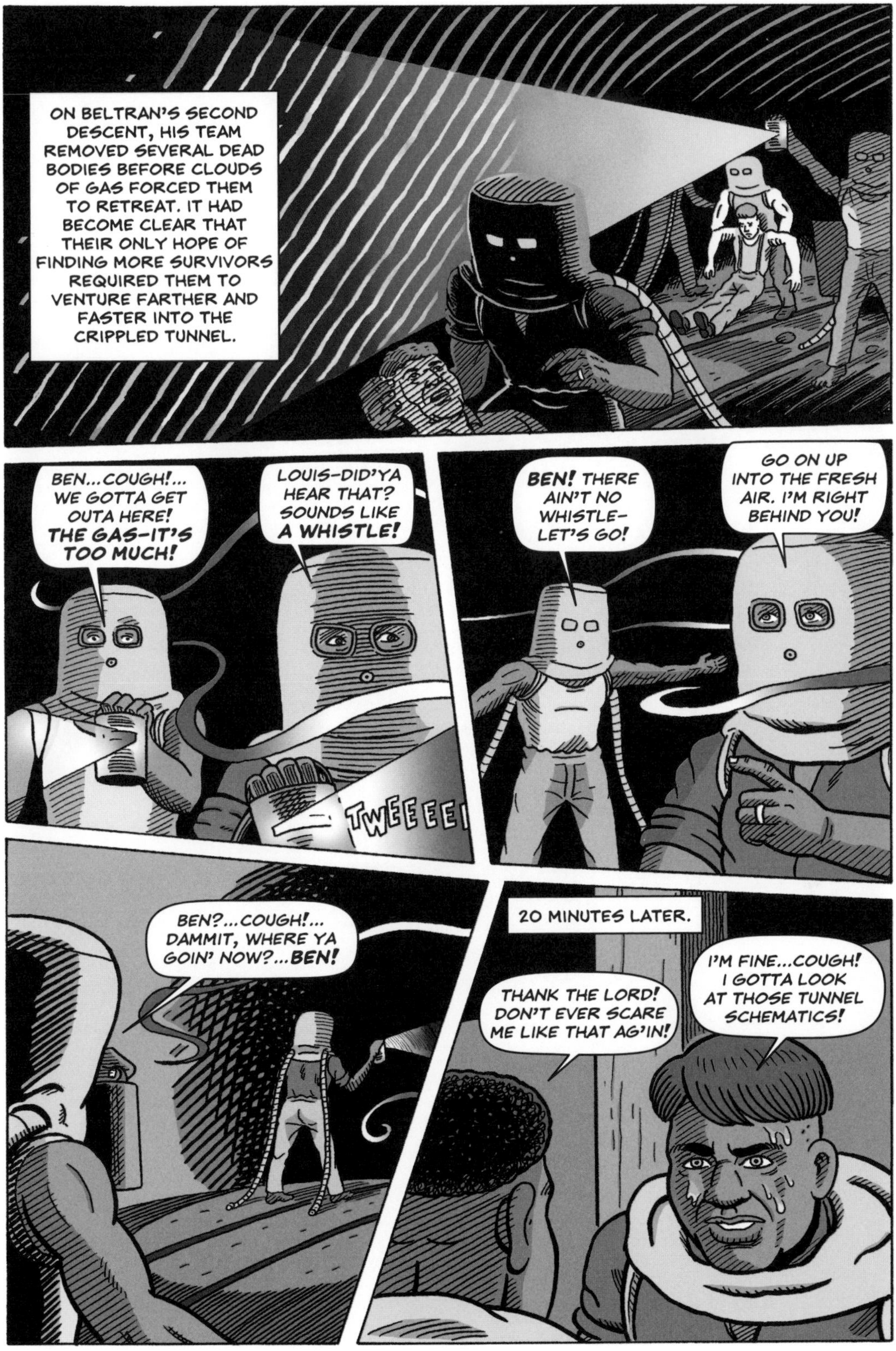

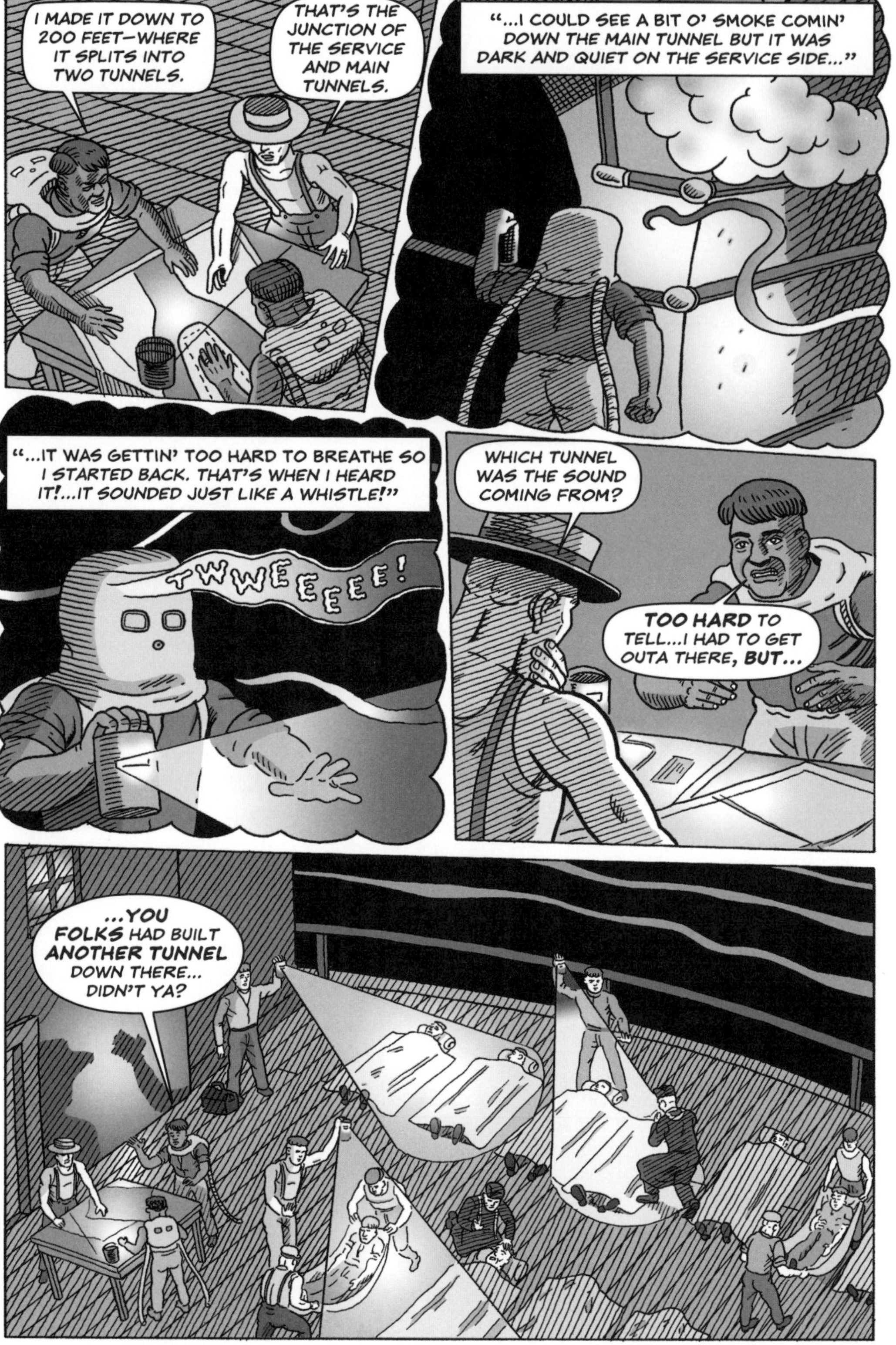

I MADE IT DOWN TO 200 FEET—WHERE IT SPLITS INTO TWO TUNNELS.

THAT'S THE JUNCTION OF THE SERVICE AND MAIN TUNNELS.

"...I COULD SEE A BIT O' SMOKE COMIN' DOWN THE MAIN TUNNEL BUT IT WAS DARK AND QUIET ON THE SERVICE SIDE..."

"...IT WAS GETTIN' TOO HARD TO BREATHE SO I STARTED BACK. THAT'S WHEN I HEARD IT!...IT SOUNDED JUST LIKE A WHISTLE!"

TWWEEEEEE!

WHICH TUNNEL WAS THE SOUND COMING FROM?

TOO HARD TO TELL...I HAD TO GET OUTA THERE, **BUT...**

THERE **WAS** A TUNNEL. HOW'D YOU KNOW THAT, BELTRAN?

THE OLD SERVICE TUNNEL WAS ON THE RIGHT OF THE MAIN. WE SHUT IT DOWN AND SEALED IT OFF **HERE** WITH A BULKHEAD.

WHY WAS IT SHUT DOWN?
THEY HIT A SERIES OF GAS POCKETS... AND THE SOIL WAS VERY UNSTABLE.

WHAT'S THIS CHANNEL **HERE?**
IT'S A CROSSOVER BETWEEN THE OLD SERVICE AND MAIN. WE SEALED THAT OFF, ALSO.

NO, THEY DIDN'T! CLARKE ORDERED THOSE MEN TO EVACUATE BEFORE IT COULD BE CLOSED. **IT'S STILL OPEN!**

"CLARKE" AGAIN... THIS CAN'T BE HAPPENIN' TO ME!
BELTRAN, WHAT'S THE MATTER? WHAT ARE YOU HOLDING?

IT'S CLARKE'S CAP...I FOUND IT AT THE JUNCTION LEADING INTO THE MAIN TUNNEL.
R. CLARK

I CAN'T PUT MEN'S LIVES AT RISK ON THE BASIS OF A FOUND CAP.

THE LAST MAN TO SEE CLARKE ALIVE SAID HE WAS HEADED DOWN THE TUNNEL WEARING THAT CAP AND BLOWING ON HIS...

WHISTLE!

MR. BELTRAN, YOU'RE TAKING TERRIBLE CHANCES. YOU DON'T OWE US ANYTHING.
"MISTER" BELTRAN? CALLING THAT SON O' DARKNESS "MISTER"! D'YA BELIEVE THAT!

HEY, EDDIE! HAND MCCOY ONE OF MISTER BELTRAN'S HELMETS. HE JUST JOINED THE RESCUE EFFORT!
HUH?

I AIN'T GOIN' INTO THAT DEATH TRAP!!
YOU WILL, OR YOU'LL BE SWIMMING BACK TO SHORE!

LOUIS, I WANT YOU TO SIT THE NEXT ONE OUT. YOU'VE DONE YOUR SHARE.
AIN'T NO WAY!

BEN, A DAY AIN'T GONE BY THAT I DIDN'T WISH I WAS BY YOUR SIDE WHEN YOU SAVED THAT BABY!

YOU'RE A GOOD BROTHER, LOUIS. YOU 'N' ME ARE MAKIN' HISTORY TONITE. I'M GLAD YOU'RE WITH ME.

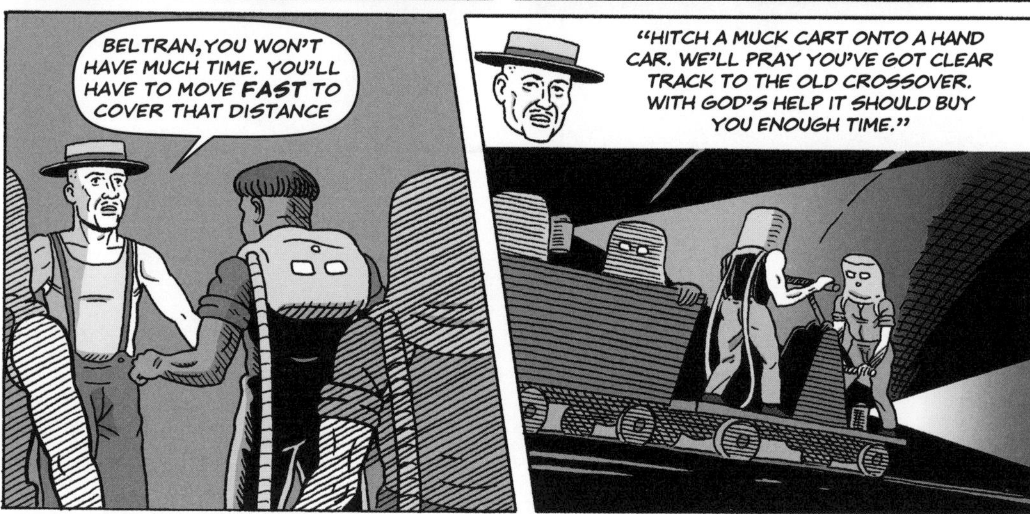
BELTRAN,YOU WON'T HAVE MUCH TIME. YOU'LL HAVE TO MOVE FAST TO COVER THAT DISTANCE
"HITCH A MUCK CART ONTO A HAND CAR. WE'LL PRAY YOU'VE GOT CLEAR TRACK TO THE OLD CROSSOVER. WITH GOD'S HELP IT SHOULD BUY YOU ENOUGH TIME."

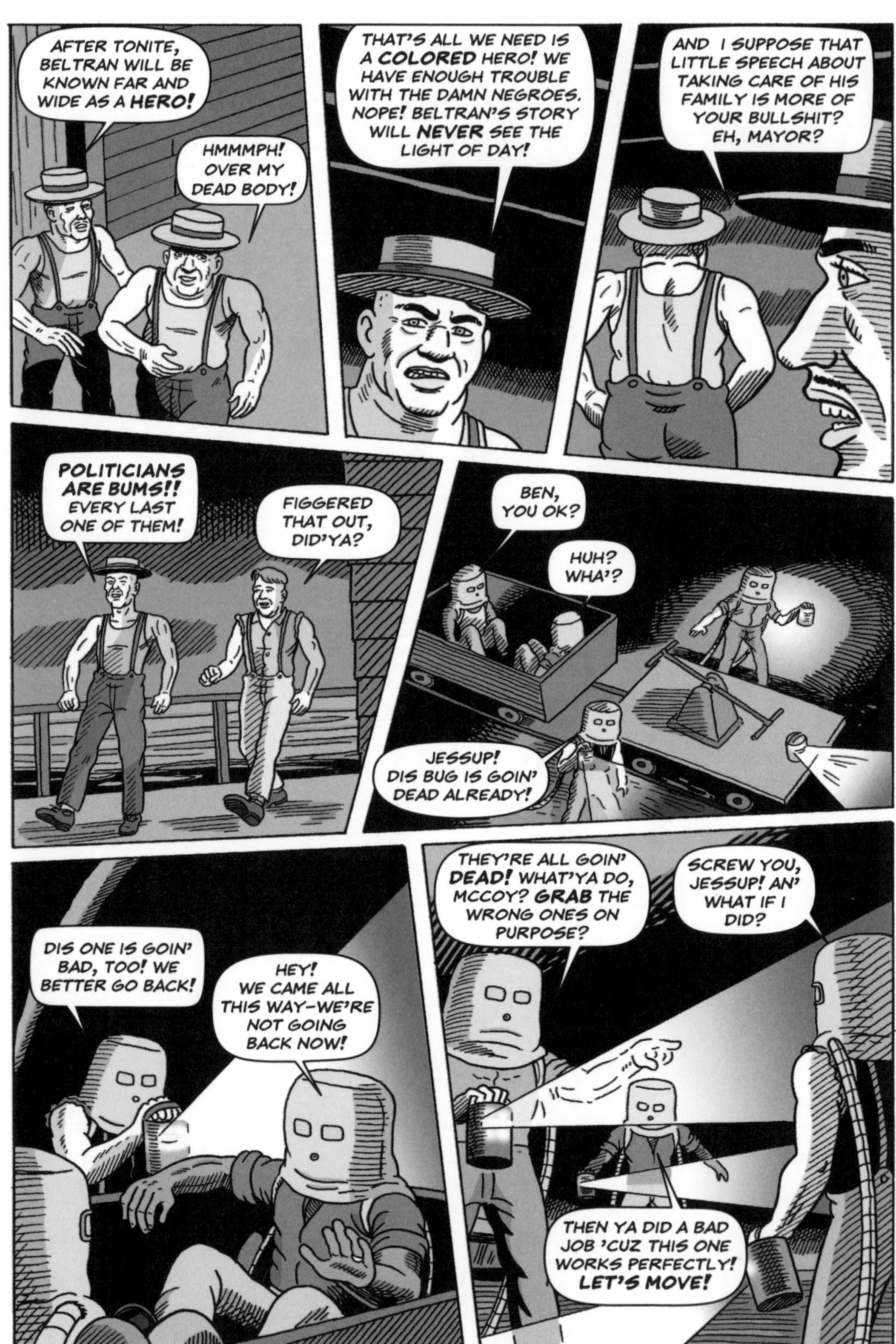
AFTER TONITE, BELTRAN WILL BE KNOWN FAR AND WIDE AS A HERO!
HMMMPH! OVER MY DEAD BODY!
THAT'S ALL WE NEED IS A COLORED HERO! WE HAVE ENOUGH TROUBLE WITH THE DAMN NEGROES. NOPE! BELTRAN'S STORY WILL NEVER SEE THE LIGHT OF DAY!
AND I SUPPOSE THAT LITTLE SPEECH ABOUT TAKING CARE OF HIS FAMILY IS MORE OF YOUR BULLSHIT? EH, MAYOR?
POLITICIANS ARE BUMS!! EVERY LAST ONE OF THEM!
FIGGERED THAT OUT, DID'YA?
BEN, YOU OK?
HUH? WHA'?
JESSUP! DIS BUG IS GOIN' DEAD ALREADY!
DIS ONE IS GOIN' BAD, TOO! WE BETTER GO BACK!
HEY! WE CAME ALL THIS WAY—WE'RE NOT GOING BACK NOW!
THEY'RE ALL GOIN' DEAD! WHAT'YA DO, MCCOY? GRAB THE WRONG ONES ON PURPOSE?
SCREW YOU, JESSUP! AN' WHAT IF I DID?
THEN YA DID A BAD JOB 'CUZ THIS ONE WORKS PERFECTLY! LET'S MOVE!

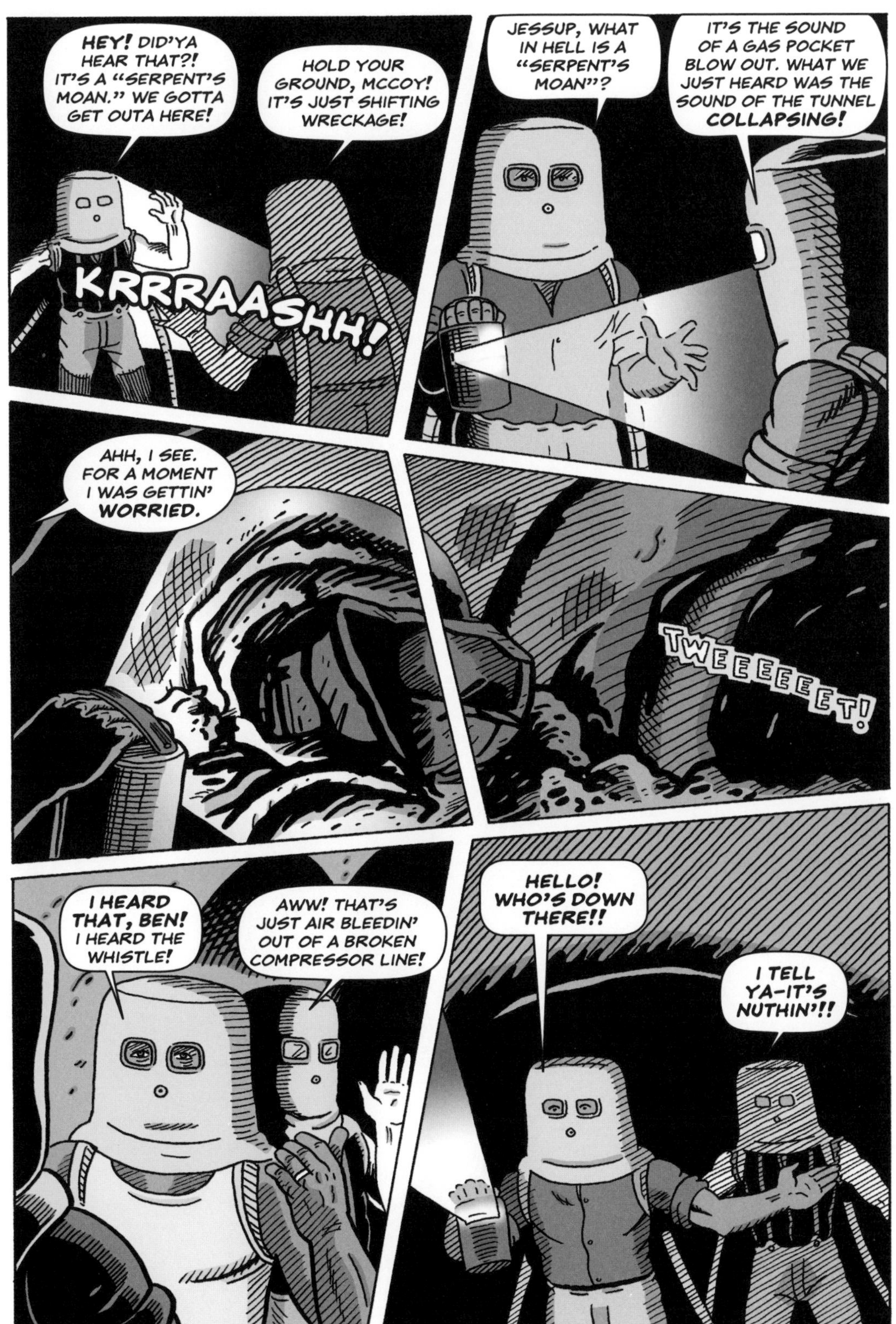
HEY! DID'YA HEAR THAT?! IT'S A "SERPENT'S MOAN." WE GOTTA GET OUTA HERE!
HOLD YOUR GROUND, MCCOY! IT'S JUST SHIFTING WRECKAGE!
KRRRAASHH!
JESSUP, WHAT IN HELL IS A "SERPENT'S MOAN"?
IT'S THE SOUND OF A GAS POCKET BLOW OUT. WHAT WE JUST HEARD WAS THE SOUND OF THE TUNNEL COLLAPSING!
AHH, I SEE. FOR A MOMENT I WAS GETTIN' WORRIED.
TWEEEEEEET!
I HEARD THAT, BEN! I HEARD THE WHISTLE!
AWW! THAT'S JUST AIR BLEEDIN' OUT OF A BROKEN COMPRESSOR LINE!
HELLO! WHO'S DOWN THERE!!
I TELL YA–IT'S NUTHIN'!!

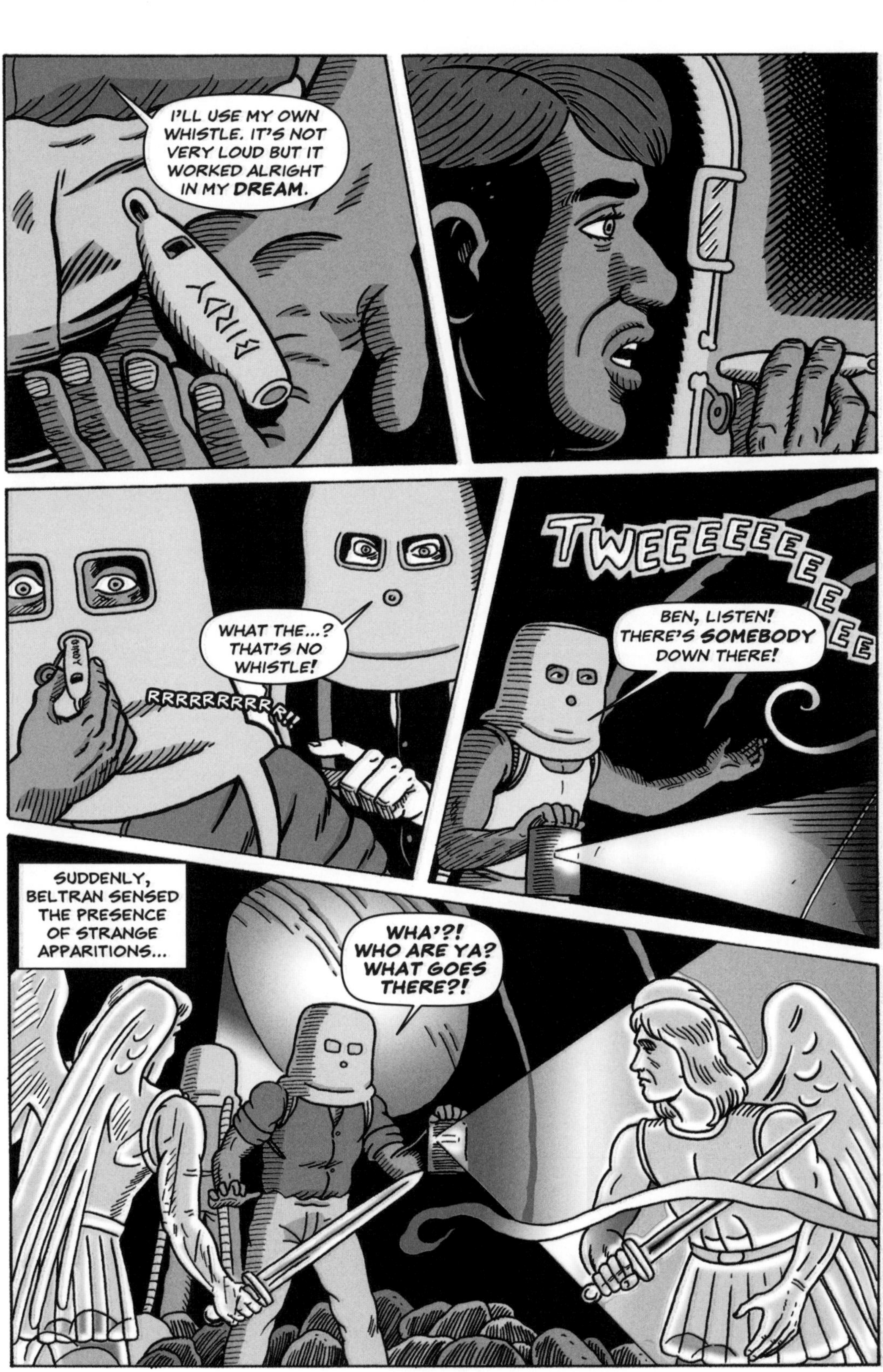

WHAT THE...? THAT'S NO WHISTLE!

RRRRRRRRRR!!

TWEEEEEEEEEEEE

BEN, LISTEN! THERE'S **SOMEBODY** DOWN THERE!

SUDDENLY, BELTRAN SENSED THE PRESENCE OF STRANGE APPARITIONS...

WHA'?! WHO ARE YA? WHAT GOES THERE?!

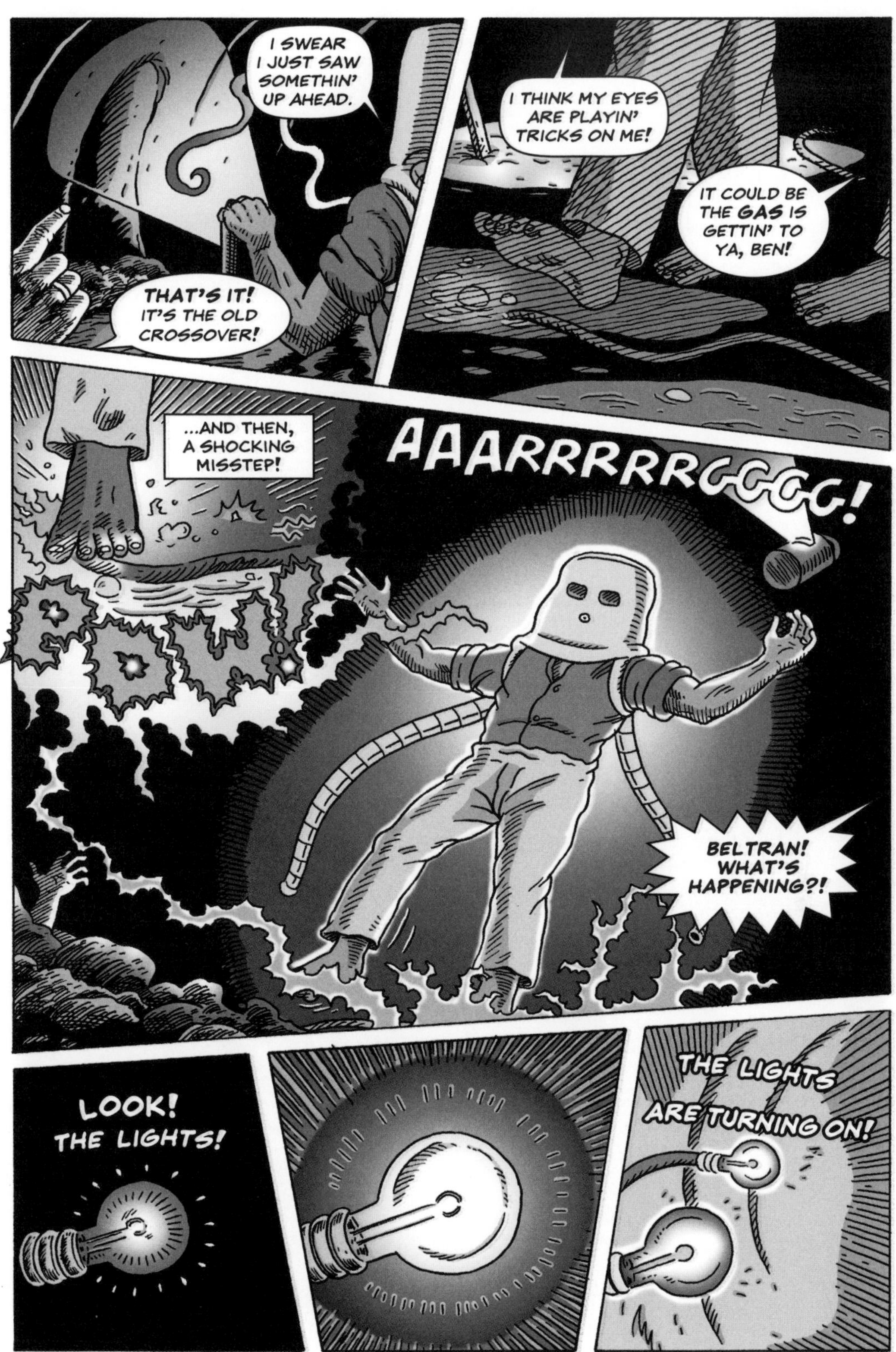
I SWEAR I JUST SAW SOMETHIN' UP AHEAD.
THAT'S IT! IT'S THE OLD CROSSOVER!
I THINK MY EYES ARE PLAYIN' TRICKS ON ME!
IT COULD BE THE GAS IS GETTIN' TO YA, BEN!
...AND THEN, A SHOCKING MISSTEP!
AAARRRRRRGGGGG!
BELTRAN! WHAT'S HAPPENING?!
LOOK! THE LIGHTS!
THE LIGHTS ARE TURNING ON!

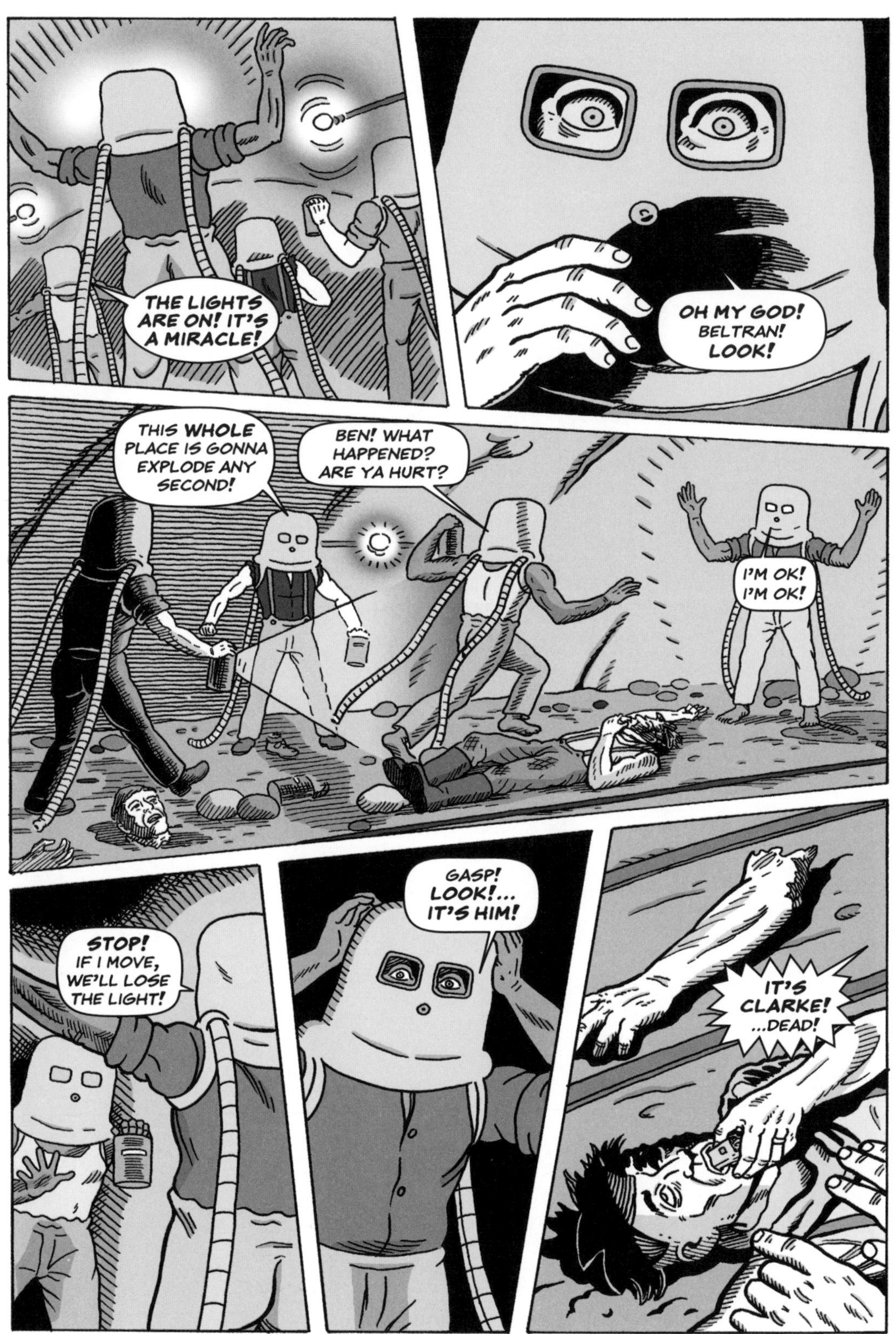
THE LIGHTS ARE ON! IT'S A MIRACLE!
OH MY GOD! BELTRAN! LOOK!
THIS WHOLE PLACE IS GONNA EXPLODE ANY SECOND!
BEN! WHAT HAPPENED? ARE YA HURT?
I'M OK! I'M OK!
STOP! IF I MOVE, WE'LL LOSE THE LIGHT!
GASP! LOOK!... IT'S HIM!
IT'S CLARKE! ...DEAD!

IT WAS HIS WHISTLE THAT LED US HERE!
"...HE CALLED US FROM THE OTHER SIDE!"
HELP! PLEASE HELP US!!
WAIT! D'YA HEAR THAT? ...VOICES!
BELTRAN! YOU ARE NOT GOING TO BELIEVE THIS!
MCCOY! MOVE YOUR ASS AND HELP JESSUP WITH THOSE MEN! LOUIS!...GET A MUCK CART UP HERE...HURRY, BROTHER!
THAT'S THE LAST ORDER I'M TAKIN' FROM YOU! JUST WHO THE HELL D'YA THINK Y'ARE?

WHO THE HELL AM I? JUST A SIMPLE, ORDINARY MAN, I GUESS! WHO THE HELL ARE YOU!?
YA DON'T BELONG DOWN HERE, YA GODDAM NIG...
LISTEN UP, MCCOY! COLORED PEOPLE "BELONGED" WELL BEFORE YOU WHITES SHOWED UP... AND WE'LL BE HERE LONG AFTER YOU'RE GONE. BEST GET USED TO THE IDEA OF US...CUZ' WE AREN'T GOING ANYWHERE!
KRRREEEEAAAAAGGORRRRR!
UH-OH... WHAT'S HAPPENIN'!!
GET MOVIN', MCCOY! WE'RE RUNNIN' OUTA TIME!
WE'RE GONNA DIE!
BETTER HURRY, BOYS! I CAN'T HOLD THIS POSITION MUCH LONGER!
LOUIS! WHERE THE HELL IS THAT GODDAM CART!!!
GOT IT!!

JESSUP! WHAT'S THE HOLDUP OVER THERE?!
THE TUNNEL COLLAPSED ONTO THIS MAN'S LEGS! HE'S PINNED!
PULL, LOUIS! PULL!!
ARRGHH!
HE'S COMIN' LOOSE, JESSUP! WE GOT 'IM!
KRRRAAACCKKK!
OH GOD! CAVE IN!!
AIEEEEEEE!!
JESSUP!! LOOK OUT!!
UNHH!!
THUD!

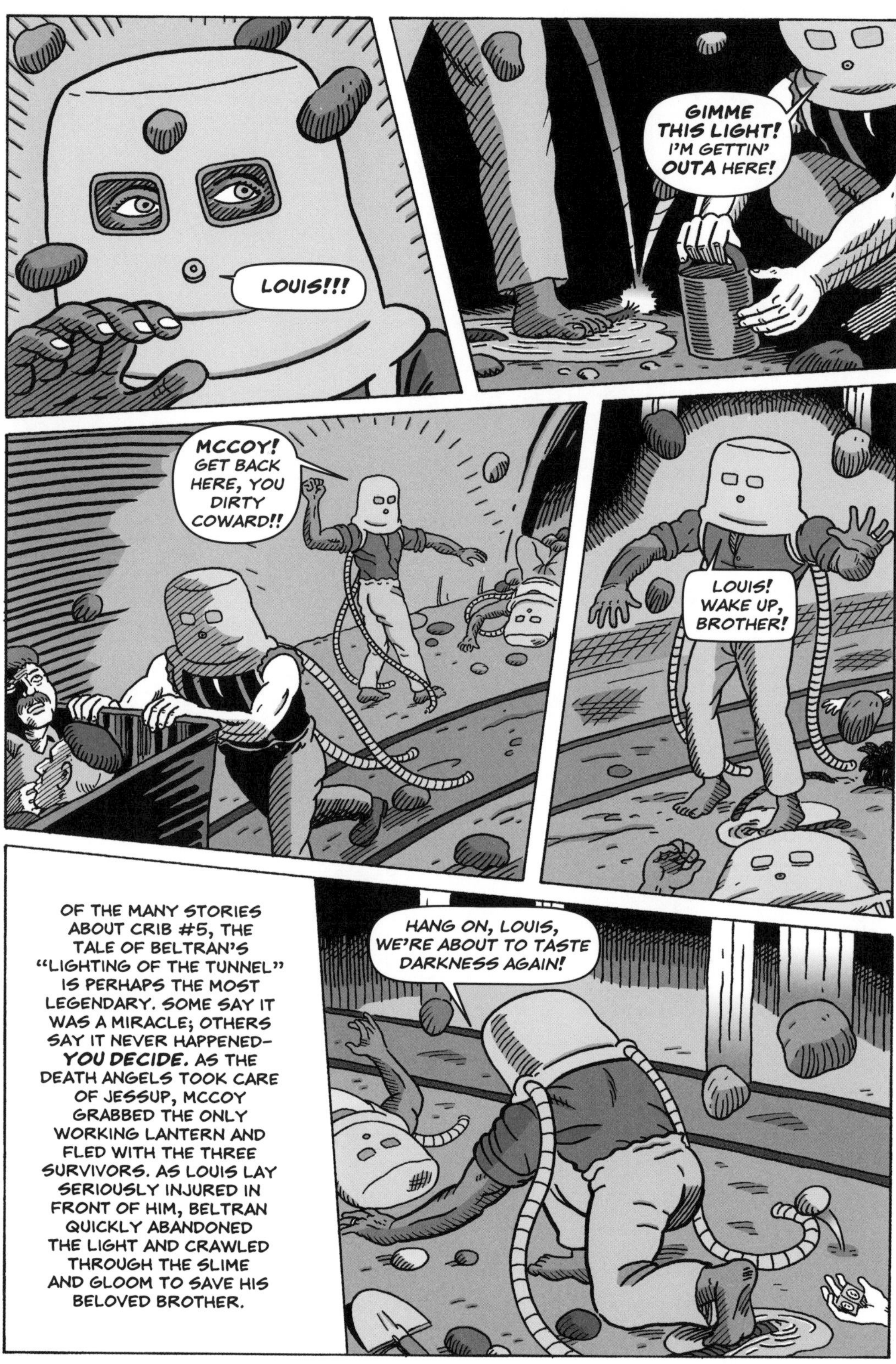
LOUIS!!!
GIMME THIS LIGHT! I'M GETTIN' OUTA HERE!
MCCOY! GET BACK HERE, YOU DIRTY COWARD!!
LOUIS! WAKE UP, BROTHER!
OF THE MANY STORIES ABOUT CRIB #5, THE TALE OF BELTRAN'S "LIGHTING OF THE TUNNEL" IS PERHAPS THE MOST LEGENDARY. SOME SAY IT WAS A MIRACLE; OTHERS SAY IT NEVER HAPPENED- YOU DECIDE. AS THE DEATH ANGELS TOOK CARE OF JESSUP, MCCOY GRABBED THE ONLY WORKING LANTERN AND FLED WITH THE THREE SURVIVORS. AS LOUIS LAY SERIOUSLY INJURED IN FRONT OF HIM, BELTRAN QUICKLY ABANDONED THE LIGHT AND CRAWLED THROUGH THE SLIME AND GLOOM TO SAVE HIS BELOVED BROTHER.
HANG ON, LOUIS, WE'RE ABOUT TO TASTE DARKNESS AGAIN!

HERE I COME, READY OR NOT!

WHILE BELTRAN WAS HELPING LOUIS, THE FIRE DEPARTMENT HAD FINALLY ARRIVED ON THE CRIB PLATFORM.
YE BOYS MADE IT AT LAST!! THANK JAYSUS!

MR. NORTON! CAPT. CASEY! SOMEONE IS COMING UP THE SHAFT!!

IT'S McCOY!!...AND HE'S GOT THREE LIVE SANDHOGS WITH HIM!!

HOORAY!
HOORAY!
HOORAY!

YOUNG MAN, I'M GOING TO PIN A MEDAL ON YOUR CHEST!
HOLD YER HORSES!
WHERE'S THE REST O' YER TEAM? WHERE'S BELTRAN?

I WAS ABOUT TO TELL YA... JESSUP AND ANOTHER GUY WERE KILLED IN A CAVE-IN. IT WAS HORRIBLE!
AND...THE BELTRANS? WHAT O' THEM? SPIT IT OUT!

BELTRAN'S BROTHER WAS HURT, BUT BOTH WERE ALIVE WHEN I LAST SAW 'EM.
Y'MEAN YE LEFT 'EM?

YE DESERTED 'EM DIDN'T YE?!
COUGH!... THAT MCCOY IS A COWARD!

HEY! IS THAT THE THANKS I GET FOR SAVIN' YER LIFE?
IT'S A CRIME!... COUGH!...MCCOY LEFT THOSE GUYS TRAPPED DOWN THERE!

LOOK, I HAD TO SAVE THESE MEN, RIGHT? WHAT'S THE USE IN ALL O' US DYIN'?
WELL, BOYO, GET THAT HOOD ON 'CUZ YER GOIN' BACK DOWN THERE!

WE HAVE TO HURRY! THOSE TWO BROTHERS CAN'T SAVE THEMSELVES WITHOUT US!

UNHH...HUH! WHAT?! BEN! BEN!!

WELCOME BACK, LOUIS, EASY NOW...COUGH!... I WAS AFRAID I LOST YA!

HAVE I GONE BLIND, BEN? I CAN'T SEE NUTHIN'.

GATHER YOUR SENSES, LOUIS. I GOT US IN TROUBLE AGAIN AND WE'LL NEED MORE THAN A COW THIS TIME!

MEANWHILE... AT THE TUNNEL FACE, GAS AND AIR HAD RECONCENTRATED TO EXPLOSIVE LEVELS. IF IGNITED, A BOLUS OF FLAME WOULD STREAM DOWN THE TUNNEL LIKE A LOCOMOTIVE. TRAPPED IN TOTAL DARKNESS BELTRAN WAITED IN DREAD FOR THE SOUND OF THE "SERPENT'S MOAN." HE DIDN'T HAVE TO WAIT VERY LONG.
TWEEEEET!
...COUGH!...I FINALLY FIGURED OUT THE MYSTERY OF CLARKE'S WHISTLE WHILE WAITIN' FOR YOU TO WAKE UP.
COUGH...FLUCTUATIONS IN AIR PRESSURE CAUSE IT TO GO OFF LIKE OLD FAITHFUL EVERY ONE HUNDRED SECONDS OR SO.
LET'S GET YA TO YOUR FEET! EASY DOES IT!
HEY! YOU HEAR THAT?
IS THAT THE SOUND THEY WERE TALKIN' ABOUT? THAT "SERPENT" THING?
IF IT IS...THEN WE'LL HAVE TO MOVE FAST!
POW!
GWAAAARRROOOOOOO

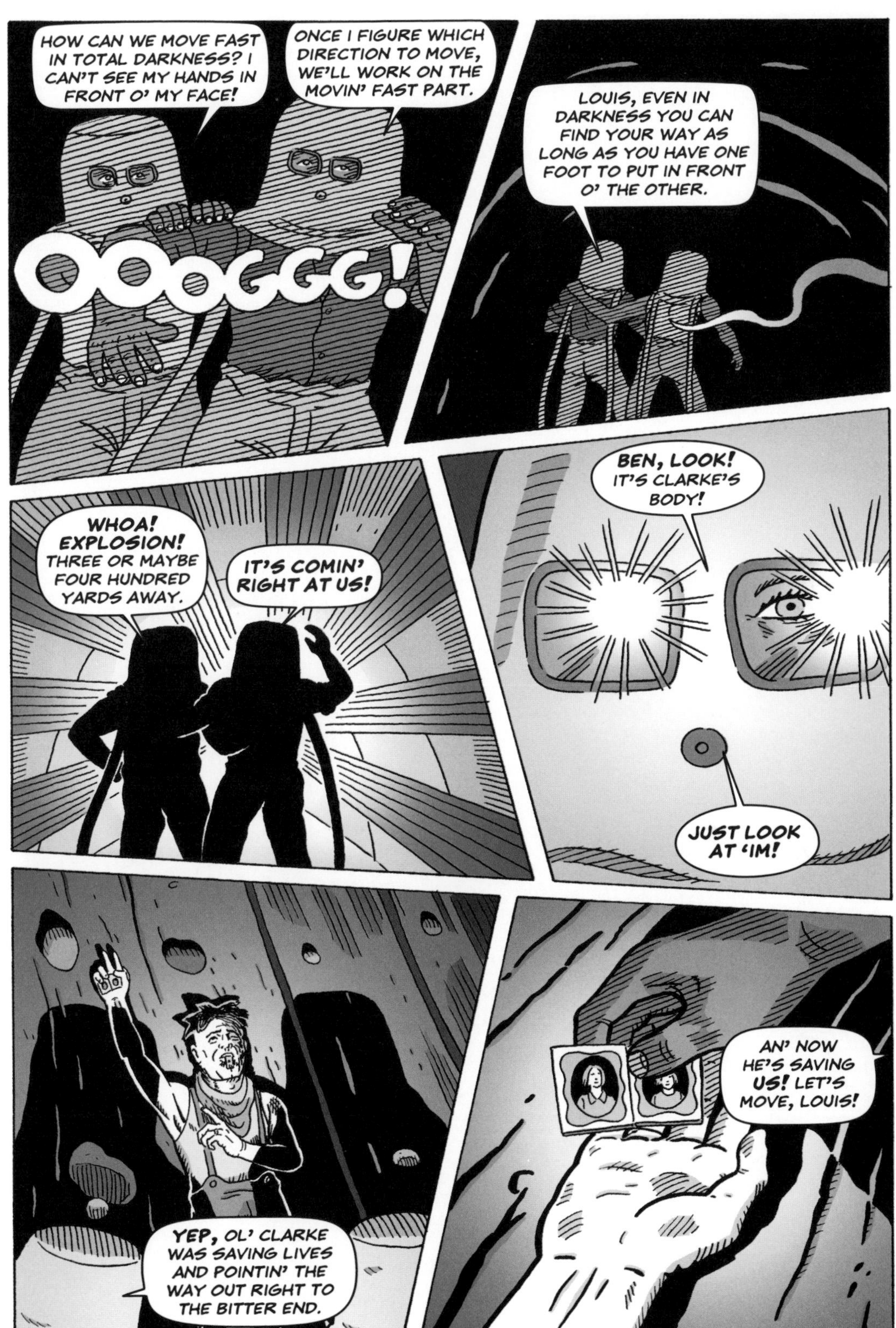
HOW CAN WE MOVE FAST IN TOTAL DARKNESS? I CAN'T SEE MY HANDS IN FRONT O' MY FACE!
ONCE I FIGURE WHICH DIRECTION TO MOVE, WE'LL WORK ON THE MOVIN' FAST PART.
OOOGGG!
LOUIS, EVEN IN DARKNESS YOU CAN FIND YOUR WAY AS LONG AS YOU HAVE ONE FOOT TO PUT IN FRONT O' THE OTHER.
WHOA! EXPLOSION! THREE OR MAYBE FOUR HUNDRED YARDS AWAY.
IT'S COMIN' RIGHT AT US!
BEN, LOOK! IT'S CLARKE'S BODY!
JUST LOOK AT 'IM!
YEP, OL' CLARKE WAS SAVING LIVES AND POINTIN' THE WAY OUT RIGHT TO THE BITTER END.
AN' NOW HE'S SAVING US! LET'S MOVE, LOUIS!

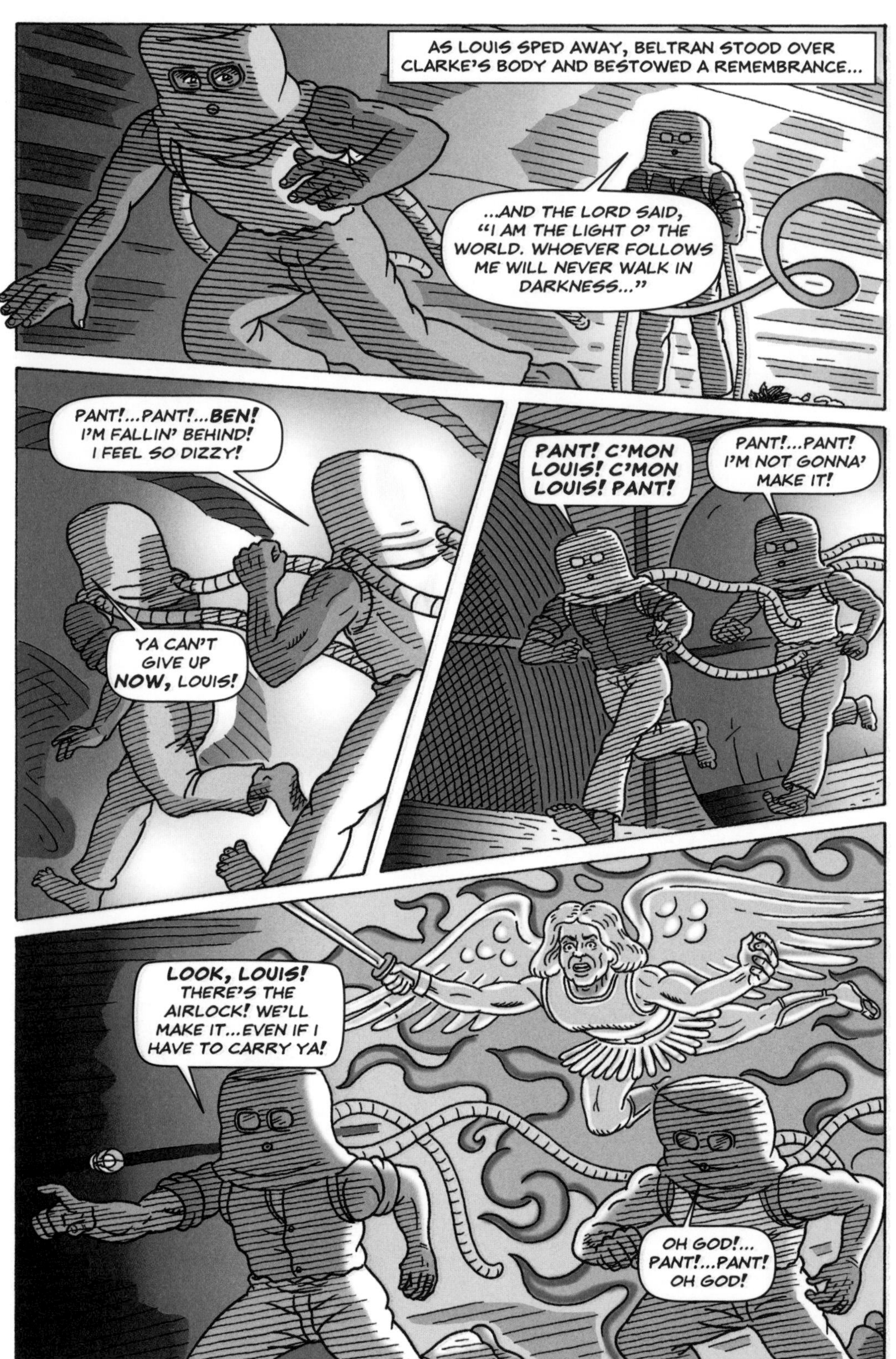
AS LOUIS SPED AWAY, BELTRAN STOOD OVER CLARKE'S BODY AND BESTOWED A REMEMBRANCE...
...AND THE LORD SAID, "I AM THE LIGHT O' THE WORLD. WHOEVER FOLLOWS ME WILL NEVER WALK IN DARKNESS..."
PANT!...PANT!...BEN! I'M FALLIN' BEHIND! I FEEL SO DIZZY!
YA CAN'T GIVE UP NOW, LOUIS!
PANT! C'MON LOUIS! C'MON LOUIS! PANT!
PANT!...PANT! I'M NOT GONNA' MAKE IT!
LOOK, LOUIS! THERE'S THE AIRLOCK! WE'LL MAKE IT...EVEN IF I HAVE TO CARRY YA!
OH GOD!... PANT!...PANT! OH GOD!

WITH FIRE LICKING AT THEIR HEELS, THE EXHAUSTED BROTHERS MADE A DESPERATE LEAP INTO THE OPEN AIRLOCK...
...LEAVING WHAT AIR THERE WAS LEFT TO BE CONSUMED BY THE HUNGRY FLAMES!
WHILE UP ABOVE...
MAYBE YOU BETTER HOLD UP, CHIEF! THE FIRE IS BACK!
HOLD UP?? ONLY IRISH WHISKEY AND RICH WIDOWS HOLD US UP, BUCKO!

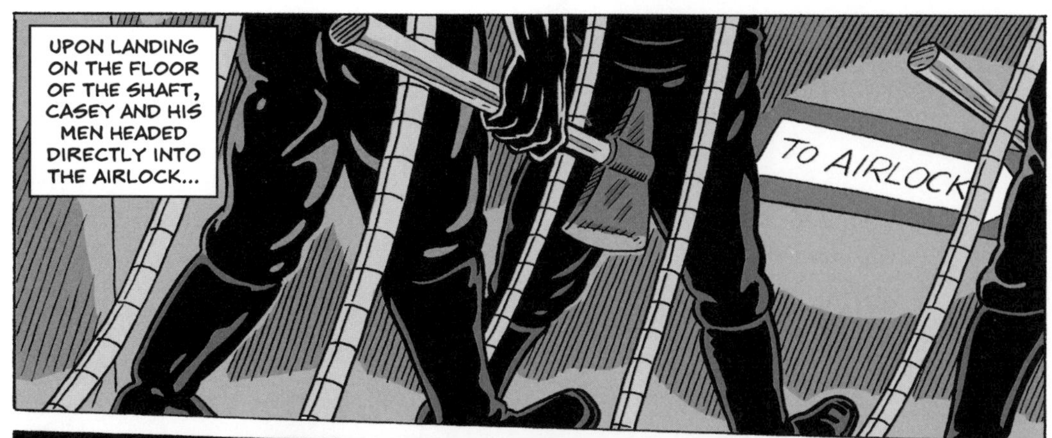
UPON LANDING ON THE FLOOR OF THE SHAFT, CASEY AND HIS MEN HEADED DIRECTLY INTO THE AIRLOCK...
TO AIRLOCK

...AND, WITHOUT A MOMENT TO SPARE...
I'LL TAKE THIS MAN ME'SELF! PANT!...I OWE 'IM THAT MUCH!

...THE FIREMEN HAD WRESTLED BOTH BROTHERS FROM THE OUTSTRETCHED ARMS OF THE DEATH ANGELS...
WE NEED A PULMOTOR! C'MON, THIS MAN NEEDS HELP!

YOU'LL MAKE IT, BEN! YER A HERO, BOYO! A REAL HERO!

CHAPTER 9: AFTERMATH:
"THE SIGNIFICANCE OF THINGS AS LARGE AS LAKES"

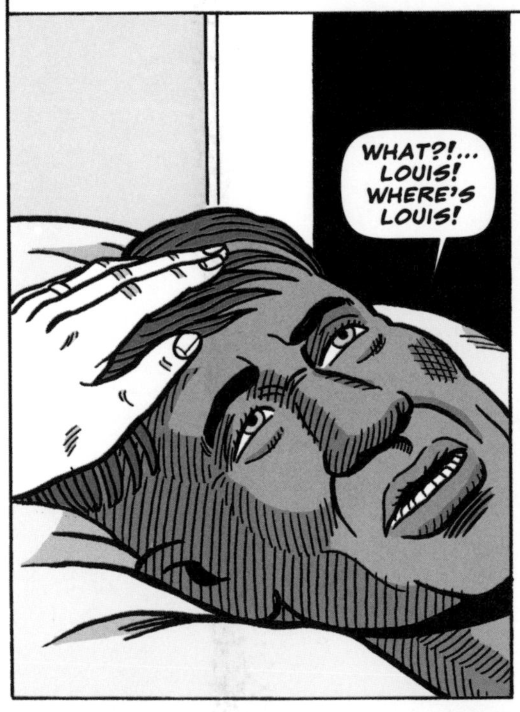

WHAT? WHY ARE YOU LOOKIN' AT ME LIKE THAT?

BEN, CAPT. CASEY SAID THE MAYOR WON'T LET THE PAPERS CARRY YOUR STORY.

IT'S AS THOUGH YOU AND LOUIS WEREN'T EVEN THERE...
WHAT!? AHH, THAT HACK SONOVABITCH! THIS IS HOW HE TAKES CARE O' ME?... WHITE MAN'S IGNORANCE, FRIEDA. IT'S PURE, IT'S SIMPLE, AN' IT'S EVERYWHERE!

THEY'RE THE SAME KIND O' MEN THAT TURNED A GREAT LAKE AND RIVER SO FILTHY THAT OTHERS HAD TO DIE FOR THE CAUSE OF CLEAN DRINKIN' WATER. JUST THINK ABOUT THAT FOR A SECOND!

AS LONG AS WE ARE LED BY PEOPLE UNABLE TO UNDERSTAND THE SIGNIFICANCE OF THINGS AS LARGE AS LAKES...OR AS SMALL AS THE COMMON MAN...
... WHAT CHANCE DOES ANY OF US REALLY HAVE?

WHAT ABOUT THAT WATERWORKS BOSS, NORTON?! HE KNOWS WHAT WE DID! WHY WON'T HE SPEAK UP?
'CUZ HE'S DEAD!
CLEVELAN

CHIEF CASEY! SEEMS LIKE YOU ARE ALWAYS ON HAND TO SEE ME HIT BOTTOM.
BE NICE TO THIS MAN, BEN. HE SAVED YOUR LIFE! DID YOU SAY NORTON WAS DEAD?
CLEVEL

DEAD AS A BRICK! KILLED HIMSELF. HE STAYED OUT THERE ON THE CRIB 'TIL THE LAST MAN WAS OFF-LOADED...

"...AND THEN HE PUT A GUN TO HIS HEAD AND BLEW HIS BRAINS OUT IN FRONT OF JAYSUS, THE TUGBOAT, AND THE HOLY GHOST."

AT THE PIER THE MAYOR TOLD THE REPORTERS THERE WERE THREE HEROES TO WRITE ABOUT!
CLEVELAND GAZETTE

ONLY THREE, HUH? AN' WHICH THREE ARE WE TALKIN'?
VAN DYKE, WHO WAS THE MAN YE SAVED, MCCOY, THE ROTTEN SKUNK WHO DESERTED YE, AN' LAST BUT NOT LEAST...
GAZETTE

...THE VILLAGE EEDJIT HIMSELF, TOMMY GALLAGHER!
LEVELAND GAZET
WATERWORKS DISASTER
INQUEST STARTS TOMORR
TUNNEL HERO TO TESTIFY
Thomas Van Dyke

THE "STAR" WITNESS TOMMY GALLAGHER
YEA, SO IT WAS JUST ME ALONE THAT HAD ALL THE GUTS. I SAVED THE WHOLE SMASH BY MYSELF WITH THE OBLIGING HELP O' A COUPLE SHINERS!
MR. GALLAGHER, WHAT EXACTLY IS A "SHINER?"
UH...GOLLIWOGS, OR...Y'KNOW... DARKIES!
AH, YES...HOWEVER, THOSE OF US THAT ACTUALLY LIVE IN THE 20TH CENTURY PREFER TO CALL THEM "NEGROES."

YEA! RIGHT! WELL, ANYWAYS THOSE TWO SHINERS WAS REAL SCARED, BUT, I KEPT 'EM IN LINE. I SAVED WILLY, AND THE REST IS HISTORY!

MEANWHILE, OUTSIDE THE COURTROOM...
NO ADMIT WHILE HEARING IN SESSI
HOLD UP! WHAT'S THIS ABOUT, PADDY?
LET US IN THERE! THIS IS BEN BELTRAN, THE REAL HERO OF CRIB #5!
STAY HERE WHILE I CHECK WITH THE MAYOR!

A FEW MINUTES LATER...
YOU CAN GO IN, BUT BELTRAN HAS TO WAIT UNTIL CALLED!
WHAT?! WHY CAN'T HE GO IN?

GO ASK THE MAN YERSELF! MEANWHILE, HE TAKES A SEAT OVER THERE!
AWW, JAYSUS! BEN, HAVE A SEAT. I'LL BE RIGHT BACK!

PLEASE STATE YOUR NAME FOR THE RECORD.
VILHELM VAN DYKE.
HISSS!
BOOO!
BOOO!
HISSS!

MR. VAN DYKE, HOW LONG HAVE YOU BEEN THE CRIB SUPERINTENDENT?
TOO LONG!!
TEN YEARS!

PROMOTED TO THE POSITION AFTER SAVING A MAN'S LIFE, **CORRECT?**
YAA...YOU BETCHA!

DID YOU FIND IT IRONIC THAT THE ORDER TO RESUME DIGGING RESULTED IN THE DEATH OF THE **VERY SAME MAN**...ALONG WITH TWENTY OTHER MEN?
YAA, SURE! ...VAT'S AN "IRONIC?"

...AND THAT THIS ORDER WAS THE KIND OF ORDER THAT COULD HAVE ONLY COME FROM YOU!
NOT TRUE! I TOLD CLARKE TO GO DOWN AN' TAKE 'ER A LOOK...AN' NOTTINK ELSE!

CLARKE TAKES A TEAM OF SIXTEEN MEN 200 FEET UNDERNEATH A LAKE...
TO MERELY, "TAKE 'ER A LOOK"? ARE YOU SURE YOU WANT TO STICK TO THAT STORY?
CLARKE **KNEW** THE DANGERS! HE SHOULD HAFF KNOWN BETTER!

CLARKE **DID** KNOW BETTER **AND SO DID YOU!** IN FACT, YOU AND CLARKE KNEW "THE DANGERS" BETTER THAN ANYONE ELSE ON CRIB #5!
MEBBE' HE VAS DRUNK! HE VAS **IRISH** Y'KNOW!

YA LYIN' DIVIL'!
AAAK!

THROW THAT MAN OUT! THERE WILL BE ORDER IN THIS COURT!

EVERYONE BE SEATED!! THAT INCLUDES YOU, TOO MADAM. PLEASE TAKE YOUR SEAT!

I'M MRS. CLARKE, AN' I WILL NOT BE SEATED! NOT AS LONG AS THIS CREATURE CAN SIT HERE AN' TELL HIS DURTY LIES 'BOUT ME DEAD HUSBAND WHO CANNO' DEFEND HIMSELF!

GOBSHITE!
CRACK!
EEEEK!!

HERE'S TH' BLOOD MONEY YE PAID ME HUSBAND!

THIS IS THE PIECE OF PAPER THAT KILT ALL THOSE MEN!
WHAT IS IT?

ASK HIM!! IT'S WRITTEN IN THAT DIVIL'S OWN HAND!!
We dig tonite-Wet Rags
I NEVER SEEN DOT BEFORE IN MY LIFE!

IT WAS HAND DELIVERED TA ME HUSBAND BY VAN DYKE'S CURSED TOADY, P.J. SWEENEY!
HEY! I DON'T KNOW NUTHIN'!

MR. VAN DYKE, DO YOU DENY WRITING THIS LETTER? WHAT IS THE MEANING OF "WET RAGS?"
HOW VOULD I KNOW? DOT'S NOT MY LETTER!

HA! MORE BULLSHITE! EVERYBODY KNOWS ABOUT "WET RAGS"!
VAN DYKE HAS US COVER OUR FACES WITH WET TOWELS WHEN THERE'S GAS IN THE TUNNEL!

YA, VELL MEBBE' I HEARD ABOUT "VET RAGS" BUT I NEFFER WROTE DOT LETTER!
SEE WHAT HE CARRIES IN HIS MONEY BELT! THAT'S WHERE HE KEEPS ALL HIS SECRETS!

MONEY BELT? I'M NODT VEARING A MONEY BELT!
SHOW US! LET'S SEE IF HE'S TELLIN' THE TRUTH!

BACK OFF ALL O' YEZ!! ANYBODY GOES NEAR WILLY'S MONEY BELT GETS A SOCK IN THE JAW!!
SO HE DOES HAVE A MONEY BELT! GET IT!

GET YER HANDTS OFFA ME!
CLEAR THIS COURTROOM!
CRACK!
AGGG!!
GIMME THAT!
C'MON, LADIES— THIS IS NO PLACE FOR YOU!

BEN!! FRIEDA!! I NEED YER HELP!!
WHAT ON EARTH IS GOIN' ON IN THERE?

PLEASE TAKE CARE OF THESE BRAVE LADIES WHILE I GO PUT OUT A FIRE!

LAY DOWN HERE...TRY TO CALM YOURSELF
I'LL GET HER SOME SORT OF PILLOW.
LAY DOWN, MA!

MY GOSH!...I'VE SEEN YOU LADIES BEFORE. I KNOW BOTH O' YOU!

MY NAME IS BEN BELTRAN. I WAS ON THE CRIB #5.
DID'YA KNOW ME HUSBAND?

NO, NOT EXACTLY. Y'SEE I HAVE SOMETHIN' HERE FOR YA...

...SOMETHIN' THAT BELONGS TO YOU.
GASP!

YOU?...YOU WERE THERE? WAS HE...? DID HE...?

HE WAS CLUTCHIN' THIS IN HIS HAND. YOU **BOTH** WERE IN HIS LAST THOUGHTS. I HOPE YOU DON'T MIND THAT I BROUGHT IT BACK.
YE BROUGHT US HIS LAST MOMENTS ON EARTH...THAT'S EVERYTHIN' FER US.
SHE'S SO PALE. LET'S HAVE HER LIE DOWN AGAIN.

30 MINUTES LATER
BEN!...I NEED A WORD WIT'YA PLEASE.
THERE YOU GO. THAT'S BETTER.

IT'S OVER, BEN. THE INQUEST IS CLOSED.
WHAT?! WITHOUT MY TESTIMONY?

THE TUNNEL BOYS RIPPED AWAY VAN DYKE'S CLOTHES TO GET AT HIS INFERNAL **MONEY BELT...**
EUREKA!

...THE MAYOR AND JUDGE LOOKED THRU IT AN' FOUND ALL MANNER O' THINGS: MONEY, NOTES, AN' A LEDGER LIST O' PAYOFFS...

...THE WRITIN' ON THE LEDGER MATCHED VAN DYKE'S NOTE TO CLARKE, PROVIN' THEY **KNEW** THERE WAS GAS IN THE TUNNEL.
tonight
Extra

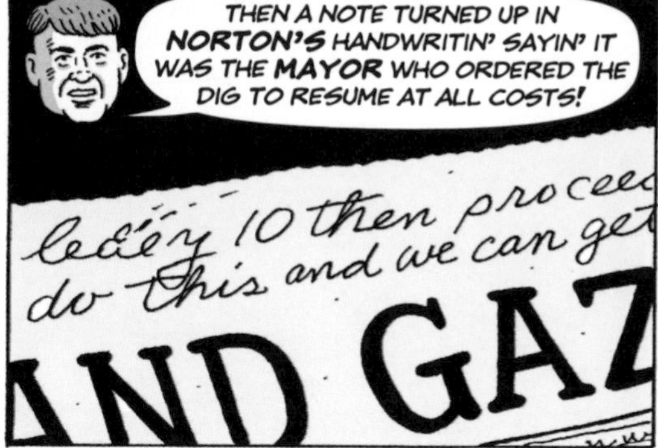
THEN A NOTE TURNED UP IN **NORTON'S** HANDWRITIN' SAYIN' IT WAS THE **MAYOR** WHO ORDERED THE DIG TO RESUME AT ALL COSTS!
10 then procee
do this and we can get
AND GAZ

...THE MAYOR READ THE NOTE AN' STARTED YELPIN' LIKE A SPANIEL! THEN HE TORE IT TO PIECES AN' CALLED IN THE PRESS!
THIS ACCIDENT WAS AN ACT OF GOD. NO ONE IS TO BLAME.
THIS INQUEST IS CLOSED!
WHAT? MAYOR, YOU HAVEN'T JURISDICTION TO CLOSE THIS!

THERE GOES THE HORSE'S ASS NOW!
THAT HORSE'S ASS WILL PROBABLY BE GOVERNOR SOMEDAY.

I DON'T GET IT, CHIEF. SOUNDS LIKE CLARKE WAS A GOOD MAN. HOW'D HE GET MIXED UP IN THIS?
CLARKE'S BUM LEG SHOULDA COST HIM HIS JOB. HE COLLECTED HIS PAY AS LONG AS HE FOLLOWED VAN DYKE'S ORDERS. HE WAS AS DESPERATE AS THEY COME.

SOMETHIN'S GOTTA CHANGE WHEN FOOLS ARE GIVEN THE POWER O' LIFE AND DEATH. WHO'S GONNA REMEMBER THESE POOR MEN AND ALL O' THEIR SACRIFICES?
IF THE STORY OF THE BELTRAN SMOKE HELMET EVER COMES OUT, THEN EVERYBODY WILL!

BEN, WE NEED TO GET MARY TO THE HOSPITAL. SHE'S IN BAD SHAPE!
LEAVE IT TO ME! I'LL GET AN AMBULANCE!

OH BEN, WHAT HAPPENS TO THEM? THEY'VE LOST EVERYTHING...IT BREAKS MY HEART.
NEVER BET AGAINST THE IRISH, FRIEDA. THEY'RE A RACE O' SURVIVORS... JUST LIKE MINE!

YOUNG MISS, I'D LIKE TO GIVE YOU SOMETHIN'.
WHAT IS IT?

JUS' AN OL' WHISTLE TO CARRY FOR GOOD LUCK.
BIRDY

BIRDY
RRRRRR!!

UH-OH, IT'S BUSTED!

TREAT 'ER LIKE FINE CHINA, LADS.
IT'S A SPECIAL WHISTLE, DARLIN'.

ONLY YOUR DADDY CAN HEAR IT. WHENEVER YOU ARE AFRAID OR LONELY, BLOW ON THE WHISTLE AND YOU'LL FEEL HIM RIGHT BESIDE YOU.
THEY NEED HELP. I'M GOING TO THE HOSPITAL WITH THEM.

BEN, I GOTTA GO. I DID PUT IN ANUTTER REQUEST FER THE SMOKE HELMETS. LET'S HOPE FER THE BEST AN' EXPECT THE WORST, EH, BOYO?
OK, CHIEF, AN' BY THE WAY, **THANK YOU** FOR SAVIN' MY LIFE.

AHHH...IT'LL BE NICE TO SLEEP IN MY OWN BED TONITE...EH...?

HMMM...CAN I HELP YOU GENTLEMEN?

THANK YOU!
DEKUJI!
GO RAIBH MAITH AGAT!
DANKE!
GESTENA!
GRAZIE!
EFCHARISTO!
DAKUJEM!

ARE WE STILL GONNA GET MEDALS, WILLY?
DOTS VAT NEWSPAPERS SAY!

"DA HEROES UFF CRIB #5" DEY CALLED US!
YEA! CUZ' WE HAD ALL THE GUTS!

THEY'RE COMINK AFTER US! RUN!!
EEEEE!!

BELTRAN LIMPED PAINFULLY FROM THE COURTHOUSE TO THE STREETCAR THAT TOOK HIM HOME. EXHAUSTED AND UNWELL, HE COLLAPSED INTO HIS FAVORITE CHAIR AND DRIFTED INTO ANOTHER "UNQUIET" DREAM...
ZZZZZ
DIPLOM

BENJAMIN BELTRAN PREFERRED TO FLY IN HIS DREAMS...

IT WAS EASIER THAN WALKING AND THE VIEW WAS WONDERFUL...

BUT, NO WALKING MEANT NO SCUFFLING...

...AND NO SCUFFLING MEANT THAT HE WAS DREAMING.

"ONCE IN A DREAM," BELTRAN SAID IN A SPEECH, "I WAS ALL ALONE WITH A GREAT FORCE HEADING RIGHT TOWARD ME..."

"...IT SWEPT ME UP AND TOOK ME PLACES I BARELY KNEW EXISTED..."
STOP
GO
GO

"... PLACES WHERE THE RIVERS CAUGHT FIRE AND WHERE PROGRESS WAS MEASURED..."

"...BY THE SOOT AND SADNESS ON TIRED FACES OF THE POOR AND VULNERABLE AMONG US..."

"...AND, BY THE MILES OF TUNNELS THAT BURROWED BENEATH LOGIC AND ENABLED GREED TO PROSPER AT THE EXPENSE OF OUR COMMUNITY'S HEALTH AND SAFETY."

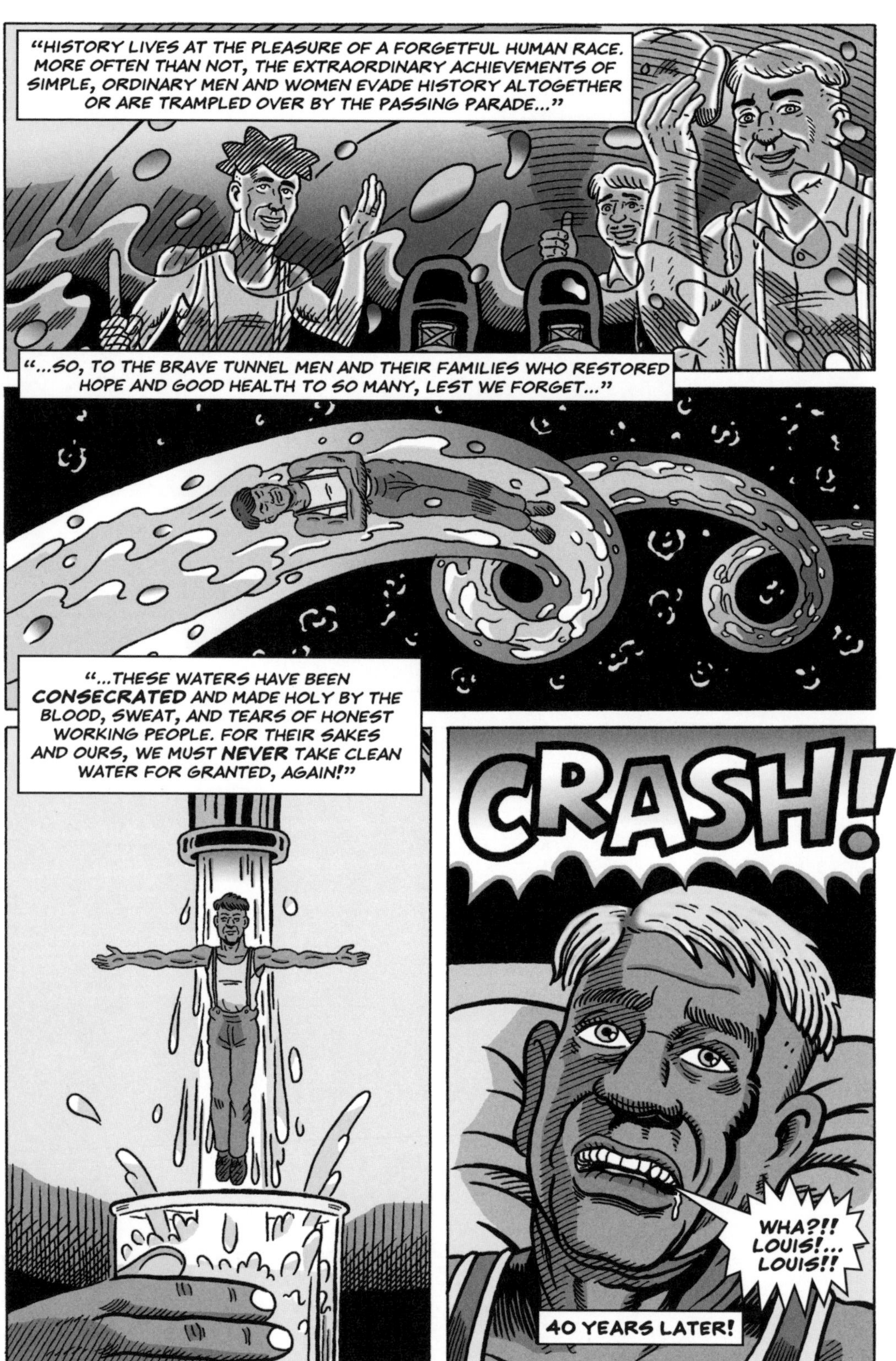
"HISTORY LIVES AT THE PLEASURE OF A FORGETFUL HUMAN RACE. MORE OFTEN THAN NOT, THE EXTRAORDINARY ACHIEVEMENTS OF SIMPLE, ORDINARY MEN AND WOMEN EVADE HISTORY ALTOGETHER OR ARE TRAMPLED OVER BY THE PASSING PARADE..."
"...SO, TO THE BRAVE TUNNEL MEN AND THEIR FAMILIES WHO RESTORED HOPE AND GOOD HEALTH TO SO MANY, LEST WE FORGET..."
"...THESE WATERS HAVE BEEN **CONSECRATED** AND MADE HOLY BY THE BLOOD, SWEAT, AND TEARS OF HONEST WORKING PEOPLE. FOR THEIR SAKES AND OURS, WE MUST **NEVER** TAKE CLEAN WATER FOR GRANTED, AGAIN!"
CRASH!
WHA?!! LOUIS!... LOUIS!!
40 YEARS LATER!

GOOD GOD! WHAT A STARTLE!

OOPS!
HEY! WHAT IN BLAZES IS GOIN' ON IN THERE!

AWARD
HOLD ON, BOY! LET YOUR GRANDPA COME HELP YOU!
ALRIGHT.

A FEW MINUTES LATER...
C'MERE, SON. SIT WITH YOUR OL' GRANDDAD FOR A MINUTE.

I WANNA TELL'YA SOMETHIN' ABOUT THAT GLASS O' WATER. D'YA KNOW WHERE OUR WATER COMES FROM?
OUR WATER COMES FROM LAKE ERIE, GRANDPA.

THAT'S 'ZACTLY CORRECT! WHERE'D YOU LEARN THAT?
IN SCHOOL. IT COMES FROM A TUNNEL UNDER THE LAKE.

YES!...RIGHT AGAIN! MY, MY, THAT'S A MIGHTY GOOD SCHOOL YOU GOT THERE!
...UMM, GRANDPA?

TEACHER TOLD MY WHOLE CLASS...WELL, SHE SAID YOU SAVED THOSE WATER MEN UNDER THE LAKE WITH A GAS MASK! IS IT TRUE?
MOSTLY TRUE, YES. I DID SAVE MEN THAT NIGHT WITH THE HELP OF YOUR GREAT UNCLE LOUIS, GOD REST HIS SOUL.

WHY'D YOU DO IT? WEREN'T YOU SCARED?!
HMMPH! SCARED? YOU BEST BELIEVE IT. I WAS VERY SCARED!

BUT, EVERYBODY SHOULD TRY TO SAVE **SOMEONE** ALONG THE WAY. GOD KNOWS THE OPPORTUNITIES ARE ALWAYS THERE. I KNEW MY INVENTION WORKED, AND SO I USED IT TO HELP MY FELLOW MAN. I'M SO PROUD THAT I CAN SAY THAT!

BUT OLD PEOPLE LIKE ME, WELL... WE'RE OUTA TIME AND LEAVIN' BEHIND A BIG JOB FOR THE NEXT GENERATION TO FINISH.

IT'LL BE THE JOB OF YOU YOUNG PEOPLE TO RESPECT AND PROTECT THE WATER. YOU'LL JUST HAVE TO DO IT. Y'SEE, 'CUZ...WATER, **IT IS SO PRECIOUS...**

IT'S AS PRECIOUS... **AS LIFE ITSELF.**
THE END

GARRETT A. MORGAN A MAN FOR ALL TIMES

Courtesy of The Cleveland Press Collection, Michael Schwartz Library, Cleveland State University

Benjamin Beltran, the protagonist and hero of *Fire on the Water*, is not fully a product of my imagination. Rather, Beltran's journey echoes that of the man who inspired his character: the great Garrett Augustus Morgan.

Today, Garrett Morgan is known as one of America's greatest African American inventors, but it's the exceptional "content of his character" our graphic novel strives to impart upon the reader. Morgan is primarily known as the inventor of an innovative breathing mask used in firefighting and for an early tricolor traffic signal. His greatest invention, however, was himself. To this day, his adopted city of Cleveland, Ohio, a beautifully situated American city ever striving for greatness, mostly fails to recognize one of the greatest Clevelanders it ever had.

Morgan was born in Paris, Kentucky, twelve years after the American Civil War ended. His parents were poor sharecroppers who worked dawn to dusk on their hardscrabble farm and struggled to feed their eleven children. Young Morgan received a few years of education before he had to quit school and earn his keep on the farm. Yearning for a better future, he packed up his meager belongings and walked away from the dead-end cycle of poverty and sought out something new. He headed north and never looked back, and he was only fourteen years old.

Young Morgan had a natural understanding of all things mechanical. His abilities landed him a job as a handyman on a farm near Cincinnati, Ohio. He used some of the money he earned to hire tutors who helped him further his education. Then, in 1895, he hopped a train and rode the boxcar rails north to Cleveland, Ohio. He arrived in the city with only ten cents in his pocket. He was eighteen, broke, homeless, and brimming with positive energy.

By 1895, Cleveland's population was exploding through an influx of immigrants and rural Americans who'd been drawn to the city's industrial growth and the promise of plentiful employment opportunities. Cleveland's primary industries, including steel, oil, and manufacturing, were running at full tilt. Morgan found steady work as a janitor for a large clothing factory. This menial job would lead to new opportunities and change his life in several ways.

Garment-manufacturing sweatshops were common in those days. Greedy business owners packed their employees (mostly young women) into poorly ventilated fire traps where they worked under Dickensian conditions. It was in the clothing factory that Morgan realized one of his first inventions.

The churning sound of industrial sewing machines was music to Morgan's ears. Upon observing how the leather drive belts that powered the sewing machines kept snapping, young Morgan invented an improved and more reliable belt. His pluck and ingenuity earned him a promotion from lowly janitor to sewing-machine repairman. It was during this same period of his life that the upwardly mobile inventor had decided to marry, but it didn't last. After his divorce, he met another woman who worked as a seamstress in the same clothing factory. Her name was Mary Anne Hasek. She and Morgan fell in love and married. Though their marriage was a successful one, it was highly controversial because it was the turn of the twentieth century, and Mary Anne was a white woman and Morgan was a black man.

Together they left the clothing factory and formed their own dressmaking and tailoring business that provided training and employment to more than thirty people from their community. Despite earning the ire of whites who opposed interracial marriage and the disapproval of their own families, Garrett and Mary Anne were quite the team.

Leveraging his skills as an inventor, Morgan created several businesses. One was the G. A. Morgan Hair Refining Company, which sold a line of beauty products that included a hair-straightening cream Morgan had invented by accident. In 1914, Morgan founded the National Safety Device Company. The company's flagship product was the Morgan Safety Hood and Smoke Protector. The patented safety hood was a type of breathing mask that made it possible for firemen to work inside smoke-filled structures. Although he was a natural at product promotion, Morgan's attempts to market his inventions were undermined by racial prejudice. Cleveland's mainstream newspapers refused to advertise products and services offered by black-owned businesses. Morgan promoted sales by performing live demonstrations of the safety hood locally and around the country. The going was rough.

As the son of slaves, Morgan understood the limitations of the time and worked hard to carefully circumvent Jim Crow "separate but equal" barriers rather than challenge them directly. He understood that if city mayors and fire chiefs discovered the safety hood had been created by a "negro," they would reject it outright, regardless of its benefits. Not to be denied, Morgan devised a simple scheme to sell his invention. He hired a white actor to portray the inventor while Morgan presented himself as a Native American nicknamed Big Chief Mason. During a typical demonstration, the white actor would first enthrall the crowd with his pitch for the safety hood, and then he would order Big Chief Mason to don the device and go into a tent filled with dense smoke. Audiences would marvel at the sight of the man behind the mask emerging unscathed after twenty minutes, long past the time anyone could survive such lethal conditions without the firefighting apparatus. The inventor's clever ruse resulted in sales, but the systemic discrimination that forced Morgan to disassociate himself from his own invention would have destroyed the pride and dignity of an Edison or a Tesla. For Garrett A. Morgan, it was just another day at the office.

In the early years of the twentieth century, Cleveland's growing population made it one of the largest cities in the United States. As a result, the city's water and sewer infrastructure needed to be upgraded quickly in order to meet the growing demand for safe, clean drinking water. Typhoid, cholera, and a host of other waterborne illnesses sickened or killed hundreds of Clevelanders annually. Hundreds of babies died each year from inflammatory bowel diseases traced back to city water. The central cause for these plagues hid in plain sight. Cleveland's astonishing growth and inadequate water sanitation systems had completely polluted Lake Erie. The eastside and westside water intakes that provided drinking water were constantly being tainted by contaminants pooling along the fetid shorelines and from the hideously toxic effluents that spilled down the city's infamous (and occasionally flammable) Cuyahoga River.

In order to capture the cleanest water possible, the city had to extend the water intakes from their near-shore positions to several miles out and under Lake Erie. For this, the city needed new tunnels, and it needed them fast. The project's plans and costs were anticipated in advance, but the sacrifices and price of human lives were not.

By 1904, extension of the eastside water tunnel had been completed. The human carnage suffered during construction was sobering. The exact numbers of dead and injured vary in the historical accounts, but it's generally accepted that between fifty and seventy men were killed while building the eastside tunnel. This doesn't even take into account the unknown number of men who were injured and maimed or died years later from the chronic nature of their injuries.

The sacrifices of the tunnel builders paid off, however. After 1904, the extended eastside water tunnel had significantly reduced illnesses caused by drinking water. When the start of the westside tunnel project was announced, city and waterworks officials claimed they had learned great lessons from the mistakes that killed and injured so many men building the eastside tunnel. Cleveland politicians erroneously promised their constituents that the same mistakes would not be repeated.

The first two years of the five-year project were relatively uneventful and in line with the city's promise. But at approximately 10 p.m. on July 24, 1916, the worst accident in the history of the Cleveland water-tunnel construction projects began to unfold.

Early that morning, Garrett and Mary Anne Morgan were awoken by a series of phone calls to their Harlem Avenue home. Cleveland mayor Harry L. Davis desperately needed Morgan to join an ongoing rescue operation taking place on Water Crib #5. They told him that an enormous gas explosion had caused a tunnel under the lake to cave in, trapping more than twenty sandhogs (tunnel workers). Morgan was directed to bring as many of his safety hoods as he could carry.

Garrett Morgan had every reason to refuse the request. Everyone knew the tunnels were deathtraps. Why should Morgan risk his life? Luckily for everyone on Crib #5, Garrett Morgan wasn't the kind of man to ignore a plea for help. He recognized that he had been handed a golden opportunity to prove the merits of his safety hood while he helped his fellow man. His response was to run out of his house barefooted, wearing only his pajama bottoms. On his way to the Cleveland piers, he picked up his brother, Frank, and together they boarded the tugboat *George A. Wallace* for the four-mile voyage to the Crib #5 platform.

Garrett Morgan wearing his Morgan Safety Hood breathing device invention in 1916.

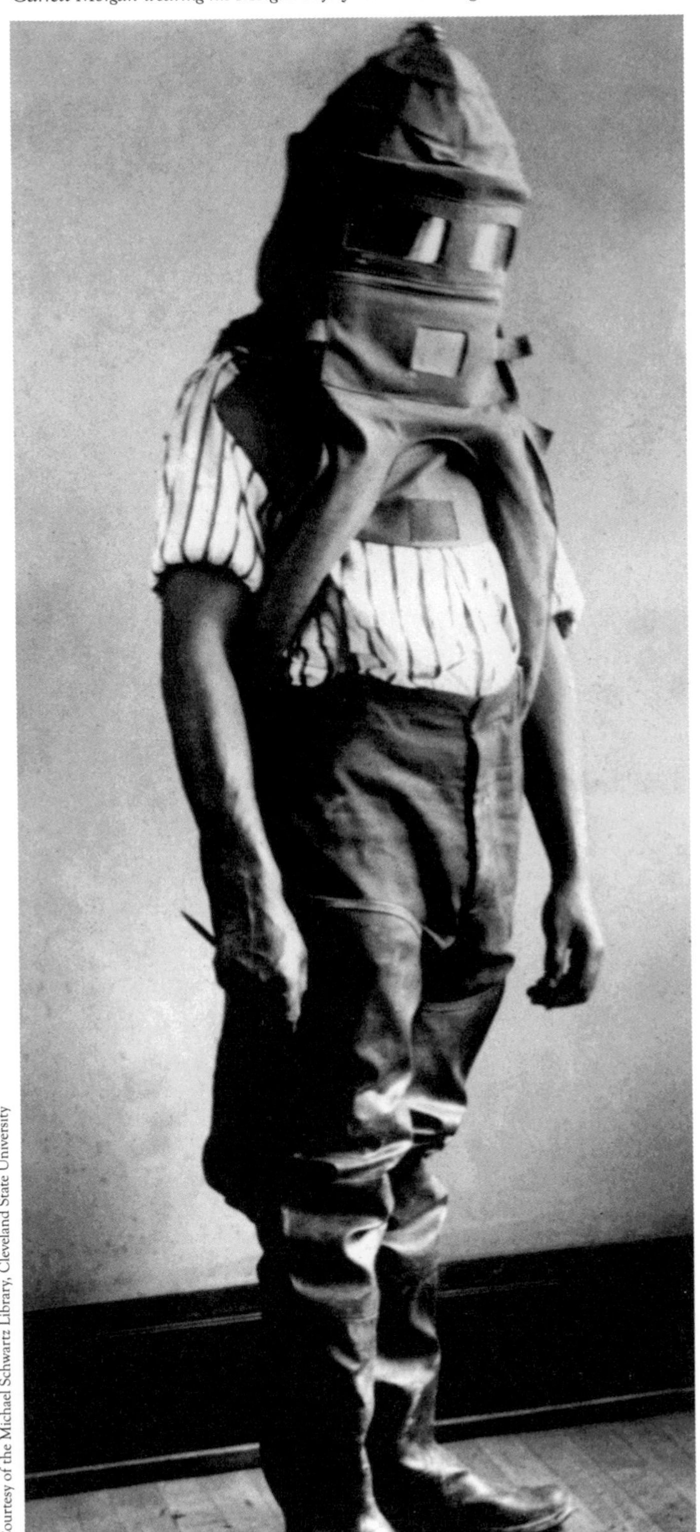

Courtesy of the Michael Schwartz Library, Cleveland State University

As Morgan stepped onto the lake platform, he saw fear and panic in the faces of the sandhogs. Morgan was initially unable to convince volunteers to accompany him and his brother into the tunnel. Finally, two men, Tom Castleberry and Tommy Clancy, bravely stepped forward and joined the Morgan brothers. Just before the sandhogs descended down the tunnel shaft, Mayor Davis assured them that, in the event of their death, the city would take care of their families for life. The mayor was lying, of course.

Tommy Clancy wasn't just any volunteer. He was the mercurial stepson of the crib construction superintendent, Gustav (Gus) Van Dusen. Four hours before the Morgan brothers arrived on deck, Van Dusen and his entire rescue team had disappeared in the gas-filled tunnel and were presumed dead. Ironically, Van Dusen could have easily prevented the tragedy. On July 22 or 23, 1916, the sandhogs working in the tunnel ran for their lives after roaring natural gas breaches erupted at the tunnel face. Water Commissioner Charles Jaeger gave Van Dusen strict orders to install a ventilator at the 650-foot mark and suspend all work until the tunnel atmosphere was clear of gas. However, on the night of July 24, 1916, despite the commissioner's unambiguous orders, crib superintendent John Johnston allowed civil engineer Harry Vokes and a team of eight sandhogs to descend into the tunnel.

The sad conclusion consistent in all accounts of the tragedy was that Vokes and his team never knew what hit them. While digging at the tunnel face, they'd struck the mother of all gas pockets. The entire crew suffocated where they stood and were blown to smithereens after sparks from a shattered light bulb ignited the gas. Workers up top on the crib platform weren't initially aware that anything had happened until the operator of the tunnel air compressor witnessed his pressure gauges suddenly go haywire. Then, John Johnston detected gas arising from the tunnel shaft. They all realized that something terrible had just happened. Johnston immediately led a rescue mission of eight men into the tunnel. Before long they became asphyxiated from the gas. Johnston and two others barely survived and had to be hospitalized. The remaining five rescuers all perished. After Gus Van Dusen led his own doomed team down the shaft and they were presumed dead, chaos reigned on Crib #5. In that desperate moment, a policeman at the scene had recalled a demonstration he'd witnessed of the Morgan safety hood. Better yet, the man who invented it was a Clevelander! What did they have to lose? It was then, at four o'clock in the morning, that the mayor dispatched a messenger to go ashore and summon Garrett Morgan to the crib.

After Mayor Davis had finished making his hollow promises to Morgan, the two brothers along with Clancy and Castleberry descended into what had become a tunnel to hell. Accounts vary widely as to what exactly happened once they'd broken through the tunnel airlock seals. We know that on his first of several trips into the tunnel, Morgan and his team tripped over multiple dead bodies. Then, a miracle occurred. Gus Van Dusen was found alive after four hours in the gas. As reported in the January 1917 *Engineering News*, Van Dusen had somehow staggered 650 feet down the tunnel and was kept alive by the air ventilator he'd installed two days earlier. Why only Van Dusen and not other members of his rescue team shared in the miracle, we will never know.

The remarkable moment when Van Dusen was brought to the surface alive was captured by a newspaper photographer. The picture shows Garrett Morgan, his safety hood pulled back over his shoulders, cradling the slime-covered Van Dusen while surrounded by sandhogs and city officials.

The picture is among the few vestiges of physical proof of Morgan's involvement in the rescue efforts. Mayor Davis had been firmly in control of the newspaper accounts of the accident. In what would turn out to be the greatest injustice of Morgan's life, the mayor made sure that all mentions of Morgan's role in the rescue efforts were scrupulously omitted from the official accounts. Davis was not about to give Cleveland's black community a hero to look up to during that dark and unmerciful era.

An elated Tommy Clancy left the scene and accompanied his stepfather onto the tugboat and to the hospital. Once back onshore, Van Dusen had the wherewithal to dispatch his daughter-in-law (Tommy Clancy's wife) to Lakeside Hospital and instruct John Johnston to keep his mouth shut. Obviously, they needed to get their stories straight. The cover-up had begun.

Back on the crib, anxious sandhogs were emboldened by the success of Morgan's safety hood, and they joined in the rescue efforts. In all, Morgan and his brother made four trips into the tunnel and brought back at least nine more men either dead or alive before the decision was made to call off the rescue. The long, horrible night was finally over, but the damage had been done. In all, nineteen souls had perished and another nine had been injured. Morgan and his brother suffered from exposure to gas that had leeched into their masks. Nonetheless, the safety hood had been a game changer. Without it, no one would have been saved.

Back on shore, John Johnston followed Van Dusen's instructions to the letter. He was so tight-lipped that the city's coroner and prosecutor placed him under house arrest in his hospital bed after he stubbornly refused to answer their questions. When the sandhogs heard about Johnston's arrest, they wrongly assumed that he was to blame for the disaster and threatened his life. At the same time, the newspapers prematurely anointed Van Dusen, Tommy Clancy, and a few others as the great heroes of Crib #5.

The Morgan brothers' role in the rescue continued to be omitted during the days that followed, and the safety hood that saved the day received scant mention in the various newspaper accounts. Van Dusen went as far as claiming that the late civil engineer, Harry Vokes, had disobeyed the commissioner's orders.

The inquest that followed the disaster was a joke. The only good that arose was when the pregnant widow of Harry Vokes stood up in the courtroom to defend her husband and called out Van Dusen for the liar that he was. During the confrontation, Van Dusen was forced to change his story. He admitted that he did not adequately convey to Johnston or Vokes the commissioner's strict orders to stay out of the tunnel. Mayor Davis was a wily politician who'd become increasingly alarmed as evidence of negligence and incompetence related to the tunnel projects kept pointing toward city hall in general and specifically to him. He decided to shut down the inquest abruptly—after only one day—and declared that "no one was to blame."

It must have been extremely difficult for Morgan in the face of such injustice. However, true to his character, he didn't take it lying down. He furiously took to the marbled hallways of Cleveland's city hall for many of the years that followed, seeking recognition and payment for the services he and his brother rendered on the crib. In his 1917 letter to Mayor Davis, Morgan wrote,

July 25, 1916: The scene on Crib #5 following Garrett Morgan's live rescue of Superintendent Gustav Van Dusen from the crippled water tunnel.

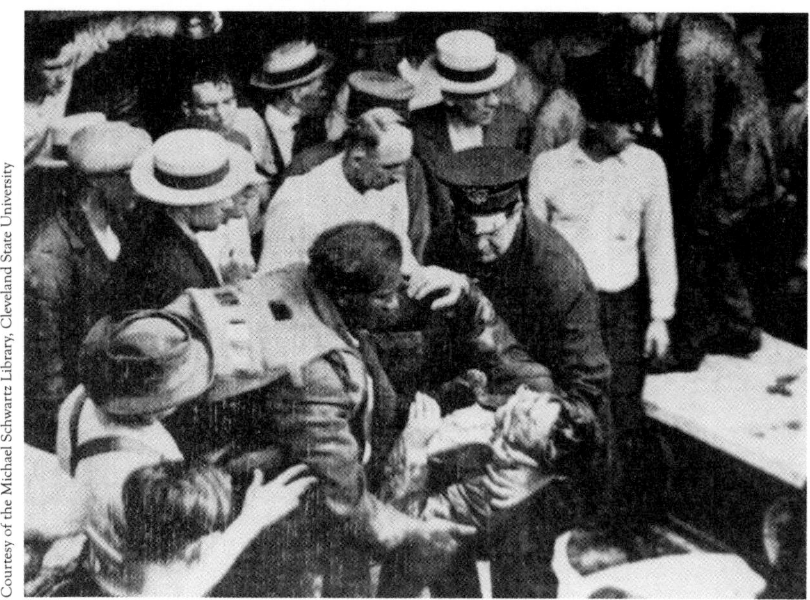

Courtesy of the Michael Schwartz Library, Cleveland State University

> I have voted and worked for your election to public office each time you have been a candidate . . . Why was it you remained silent and allowed awards to men who either followed me into the tunnel, or if they went in at all, went in after my return in your presence with dead and alive bodies . . . when I returned you congratulated me and told me you would see that I was treated fairly and would be commended for my bravery . . . The treatment accorded me in the particulars set out . . . above is much as to make me and the members of my race to feel that you did not give a colored man a square deal.

The Davis administration stubbornly refused to acknowledge the Morgan brothers' heroism or to pay them for their time, materials, and the medical care they required after the accident. During the months and years following the 1916 tragedy, stories of Morgan's heroism and his safety hood finally began to reach other parts of the country and the world. Numerous civic groups, local business associations, and the NAACP recognized him as a bona fide and unsung hero of the waterworks Crib #5 disaster.

Unfortunately, this belated recognition came with a downside. Once it became understood that the inventor of the Morgan safety hood was an African American, sales of the device plummeted, just as Morgan had feared they would. His fortunes changed, however, when the US Army bought the patent and modified the safety hood for use during World War I.

By 1917, Morgan had become fed up with the lack of good, honest newspaper representation for Cleveland's African American community, He decided to do something about it. With the help of a group of investors, Morgan created a new newspaper known as *The Cleveland Call*. The paper went through a bumpy growing period, and Morgan often had to keep the paper afloat with his own money. Then, in 1927, *The Call* merged with *The Cleveland Post* to become *The Call and Post*. The *C&P* is still published to this day, serving the community for which it was created.

Morgan's inventing didn't end with the safety hood. In 1922, after witnessing carnage on the streets of Cleveland involving an automobile and a horse-drawn wagon, Morgan invented a unique, three-element traffic signal that directed the movement of street traffic in a more safe and organized manner. He later sold the device to General Electric for the then tidy sum of $40,000.

In 1934, Morgan's nemesis, Harry L. Davis, returned to Cleveland after a stint as governor of Ohio from 1921 through 1923, and was again elected the city's mayor. That same year, Garrett's brother, Frank, was dying from a chronic lung condition that he blamed on the exposure to gas during his night in the tunnel. Morgan again camped out at city hall and demanded that something be done to help his brother. He applied to the city for a $25,000 pension in recognition for their heroism. Davis refused to meet Morgan personally and the pension claim was denied. Finally, the mayor acquiesced to one of Morgan's demands and provided Frank with a gravesite paid for by the city. Frank succumbed to his lung condition on April 5, 1934. He was fifty-two years old.

Morgan pushed on and devoted the rest of his life to business and community activities. He sued a Cleveland radio station in 1937, asserting that their broadcasted reenactment of the 1916 crib disaster had failed to include one important character. Him!

His final years weren't easy. Morgan was beset by illnesses and incremental blindness that he attributed, in part, to the injuries sustained in the tunnel. However, he never stopped fighting Cleveland's city hall for the recognition denied him and his brother. Unhappily, Garrett Morgan's good fight ended, without success, on July 27, 1963. When he died, he'd been working on his newest and last invention, a self-extinguishable cigarette.

To the end, he was still seeking out solutions for the common man's problems. Garrett and Mary Anne are buried in Cleveland's beautiful Lake View Cemetery near other prominent Clevelanders, including John D. Rockefeller, President James Garfield, Eliot Ness, Harvey Pekar, and Ernest Roland Ball, the man who wrote, "When Irish Eyes Are Smiling."

Twenty-eight years after his death, the Cleveland waterworks renamed its Division Avenue filtration and pumping plant the Garrett A. Morgan Water Treatment Plant in belated recognition of Morgan's heroism inside the water tunnel that still supplies the plant to this very day. A school was named in his honor, and the city erected a plaque commemorating his life in proximity to where his Harlem Avenue home once stood.

Despite these recognitions, there is no statue to honor Cleveland's brilliant inventor, good citizen, and forgotten hero. Among the most poignant attempts to preserve Morgan's memory were those mounted by a Cleveland schoolteacher named Tyrone Williams. For many years on July 25, Williams marked the anniversary of Morgan's heroics on Crib #5 with a one-man wreath-laying ceremony on the same pier that Morgan and his brother awaited their tugboat ride into history.

Like Tyrone Williams, *Fire on the Water* strives to inspire a new interest in Morgan's story so that future generations will take note of this great American. The futility of racism and the long-term rewards of racial justice are lessons that can be discovered by studying the rich tapestries of Morgan's life. His is a resonant story that needs to be told now more than ever. Tyrone Williams expressed it well during a 1990 interview with the *Cleveland Plain Dealer*: "If I wasn't fighting for him, he'd be forgotten," said Williams. "He wasn't just for blacks, he was for everyone."

Perhaps no one said it better than Morgan himself, with the words that he'd stipulated to be carved onto the stone that marks his final resting place: "By His Deeds He Shall Be Remembered."

—Scott MacGregor, Lakewood, Ohio

BIBLIOGRAPHY

The story of Garrett A. Morgan is a perfect example of how the history we're taught is not necessarily the history that happened. That's because the story of Morgan's heroics on the night of July 25, 1916, was, thanks to systemic racism, erased in the same way one erases a wipe board or an email. As a result, he was forced to spend the rest of his life fighting his brave and lonely fight for his rightful place in history. It was a fight he ultimately won, just not during his lifetime.

After Morgan died in 1963, it became the job of his family members, various biographers, documentarians, culture creatures, and graphic novelists to cobble together and return the elusive and hard-earned facts of his storied life to the bright light of truth.

This essay has drawn its facts from several sources and they encompass the following:

BIOGRAPHICAL WORKS: Jackson, Garnet Nelson and Thomas Hudson, illustrator. *Garrett Morgan:* Inventor (New York: Modern Curriculum Press, 1993); Kulling, Monica and David Parkins, illustrator. *To The Rescue! Garrett Morgan Underground* (Toronto, ON: Tundra Books, 2017); Murphy, Patricia J. *Garrett Morgan: Inventor of the Traffic Light and Gas Mask* (Berkeley Heights, NJ: Enslow Publishers, Inc., 2004); Oluonye, Mary N. *Garrett Augustus Morgan: Businessman, Inventor, Good Citizen* (Bloomington, IN: Author House, 2008). **DOCUMENTARY WORKS**: Bellamy, John Stark, II. *They Died Crawling, and Other Tales of Cleveland Woe* (Cleveland, OH: Gray & Company, Publishers, 1995); Dubelko, Jim. "The 1916 Waterworks Tunnel Disaster," Cleveland Historical, https://clevelandhistorical.org/items/show/736, accessed August 21, 2019. **ACADEMIC WORKS**: Cook, Lisa D. "Overcoming Discrimination by Consumers during the Age of Segregation: The Example of Garrett Morgan." *Business History Review* 86 (Summer 2012) http://econ.msu.edu/papers/Overcoming_Discrimination_by_Consumers.pdf, accessed August 21, 2019; Kish, Jeanne, "Garrett Morgan and the 1916 Waterworks Disaster," *Ohio Social Studies Review,* 39, no. 1 (Summer 2003): 32–39; Bernstein, Margaret. "Inventor Garrett Morgan, Cleveland's Fierce Bootstrapper." June 13, 2012. Teaching Cleveland Digital, http://teachingcleveland.org/inventor-garrett-morgan-clevelands-fierce-bootstrapper-by-margaret-bernstein, accessed August 21, 2019; Daniel Dana. "Report on the Sanitary Condition of The Cleveland Water Supply." University of Michigan Library. 1912. **CIVIL ENGINEERING**: "Cleveland's New Water-Intake Tunnel Under Lake Erie Completed." *Engineering News* 77 (January–March 1917): 94–99. **NEWS MEDIA**: *The Cleveland Plain Dealer*: various articles, 1916–1990.

ABOUT THE AUTHOR AND ILLUSTRATOR

Photo credit: Maureen MacGregor

SCOTT MACGREGOR has been writing comic book stories for more than thirty years. This is his first full-length graphic novel. Scott lives in Cleveland, Ohio.

GARY DUMM is a lifelong resident of Cleveland and an artist who worked extensively with Harvey Pekar on *American Splendor*. Dumm's cartoons have also appeared in *Entertainment Weekly*, the *New York Times*, the *Village Voice*, and *Le Monde*.